RULE 42
AND ALL THAT

RULE 42
AND ALL THAT

SEÁN KELLY ~

Gill & Macmillan

Gill & Macmillan Ltd
Hume Avenue, Park West, Dublin 12
with associated companies throughout the world
www.gillmacmillan.ie

978 07171 4183 8

Index compiled by Helen Litton
Typography design by Make Communication
Print origination by TypeIT, Dublin
Printed and bound in Great Britain by MPG Books Ltd,
Bodmin, Cornwall

This book is typeset in 12pt on 14.5pt Minion.

The paper used in this book comes from the wood pulp
of managed forests. For every tree felled, at least one
tree is planted, thereby renewing natural resources.

A CIP catalogue record for this book is available from
the British Library.

5 4 3 2 1

The extract from 'The Augean Stables' is taken from
Seamus Heaney's collection, *Electric Light*, published by
Faber & Faber Ltd in 2001 and reproduced on page
257 with their kind permission.

CONTENTS

ACKNOWLEDGEMENTS

John Kenneth Galbraith, the prolific and acclaimed Irish-American scholar and writer, was once asked how he managed to write so much. His reply was, 'I get up early, have a good breakfast and begin.'

Well, the opposite was true for me as I wrote this book. It could be said, 'I got home late (from work), had a good supper and began,' and I often wrote until the early hours of the morning. You see, Fergal Tobin insisted that I write *gach uile focal*, every single word, myself. He set me a target of 85,000 words, or so. I thought it an impossible task, but as it happened I wrote far too *much*—and in came the guillotine. Be that as it may, I am pleased to have written it all in longhand: 'The last of the Dinosaurs,' said Fergal.

I am most grateful to all who encouraged and helped me, especially my wife, Juliette, and family. They took no notice of me as I wrote along. Also, I would like to express my gratitude to various journalists who helped by tracing articles, and whose work I have quoted in the following pages.

It has been a labour of challenge and satisfaction, and I hope you will enjoy reading all about Rule 42—and much more besides.

Finally, probably the saddest day in the Kelly household was 12 July 1988, when my brother Pádraig died suddenly. This book is dedicated to his memory.

Yours in Sport,

Seán Kelly
August 2007

PROLOGUE

On Saturday 16 April 2005 I was seated in the Uachtarán's chair, presiding over the annual GAA Congress. Ostensibly we were focused on the business in hand, but every pair of ears was straining to hear the approach of the teller, bearing the all-important news.

At 4.05pm Paraic Duffy entered the room and walked up to the rostrum. In his hand he had a piece of paper, which he handed to me. The paper was folded. I thanked Paraig. I knew the vote before me was the result of the most contentious, and perhaps divisive, motion in the history of the GAA—the result of the Rule 42 debate on whether to open Croke Park to rugby and soccer, or to keep its gates closed forever.

As a speaker made his point from the floor, I opened the note. It contained the following information and little more:

Tá   227
Níl 97

The motion was to allow other sports to be played in Croke Park over a specified period of time; a two-thirds majority of Congress was required to pass it. The eyes of the 350 delegates, hordes of onlookers in the public gallery plus the assembled media were fixed on me.

I never blinked, even though an overwhelming sense of euphoria and relief welled up within me. Out of courtesy to the speakers to the motion at hand, I refolded the note, put it on the table in front of me and asked, 'Any further speakers to the motion?' There were one or two, but the restlessness and excitement in the hall meant that nobody was listening. I could hear people praying, 'For God's sake, take us out of our misery and give us the result.'

Many of the supporters for changing Rule 42 felt my refolding of the note and delay in calling out the result was a sign that the motion had been defeated. Martin Breheny commented afterwards in the *Irish Independent* that 'Kelly was poker-faced, gave nothing away but that an ever so slight smile came over his face as he read the contents of the note.'

When the show of hands had been taken for Motion 34, I said, 'I will now give you the result of the motion on Rule 42.' I called out the vote.

'The motion is passed.'

It was an unforgettable moment; the defining mark of my presidency of the Gaelic Athletic Association. Some say it marked it as a blighted period in the Association's history; others believe it was a moment of triumph, of progression that proved a watershed in the long story of the GAA. For me, it was the culmination of three years' hard work, of talking and debating and discussing and listening. It was a moment I had feared would never arrive, but I am very proud it was a moment that came under my watch.

After the noise in the hall had died down, I moved on to the next motion and shortly afterwards called for the next major vote of the day: the election of Uachtarán-Tofa, who would be my successor twelve months hence. My time with the GAA was on the wane, but I was quite sure now that it would never be forgotten.

PART I

The Early Years

The Farm

Knockataggle was the name of our townland, situated in the parish of Kilcummin, in Co. Kerry. In Irish it is Cnoc an tSeagail—the Hill of the Rye. Our two-storey house was halfway up the hill and had a panoramic view of the MacGillycuddy's Reeks, the famous lakes and the forests and Ireland's highest mountain, Carrantouhil, silhouetted in the distance. We could see Mangerton Mountain and the Punch Bowl, while to the east were the well-named 'Paps', overlooking Rathmore. I remember one day pointing out the Paps to an American tourist, who hitch-hiked a lift with me, and she replied, 'Is there a male equivalent?' 'If there is,' I retorted, 'I haven't seen it.' To the north lay the vast expanse of bog known locally as Foil buí (the yellow cliff). As locals, we took all this breathtaking scenery for granted. The mountains were to be scrutinised more for signs of oncoming rain than for their beauty, the bog was regarded as a source of energy and hard work, while the lovely lakes were merely a curiosity, a place where faraway boatmen fished and tourists ambled.

Almost everyone in our area worked on the farm. There was no such thing as 'tours' or even 'holidays' back then. A match, a wedding, a funeral or a christening constituted a day out—that was a holiday. My father was a great farmer, he was a natural farmer. He had attended St Brendan's College—known locally as 'the Sem'—for a few months, but had left to farm the land. He was an unbelievably strong man and a great worker. He worked night and day. When the children started to come along and there were more mouths to be fed, he trained to be a nurse and worked in a psychiatric institution called St Finian's Hospital. He worked nights at the hospital, slept for a few hours and then returned to the farm. At busy times, such as silage and haymaking, he would go for a couple of days without sleep, maybe gathering an hour or two at most.

My mother also comes from Kilcummin, from the eastern side known as Anabla. Her townland was Inchocorrigane, or Inch for short, where two families of the O'Connors still live and farm the land. As was the norm, those families were fairly big and so was ours. Seven children arrived in reasonably quick succession: Brian the eldest, then Mary, the only girl, followed by Pádraig, Lar, myself and Seamus in successive years (1950–53), and then two years later the baby of the family, Dermot, arrived to bring up the rear.

In many ways my father was a self-educated man. I often think *The Farmer's Journal* educated him. He read it assiduously and was always the first to try something new. He was the first to try silage, grew turnips and mangolds for fodder, put in the first milking machine in the area, had early grass and late grazing, bought a tractor—in short, he was methodical and innovative. We made hay in poor weather using tripods when no other farmers around had ever used them. The tripod—comprising three long timber poles tied at one end and spread out at the other, with a wire loop three-quarters of the way down—was put standing on the ground and the hay built up around it, resting on the wire loop to allow the air to circulate. The tripod kept the hay off the ground and hollow in the middle. As a result we had good hay in bad years when other farmers had 'heated' stuff. It was awfully hard work though. The poles had to be got, nailed together, the tripods made and transported to the hayfield. It also meant all the hay had to be piked into a trailer to be drawn in and piked again into the shed.

Thankfully, Finbarr Slattery, that gentle soul of agricultural and horse-racing fame, was our agricultural advisor. He advised silage. Again my father was first to try it. More hard work—initially. In the absence of walls, my father purchased railway sleepers and built them around the hayshed into which the silage was piked. It also had to be packed. Kitty the horse was used for this. Perched atop her sturdy back, the packer would reach up and stash the silage high in the barn. One of the worst frights my father ever got in his life happened one day when I was packing the silage with Kitty. The trick was to keep as close to the edges of the silage pit as possible in order to pack it properly. I was too meticulous on this occasion. The clamp of silage had risen way above the walls. I went out too far and the horse slipped. Fortunately, I grabbed an overhead beam as Kitty darted away furiously. She soon recovered and I remounted, but my mother and father, who had witnessed the would-be accident, were badly shaken. The family always remembered it thereafter as the day Seanie and Kitty nearly met their Waterloo!

A far worse accident befell my father a few years later. All the silage had been made and the hay drawn in, except for one small cock that I had made in front of the house. There were no more than a few pitchforks in it altogether. One evening I decided to draw it in. The tractor and trailer with the tipper were in the yard. I used them to draw in the haycock but then, instead of using a pike to take it from the trailer to the shed, I decided I'd use the tipper. When the hay slipped out, the tipper would not go back down for me. I threw the hay in the shed, gave up on the tipper and went in home to Mam for a cup of tea. While there, I told my father that the tipper was stuck in the vertical position.

About an hour later I went to turn in the cows for milking. It was a beautiful evening in the middle of August. I knew the cows would be thirsty for water, so I decided to fill the barrel for them. Every other time I had done this, I left the tap on, let it fill and then came back to turn it off. This evening, I was in no hurry as there was no football training. On a whim, I decided to stand on the wall dividing the yard from the field and see if I could fill the barrel to the very top and, without spilling a drop, pull out the pipe and get it over the wall so fast that no water would spill on the ground. It was just a mad notion. The barrel was nearly full when I thought I heard a noise coming from the yard above. It sounded like a cat. I said to myself, 'The cat is crying very loudly today.' I heard the cat call again, only this time it was fainter. Instinctively, and without any prior knowledge, the trailer and the tipper flashed into my mind.

I leapt from the wall like a cheetah and sprinted up to the yard. As soon as I rounded the corner I saw the tipper had come down and Daddy was trapped under it. Using all my strength I lifted the trailer with my hands and my father fell out onto the ground. Several times since I have tried lifting that trailer, but to absolutely no avail. Where I got that strength from I do not know, but men twice my strength couldn't lift it. Thank God, I did it on that occasion. If I had failed, my father would have been dead. He told us afterwards that after he had called out the second time, his lungs collapsed and he couldn't breathe anymore.

We called the doctor and the ambulance. Daddy was taken to hospital. His face was destroyed, several ribs were broken, but he was alive. And being the strong man he was, he went on to make a great recovery. My foolishness with the water had saved his life and our sorrow.

They were interesting times to live through, and so different from today. In the 1950s and 1960s huge changes were taking place in agriculture, nearly all for the better. Silage slowly replaced hay, tractors replaced the horse and milking machines replaced the hand. This was very welcome to the head milker in each household. Milking by hand was tough work, especially if the cow was cross—she could put you, the bucket and the milk flying across the shed. Irritable cows were usually spancelled, in other words the two hind legs were tied together. Sometimes the tail was tied as well; a lash of a long tail in the face would leave you sore for a while. My mother was very adept at milking cows. She never seemed to mind it and could get the last drop out of a cow—the stripping, as it was called. My brother Lar was a great milker, too. Once, when our neighbour across the valley, Mike Mangan, was sick in hospital, Lar used to go up before going to school and milk all his cows, returning again in the evenings to do the same. Lar never complained. Indeed, years later, when Lar was ordained a priest, Mike's wife Nellie was as proud of him as my own mother.

My mother was a great woman for keeping all kinds of fowl. She kept geese and turkeys for the Christmas market. They were all killed and plucked and sold to order. She kept ducks, too, as some people loved the ducks' eggs, and of course she kept loads of hens. They laid their eggs everywhere and anywhere. One of the great delights of childhood days was in discovering a hen's nest in some bushes or other and running in to tell Mam. She'd be thrilled with you for bringing the news.

Best of all, though, was when Mam had eggs to hatch, but no hatching hen, or when a hatching hen rose out of the nest. This was a kind of a wildcat strike, when a hatching hen suddenly stopped hatching, leaving the eggs in mortal danger. One or two of us would be despatched to the neighbouring farms with our tale of woe. When we returned with a lovely brown Rhode Island Red hatching hen under our oxter, Mam would be delighted. Then we'd have to tell her all the news from the neighbours.

I loved those visits to the neighbours. Not only did you procure the desired hatching hen but you were always treated to something nice, like orange and cake or lemonade and biscuits, and sometimes a few pence besides. Those women—Kate Horgan, Mary Horgan, Síle O'Connor, Bridie Horgan, Nell Tangney, Mary O'Sullivan, Nellie Mangan, Nora O'Shea, Eileen Grady and Julia Mangan—were lovely, kind women who always loved to see us coming in and always gave us a *céad míle fáilte*. They enjoyed our visits, too. I remember old Bridie Horgan often turning to her husband, Tim, and saying, 'Isn't he gas? God bless the small boy,' after I'd made some comment or other.

Along with Mam's gaggle of birds, we also kept a goat for a while. When the goat was tipping (i.e. ready to mate), we had to find a puck goat. The only puck goat was away up in the top of Cockhill, where it lived with its two owners. They were probably harmless, but we were scared stiff of them. None of us was brave enough to take the goat to the puck. Eventually, my brother Pádraig said he'd go, but only if I'd go with him. So off we went, marching our puck goat miles up the hill. When we approached the household, we did so with great trepidation. But as it was obvious we weren't up to mischief and as Pádraig spoke very politely, we were very well received—to our surprise. The job was done and we returned home very satisfied with ourselves. When they saw all was well, the other lads were sorry they hadn't come with us. The trip had a successful outcome, too, as a few months later the goat gave birth to triplets—three beautiful kids that brought us great joy.

We also kept pigs for a while. I remember a pig being killed outside the kitchen window. His eerie screeching could be heard in the next world. The pigmeat was salted and stored in a barrel and we had great meat for a long time. The nicest of all, though, was the home-made pudding. It was delicious. For good measure, Brian made a football out of the pig's bladder and so many a great evening's entertainment came from that pig—after a good feed on its meat. We also had cats and dogs, but our favourite of all was Kitty, the ould mare. She was so quiet. I remember as a small child climbing up her tail, walking between her legs, hanging off her neck, but she never complained. She was with us for a long, long time. The day Daddy told us he was taking Kitty to town to sell her because she was getting too old, we were very, very sad. But then, it would have been worse to watch her die on the farm, which my father knew was inevitable. If a dog is a man's best friend, a good horse isn't far behind.

Many visitors to our area commented on the bogs surrounding the farmland. I don't have the same longing, sentimental view of the bog as most people do. The work was too hard: cutting with the *sleán* all day; throwing it out on the bank; an odd sod falling into one of the numerous pools of water at the edge of the bank, then trying to retrieve it, but it being so soft and wet it would break in two and fall in again just as you were about to throw it on the bank; spreading the sods out on the bank; coming back to turn it; 'footing' it, reeking it, drawing it home; and putting it into the shed or making a reek of it outside. It was hard on the back, I can tell you. I found the bog very off-putting; dull purple heather everywhere, cold winds blowing and occasionally having to go 'bogging'—the worst of all scourges—when the trailer or horse sank in very soft ground. It was a big operation to free the cart or the horse. In fact, the only good thing about the bog was teatime. Mam would send me off to a nearby well—of which there were plenty—for a gallon of water. Then the men would light a fire, boil the kettle and have what is now called a picnic. After hard physical work, there's nothing nicer than a picnic, although once or twice a year is quite enough.

When you live in a small farming community, as ours was, your neighbours are very important to you. They are the people you turn to for help in all matters and you come to rely on them. We were very lucky in our neighbours—they were a great collection of characters. I was about ten years old when a new neighbour came amongst us. He was Johnny Friel, a real cool man with his own unique style. He became great friends with my father. He smoked a pipe and had a habit of repeating everything—'She won't do, Pádraig, I say, Pádraig, she won't do,' he'd say to my father. He was a very good farmer and made a great job of his own farm. He and my father often bounced ideas off one another.

Our next-door neighbours were Dan and Kate Hogan. Dan was a most amazing man. He smoked a pipe and always wore a hat, a brown hat. Nothing in the world worried Dan. He never planned for tomorrow and took it right easy for today. He left his cattle wander all over his farm—and often into ours, too. We all enjoyed his laid-back approach. At that time if you hadn't the potatoes set by the time the first cuckoo arrived, you were ridiculed by the community at large. One year Dan didn't have the manure out, not to mind the ploughing and the setting done. Himself and a neighbour were putting out the dung for the spuds when who should start singing in the bushes nearby, only the cuckoo. Knowing full well the stigma attached to same and what the neighbours would say when they heard of it, Dan shouted in the direction of the cuckoo, 'God blast you over there, you oul' bitch!' Naturally, the neighbour who was helping him told everybody and we all had a good laugh, but in reality there was no cuckoo, only one of the neighbours pretending to be one!

Even storms didn't put a stir on Dan Horgan. One day my father and a great friend of his who often worked with us, Liam Murphy (who later emigrated to Chicago), had just secured a shed on our farm when Daddy heard Dan's wife calling. 'Pádraig, Pádraig, the roof is lifting off our house,' she cried. My father and Liam ran over quickly. Sure enough, the whole roof was lifting off their stone-and-mortar house. Liam and my father drove a bar into the wall, close to the ground, then tied a rope onto the timber beam and tied it down firmly. It did the trick. But did Dan do anything about securing the roof when the storm abated? Not at all. He was quite happy with the handiwork of Liam and Dad and just left things as they were.

If Dan was lackadaisical, his wife Kate was meticulous. She was a fine woman, who also happened to be my godmother. Kate was a great cook or, more specifically, a great baker. She made a special cake of eggs and some other ingredients and it was the nicest I have ever tasted. It looked a bit like a Madeira cake. Indeed, to this day, every time I go to a club opening or a function and I see Madeira cake, I always take a slice, in the hope that it'll be as good as Kate's. It's been a fruitless search so far; in forty years no cake has even come close to Kate's special recipe.

I remember my third birthday well. Brian, Mary, Pádraig and Lar were at school when Kate arrived with a brown corduroy suit for my birthday. I sat at the top of the table, looking like a young prince. Kate and Dan didn't have much money (nobody did then), but somehow she had managed to buy that suit for me.

In many ways Kate was the exact opposite to Dan. She was always calling for him, and even got a whistle for that purpose. Sometimes Dan would get exasperated by her search for him. I might be walking over the boreen with Dan and the next thing you'd hear Kate calling, 'Dan, Dan'. He would shout back, 'I'm coming at my best.' Then he'd turn to me and say, 'Seán, we'll sit down here now, until I smoke my pipe.' Later on, when he'd go back to Kate, he'd have some yarn for her about a cow thieving, or that he'd called into Hannah Connor (my mother) or some such fib to cover his dallying. The pipe and the hat were Dan's trademarks. Even in later years, when he was dying, he insisted on wearing the hat in bed. For all his foibles, he was a tremendous character, was great company and we were all very fond of him. I often think that, with all the hustle and bustle of modern-day life, if we all had a bit more of Dan's carefree approach, we might be better off.

The place you were sure to bump into the neighbours was at the creamery, which was next to the church: the place of worship next to the place of gossip. The creamery opened for business at around 7.30am and finished its day's trading at about 11.00am. Each farmer arrived almost to the exact minute everyday. My family, Mikey Shea, Doe Sullivan and Seán O'Connor were nearly always first there. Dan Horgan was nearly always last. Every Sunday morning, during 9.00am Mass, just at the consecration we would hear Tom Galvin outside saying 'Go on' to the mare on his way to the creamery—it was that predictable!

Later on, when I was older and started going out to dances at night along with my brother Diarmuid, we would be last to the creamery—to the amazement of our neighbours. 'The Kellys last to the creamery! What's coming over the young people, at all?' the old sages would say. My father, who would have been working the night in St Finian's Hospital, wouldn't know anything about our tardiness. He wouldn't have been best pleased either, but it's not easy to get up at 6.00am to milk cows when you only went to bed a few hours before. In our defence, it didn't happen too often.

We knew our area like the backs of our own hands. Growing up in a place like Knockataggle, you got to know every bit of the landscape because it was your whole world. Nearly all our fields had Irish names, we had Páirc an Tobair, Páirc an Luaithe, Páirc na Sceach, Goirtín na Fiche, Gort na Meitheal, Páirc An Uardail, Páirc na Ráibe Lúibín na gCat and Páirc na gCaorach. Dan's fields had names like the Mullach, An Carraigh and Páirc na Crú. Between his land and ours was a tree called 'Jackie's Tree', named after a man called Jackie who used to sit under it to smoke his pipe. It was easy to become part of the landscape in those days, and a lovely way to be remembered, I think.

One of our fields was known as Danny's Meadow. It had an interesting history. Years earlier, a neighbour named Danny couldn't pay the rent he owed to the Land Commission. One night, without warning, the bailiffs came and took away all his cattle. When he awoke the next day, he had nothing—no money and no cattle. My grandfather, Brian Kelly, was the local shopkeeper and auctioneer. Danny went to him with his tale of woe. My grandfather gave him the money to pay the rent. Danny walked all the way into Killarney, got the train to Tralee, where his cattle were impounded, paid his rent and walked his cattle all the way back to Kilcummin—over 20 miles. My grandfather said nothing to anyone about this 'dig-out' and asked for nothing in return. Years later, when Danny's lot had improved somewhat, he insisted on giving a field to my grandfather by way of repayment. Thus it has been known as 'Danny's Meadow' ever since.

My father and Liam Murphy (who now lives in Chicago) spent many a hard day digging drains in Danny's Meadow afterwards, and I well remember coming home from school and being dispatched by Mam to take the tea over to them. The tea was poured into a bottle and wrapped in a wool sock to keep it warm. Daddy and Liam must have longed to see me coming across the fields as digging drains all day is hard, hungry and thirsty work.

Another back-wrenching job was picking stones. When fields were ploughed for re-seeding, all the stones had to be picked out of the ground. You picked them up, put them into a bucket, made little piles of them around the field and drew them away in a cart and trailer later.

I am particularly familiar with the pains of stone-picking. During my second year in St Brendan's ('the Sem'), I got a terrible pain in my side. I went to Winnie, the school matron, who sent me to the doctor.

They could find nothing wrong, but nonetheless sent for my father to take me to see the family doctor. Our GP was a great golfer and wonderful doctor, Dr Billy O'Sullivan.

Dr Billy could find nothing wrong with me either and wondered privately to my father whether I was just looking for a few days off school. He decided not to send me back, all the same, and sent me home with my father. Daddy, not being too pleased with me, decided to give me some work to do. He had just ploughed Gort na Meitheal field and told me to go and pick the stones off it. Mam wasn't very happy with this as she was worried about the pain in my side; I think she alone believed me.

Anyway, I set to work and I remember my father was delighted and greatly surprised when in just two days I had all the stones picked in little heaps, like drumlins, all over that 5-acre field. The pain in my side eased and I returned to the Sem halfway through study on Sunday night. Fr Clifford gave me a big welcome and Lar, in particular, was delighted to see me back again.

For years afterwards that same pain in my side returned occasionally and it bode ill for me. Only for a vigilant doctor—Dr John McCallagh—it might well have killed me. I had what is known as a rumbling appendix. It eventually burst—as it was inevitably going to do—but thankfully it happened when I was in the operating theatre in Cork Hospital in 1992. I was in good hands, the appendix was taken out and I have never looked back since. But what if it had burst while I was picking stones in Gort na Meitheal?

Gort na Meitheal is remembered in our family for another reason, too. My father was the only farmer around who grew turnips and mangolds for winter fodder. It was a lot of work: ploughing, harrowing, drill-making, seed-setting, thinning and harvesting. Thinning, now *that* was the job. There were about 200 long drills in the field and when the plants were about 4–5 inches tall they had to be thinned, so that there was only one plant every few inches. While the thinning was being done, we also weeded the drills to rid them of the straggling plants that threatened to choke the young tubers.

This is where Daddy showed himself at his enterprising best. The Killarney Races were held each July and we all loved to go. Playing on our weakness, my father would offer us twopence per drill to thin the turnips. It worked like a treat. It wasn't unusual for all six brothers to be out at 8.00am, diligently thinning turnips, and it would all be done in time for the races. We were as happy as kings when pay-day came around. The morning of the races, we would all troop off to Killarney with our half-crowns. Mam always went with us because she enjoyed the races, too. Daddy didn't come along, however, as he was either working in Finian's or at home doing farmwork.

A day at the races would have been a luxury too far for any farmer in those days. Aside from the lost hours of work, there was the ever-present danger of cow and sheep thieving. Without any electric fences, it was hard to keep the animals out of meadows. We had one cow that was expert at breaking into good meadow grass. She was a (black) Kerry cow and we called her Thief. You'd constantly be out with your saw to cut bushes to plug the gaps she had made. Even the day of my Confirmation I had to change out of my good clothes and go over to mend some fencing—and it raining into the bargain—and all because Thief had broken into the meadow yet again.

Drawing in the hay, on the other hand, was a pleasant chore because the saved hay smelled beautiful. As we often used tripods, we had to pike hay into the cart and from there into the shed. Our neighbours made wynds, or big cocks, of hay and would sling the wynds along the ground. Mike Mangan, across the valley, was an expert at this. We were envious because he, like the other farmers, had only one piking to do while we had to pike it twice: once into the cart and then into the hayshed. My eldest brother, Brian, was very good at this. He'd take half the wynd with one pike. There was always a great sense of achievement and relief once the hay was stored safely in the hayshed for the winter.

The 'litter' was a different kettle of fish altogether. The 'litter' were rushes my father had cut with the scythe in the course meadow or the bog. It was used for bedding, but because rushes are long and slippery it was hard to fill a load properly. Sometimes he'd get annoyed at us for not filling it properly: 'Keep it out at the edges,' he'd say to us. But it was difficult. I eventually became fairly handy at this, so he'd say, 'Seán, you go up on the trailer and we'll pike it up to you.' But I didn't like rushes too much—no sweet smell like hay, and very slippery.

Nettles were another pain in the arse or, more accurately, a severe sting in the legs and hands. Occasionally the parish priest would send for me and Seamus to weed his garden, which had a lovely array of fruits and vegetables. One day he gave us a half-crown and then left us to our own devices as he had an errand to run. Of course, that meant no nice tea and currant bread, which was a very attractive part of the package. It took us hours to weed the garden and we were mightily stung by the nettles. By the end of it, we were very disgruntled with our lot. Seamus decided a half-crown minus tea and currant cake didn't equal adequate wages. In order to recompense ourselves, he suggested we raid the garden to garner our own 'fruits of labour'. And that we did. The parish priest had beautiful peas—the first time we'd seen them growing—and we ate rakes of them and took more home to our mother. We did likewise with the strawberries, apples and plums, lettuce and onions. We had a feast; I blush to think that Seamus is now a priest—preaching honesty to the masses! Still, at the time we felt justified. The parish priest must have got the message, too, because in future years he stayed around, gave us tea and currant bread and quadrupled the wages. He probably reckoned it was cheaper in the long run than leaving us to our own devices.

We weren't always available to help out the neighbours with their tasks. Lambing and calving are very busy times on the farm, and often threw up unique problems. In those days there were no calving jacks and no telephones to call the vet in an emergency. It was ropes and muscles and thinking on your feet. Sheep were easy enough to handle, although occasionally one would put out the vessel. Lar and I spent many a night watching sheep like that and putting the vessel back in. The biggest problem with sheep was marauding dogs. On a number of occasions we were woken at night by the pitiful cries of the sheep and lambs coming under attack from dogs. It is a most awful sight: a poor sheep destroyed by a dog as she tried to save her young. My father would naturally be furious when this happened, and in the end he bought a gun to shoot the dogs and keep them at bay. After a while people became more vigilant about their dogs and the problem abated.

Dealing with cows having difficult calvings presented a different set of problems. On a bad day, you'd lose both cow and calf. Occasionally the vet would be called for, but often the cow was so long calving that the calf would be dead by the time the vet arrived. If he managed to save the cow, that was a bonus. The very first time we had a Caesarean section carried out on a cow, there was an unexpected repercussion. The cowshed was too dirty to perform the operation there, so it was decided to do it in the kitchen. It was in the middle of the night and the cow had to be knocked out cold. The job was done (the calf was dead, unfortunately) and my mother supplied sheets to keep the cow clean. The sheets, of course, were covered in blood. The vet headed back to Killarney and my parents went back to bed. When they got up a few hours later to milk the cows, the cow was still out cold, so they left her there on the kitchen floor, still wrapped in sheets. They went off to do the milking and other chores, pulling the door shut behind them.

As we were close to the post office, we always got our post early. If there was no one in the house, the postman went in the back door and left the letters on the kitchen table—which he did this morning. The only problem was the cow had recovered and was anxious to get out of the house. In her writhing, she had entangled the sheets around her head and body. Of course, when the postman opened the back door, she bolted straight at him, putting the poor man and his letters flying. He must have gotten an awful fright when he saw this four-legged apparition, wrapped in sheets and covered in blood, heading towards him when he opened the back door. He never said a word about it to my parents, but he never went in the back door again. We are quite convinced he must have thought it was a ghost of some kind!

As well as the odd visit from the vet, the doctor was occasionally called for, too. One night we were out late playing football with the Healys and the O'Sullivans. I was perspiring greatly. We played until it got dark, then I ran home. On the way it started raining and I got a drenching. We didn't have pyjamas then, so when I got home I hopped straight into bed, the body hot from sweat and the shirt wet from rain. My parents were already in bed, otherwise I would have been made to change and cool down before going to bed. As it was, I got pneumonia for my troubles. My temperature was dangerously high and I went deaf. My grandmother was called for first, then, when they realised how serious it was, the doctor.

Dr Billy arrived and promptly told me turn around for an injection in the bum. I didn't hear him, of course. 'Are you stupid or stubborn?' he said crossly. I didn't hear him, but my grandmother did. She flew at him. 'The boy is neither stupid or stubborn,' she lectured, 'he's deaf and you should know that. After all, you are the doctor. In fact, he's a very bright boy,' she added for good measure. Very few would have spoken to Dr Billy like that, but he took her point and spoke louder to me. I turned around and received my injection, after which he sent me straight to hospital: the Isolation unit in Killarney.

I enjoyed my stay in the hospital. The nurses and Dr Billy were very nice to me and every night my father brought me a little comic, which I loved, especially one about a dog named Lassie. I recovered to full health and never contracted pneumonia again, even though my poor mother still worries if I get a cough or a cold.

The other time I stayed in hospital in my youth was when I had to get some teeth pulled out. There were no toothbrushes then and thanks to the neighbours' sweets when I went on hatching-hen missions and other errands, my teeth had become rotten. I suffered hugely from the pain. I used to lie on the sofa and cry my eyes out, kicking and screaming. I think the combination of being so young and having so many bad teeth convinced my parents it needed more than a trip to the dentist. Like the calving cow, it was felt I should be knocked out properly. I was petrified about this prospect as I had heard stories of people going under an anaesthetic and never recovering. Early one morning my father brought me in to hospital. As I was leaving the house, I went into all my brothers and my sister, Mary, who were still in bed, woke them up, shook hands with them and said goodbye. I was certain I was going to die during the operation and never see them again. Thankfully, the dentist did a good job and it was a great relief to me, and to the entire family, when I didn't get any more toothaches. Sometime later Lar asked me why I had woken them all up and shook hands with them; I was too embarrassed to tell him the truth.

Relatives

There were the not-so-good times, but of course there were great times as well. One of the best things about the summer was the holidaying visitors, especially our cousins from Dublin. My uncle Seán lived in Blackheath Avenue, Dublin, and he and his wife, Eileen, and their children—Maria, Bríde, Fionnuala, Niamh, Brian, Noreen and Michael—came to Kilcummin every summer (as they still do). We had great fun playing together. We used to make our own swings with ropes tied to sturdy tree branches, with a bag full of hay to sit on to prevent lacerations from the rope. We played all sorts of games and had great fun. (Incidentally, Fionnuala is now married to Enda Kenny, leader of

Fine Gael. When I built my house years later, it was Fionnuala who picked out and ordered the kitchen for me. She did a good job, too, because when I got married a few years afterwards, Juliette thought the kitchen was class!)

My mother used to get great enjoyment out of my cousin Brian. He moved from Dublin down to the Sem for his secondary education. He was often out on the farm with us and developed a Kerry accent—not a bad move for a jackeen! He learned to drive the tractor and went to the creamery. He used to joke with my mother, saying, 'Auntie Hannah is always in good humour,' which had been her reply to him one day when he asked if she was in bad form. But, in truth, my mother was nearly always in good humour. As long as her husband and children were happy, she was happy. I suppose lots of mothers are like that—they forget themselves and give all their loving and worrying to their families.

My mother came from Kilcummin, from Inch, on the eastern side. She was one of the famous O'Connors of Inch, although we rarely used the 'O'—she was known as Hannah Connor mostly. Her family were farmers too and had a fierce reputation for hard work. Once when a local youth was given six months' hard labour in jail for some serious misdemeanour, Finbarr Slattery remarked: 'It wasn't half good enough for him. Six months with the Connors of Inch would put manners on him.'

Yes, the Connors were great workers, and honest workers too. It was always great to visit Inch and be treated royally by Nan and Grandda when they were alive, and then by my uncles Pat and John and their respective wives, Angela and Sheila—or Sheila small Jack, as she was known. They are nearly all dead and gone now, alas. My other uncle, James, and his wife Mary lived and farmed in Baraduf. He was the youngest son and I can remember being at his wedding and enjoying it greatly—it was the first time I saw men drinking pints and women drinking half ones.

Mam had only one sister, Eileen, and as my father had no sisters at all, Eileen was my only aunt. But what an aunt! Herself and her husband, Mick Breen (originally from Abbeydorney, Co. Kerry), lived in Mount Prospect Avenue in Clontarf, in Dublin. The day they arrived each summer was one of great joy. Mam would have everything ready and we seemed to spend an age staring fixedly out the northern window to be first to spot the car, loaded with all our cousins, rounding the corner at Tangney's Cross. We'd have great fun with them once they arrived, driving the sheep, calves, dogs and cats wild and inevitably doing some damage, but nothing too serious. Mick would ask me questions about the MacGillycuddy's Reeks and the height of Carrantouhil, about the Fianna and the Tuatha Dé Danann, while Mam and Eileen exchanged all their news in breathless chat.

Auntie Eileen was a marvellous woman and very generous. Every Christmas a big parcel arrived at the door with something in it for all of us. Considering the size of her own family and all the nephews and nieces on both sides of the Breen household, I don't know how she managed it. But manage it she did. As I said, a marvellous woman. Later, when Lar and I were boarding in St Brendan's, the occasional letter would arrive with a 10-bob note tucked inside. Later again, when I went to Dublin to study to be a teacher, I'd occasionally call to see her. She always had a great welcome for me, saying, 'Well, if it isn't Seán Kelly. Come on in, you're welcome. We thought you had forgotten us. Now, tell me all the news and how are your mother and father? You're all good, thanks be to God.' Then she'd give me advice, 'Seán, go to bed early, now, won't you and keep away from the girls.' Then she'd laugh, and make the tea and on it went.

I also loved spending time with my Uncle Seán Kelly. I was named after him. He had an All-Ireland medal and was a mighty man for the work, too. I enjoyed his company and his advice was always solid. Uncle Seán never bought a car. Everyday he walked or cycled from Clontarf to the GPO, where he worked, and walked or cycled home again in the evening. He played football for the Civil Service and it's said he should have been on the Kerry team a lot earlier, but as he was playing in Dublin the selectors never saw him play. However, with 1953 approaching—the Golden Jubilee of Kerry's first All-Ireland (1903)—Kerry made a huge effort to unearth new talent. Tom Woulfe of 'Ban' fame was involved in the Civil Service club at the time and he told the selectors that a 'Seán Kelly' was well worth a trial. On that Civil Service team at the time was Jack Lynch, the former Taoiseach—lovingly known as 'the real Taoiseach'.

Uncle Seán was picked for Kerry and on match day, when he was going into the dressing room to tog off, who was waiting for him at the gate but the great Jack Lynch. Jack was there specifically to wish Uncle

Seán well, saying, 'You should have been on the Kerry team long ago. You'll do very well.'

Occasionally my father would send for Uncle Seán to play for Kilcummin, especially if an important match was on in the East Kerry Championship (O'Donoghue Cup). When called, Uncle Seán would come down on the mail train on Saturday night. On this particular Saturday, the only other passenger on the train was Jack Lynch, who had just finished his law exams. He told Seán he didn't know whether he'd practice in law or go into politics—the country soon found out which. On that day, Jack was on his way home to play for Glen Rovers, his local club. They both had bikes for the final leg of the journey. The mail train went straight to Cork Station, which meant Uncle Seán had to get off at Mallow and cycle to Killarney. Unfortunately for him, he got a puncture on the way and as it was the dead of night, there was nothing for it but to walk, the bike in tow. At the first sign of dawn he spotted a light in a house near the Cork border and asked the farmer for assistance. The repair kit was produced, the puncture fixed and off he went to Killarney, played the game and headed back to Dublin again. A long haul, but he thought nothing of it.

Uncle Seán made the Kerry team at full-forward, was one of the top scorers in the Championship, got a Sports Star of the Week award and won the All-Ireland with Kerry in 1953. They were there again in 1954, but a great Meath team, with Paddy 'Hands' O'Brien *et al* on board, stole Sam away to the Royal County.

All in all, my childhood days were happy and full of fun with my brothers and sister. We did work hard, but that only made us enjoy our free time and games all the more. And of course, there was football—the first passion of the Kelly household. But the apron strings had to be cut sometime, and for me that heralded the start of my school life and my years at the Sem, in particular.

Primary School

School started for me when I was just three years old. I went there straight after Easter 1955. My birthday is 26 April, or at least, that's what the birth certificate says. Until I actually received a copy of the certificate when I was thirteen or fourteen, we all believed my birthday was 1 May. That was the date we celebrated it for the first twelve years of my life. What's more, my mother's birthday was celebrated on

27 April. Then in 1996 when she and Dad were going to Lourdes, she needed her birth certificate to get a passport. Guess what the birth certificate revealed? Yes, her true date of birth was also 26 April. So I share my mother's birthday. I suppose you could call it a 'Lourdes miracle' that we found out!

Anyway, at the age of three, regardless of when I had the cake and candles, off I trundled to school, with my sister Mary looking after me. I liked the teacher. She was young and good-looking and had a lovely name: Mary Grace. I assumed she was related to Princess Grace. Later, when she went off and got married and told us her name was now Mrs Ryan, I was very disappointed. It didn't sound as good, and sounds are very important to young lads. But she was still gentle and kind and taught us well. Mrs Ryan (Miss Grace) went on to teach in the school for forty-four years, retiring just a few years ago. Years later she told me that my first day at the school was very funny. She asked me to write something on the blackboard. Up I waddled, pulled up my short trousers, got up on my tip-toes and wrote the answer, barely able to reach the blackboard. She had to suppress a smile as she watched me. She taught me for the first three years—Junior Infants, Senior Infants and First Class.

Of course, it was in First Class that boys and girls made their First Holy Communion. My First Communion day was one of the happiest of my life. Dressed in a brand new suit, with the holy medal and badge fastened onto the lapel, I went around the houses and received little gifts everywhere I went—it was heaven as far as I was concerned. After the ceremony I walked to town with Mam and we had a great time. I bought a small football with my Communion money, and to this day I can still see my stampeding brothers racing towards me as I rounded Jackie's Tree, hopping and kicking the ball before me. They came thundering down the boreen and we got hours of entertainment from that football. I think it was the first real football we ever had; it was certainly one of the best investments any child ever made with his Communion money.

Seamus was a year younger than me, so he started school in 1956, the year after me. On his very first day in school I was put into the corner for some misdemeanour or other. My 'punishment' meant standing in the corner of the room, with my back to the class, for as long as the teacher deemed necessary. When I was put into the corner, Seamus didn't like it. There I was, standing in the corner, quietly idling, when he left his desk (the three classes were in one room together), walked up to me and pulled me out of the corner. This was absolutely unheard of! Despite my resistance—naturally afraid that I'd get worse punishment for his bad behaviour—Seamus' persistence won the day and the teacher let me off. For the rest of the day indignant little Seamus insisted on sitting in my desk—a strange case of the 'small' brother minding the 'big' brother.

The Brothers Kelly, like most brothers, were a sticky lot. One day when we were coming home from school a fight broke out. Lar's coat got torn. When we got home Pádraig, who had reached home before us, said we should cut across the bog so that we'd be at the cross before those responsible for tearing Lar's coat reached it. We cut across the bog, following Pádraig. Round two of the fight started in earnest. In boxing parlance, while the Kellys lost Round One, we took Round Two, so you could say the scrap finished in an honourable draw. The best outcome, however, was that very few fights broke out thereafter.

There was no central heating in those days, of course, so each of the three classrooms in our school had a fireplace. If we got wet on the way to school—everyone walked then—the fire was useful for drying and warming our coats before going-home time. But the best value of the fire was for warming the milk or cocoa we brought to school in little glass bottles. Cocoa was a hot favourite at the time: it was mainly Cadbury's when we were growing up, with Fry's being a particular favourite. (The packet had a picture showing a family of kids, all different sizes, lined up in order of size.) All the pupils' bottles were lined up in front of the open fire to be heated for lunchtime. Sometimes a bottle would overheat and explode, much to the delight of us all—except the unfortunate owner, who would have to do without. Over time, though, we got it down to a fine art: one eye on the blackboard and one eye on the row of bottles. At the first sign of boiling a posse of pupils would loudly inform the teacher, the overheating bottle would be moved to the side and the bottle on the outside moved in to give it some extra warming. It was a simple and delicious system!

Each family was expected to supply a rail of turf or a half-ton of coal for the classroom fires. Every family had a turn as the fuel supplier. It was always great to see some pupil's father arriving with a rail of turf. It meant we wouldn't be cold, our bottles of cocoa wouldn't be cold, our clothes wouldn't be wet and, best of all, it meant half-an-hour off school for the bigger boys as they threw the turf into the shed.

The Master would inform you when it was your family's turn to bring in the coal or turf. When our turn came, he duly told us to remind our parents, but we never told our father. Some time later the Master asked why the Kellys weren't bringing any coal or turf to the school and I replied, 'Last year when my father brought in coal, you gave out to him about us, so we didn't want the same happening again.' Naturally, he wasn't too pleased with that response. Indeed he was right because I was being cheeky. We eventually reminded Daddy of our duty and the load of turf arrived in the school; there were no complaints about the Kellys that year.

The Master taught fifth and sixth classes while his wife, Mrs Abina O'Connor, took the second, third and fourth classes. Mrs O'Connor was a first cousin of my father's. She was a very good teacher and very kind and *grámhar*. She used the stick sparingly, which was a blessing. It was a small, triangular-shaped stick and she used to rap your knuckles when you were writing, if you were making a poor show of it. After a while we became experts at anticipating the stroke and withdrawing our writing hand from the page just in time. Mrs O'Connor was also Lar's godmother, so I guess he got away with more than most in her class. Sometimes her daughters, who were trainee teachers, came for a few weeks' practice, which was a great novelty. When they gave us sums or some exercise to do in class, they would have a competition to see who could get the answer first. The lucky winner was rewarded with a sweet, along with a few runner-ups. No doubt those lovely girls arranged it so we all won in the end. 'Twas no wonder we had trouble with toothaches!

There was no organised football at schools level in those days, but we nearly always organised a game amongst ourselves on the school 'pitch'—a sloping field with rows of fir trees around it. Two of those upstanding trees served as the goalposts. We had good fun and developed our fielding and kicking; these were the days before hand-passing. Occasionally, but not too often, a row would break out. One day I got a punch in the temple from a bigger boy. I was knocked out cold, but I recovered. Revenge was exacted on the culprit by two of my brothers, and that put an end to that.

Once a year a challenge game was arranged with one of the other two schools in the parish: Coolick or Annabla. My very first official game of football was a challenge match between Coolick and Kilcummin. The senior, sixth-class boys organised it and picked the team. I remember my brother Pádraig and our neighbour, Tom Sullivan, picking the team. I was delighted when they selected me. Unfortunately, we were well beaten. Coolick had some fine footballers, some of whom went on to be colleagues of mine for many years, including the Healys, the O'Connors, the O'Sullivans and Liam Horan.

For cows and calves summer arrives when they are put out to pasture after the long winter indoors. Usually they go for a few gallops to express their delight at their newfound freedom. In those far-off days, summer arrived for us when we were left out of our shoes or boots—in other words, when we could go barefoot. No more tying of broken laces; the only drawback a few thorns to be plucked out of the soles now and then. Gradually our soft winter skin hardened and the soles of our feet became like leather.

We were barefoot when the road to the village was tarred for the first time. It was very prickly and sticky at first, but after a while it settled down and it was lovely to walk on the tarred sides on warm days. Electricity for the countryside arrived, too. Arriving home from school one day, I saw two men with two horses pulling long poles up to Páirc an Tobar. Soon the poles were upright and the lightbulb entered our lives. A well was dug a short distance from our house, which made trips to the well a thing of the past. Indoor toilets replaced the great outdoors and life moved along, as it always does.

Sixth Class

I had an uncle, Seamus Kelly, now passed on, who owned a chemist's shop in the Mall in Tralee. He also owned a jewellery shop at 2 Denny Street. Uncle Seamus played senior football for Tipperary, junior football for Kerry and for many years was centre half-back for Austin Stack's GAA club. He was a very stylish, but meticulously clean footballer. He was whistled only once for fouling and was very annoyed over it because he maintained the referee was wrong.

Anyway, it was decided that I would attend Tralee Christian Brothers' School (CBS) for sixth class and live with my Uncle Seamus and his wife, Lucy, for the year. It was a big change, but a great change.

For the first time I came face-to-face with 'townies' and, to my surprise, I liked them.

The new CBS had just been built in Clonalour, in Tralee, and that's where I was sent. My classroom was upstairs, the second from the end. The size of my new class amazed me: fifty-two boys and no girls at all. There would hardly have been fifty-two pupils in Kilcummin National School altogether. Brother Griffin was my new teacher and I liked him straight away. Initially, I was overawed by the townies and in the first class test, in November, I finished forty-eighth. At Christmas I had edged up to twenty-ninth place, I claimed twelfth by Easter, and by the summer I was listed in fifth place: a good achievement.

The best thing about the CBS, however, was the football. The Christian Brothers have often been credited with making the GAA, and rightly so. There were a few stalwarts in every school, and ours was no exception. Brother Dooher, in particular, was a great lover of sports. There was one young layteacher, Mícheál Hayes, who was a genius. He was about thirty years ahead of his time and, along with the late James Hobbart, he made Austin Stacks the best GAA club in Ireland. Stacks was built from the bottom up, from the primary school, and Mícheál Hayes was pivotal to that far-sighted approach. They trained the boys regularly and took them away on football weekends. The three O'Keeffes, Timmy Sheahan, Tommy Kenington and Fergal Dillon were 'big' names then, even though they were only eleven or twelve years old.

At this time Denis O'Sullivan was one of the big football stars in Tralee. He was playing with Kerry and his late brother, Albert, became a great friend of mine. We used to kick around together while they were training. Denis played for Kerins O'Rahilly's, as did the great John Dowling, former Kerry footballer and All-Ireland winning captain in 1955.

The late John Kissane was the main underage organiser in Strand Road (other name for Kerins O'Rahilly's). The town under-14 league was starting and John asked me if I would like to play for O'Rahilly's. It was like asking a fellow would he like to be a millionaire. Next to my Holy Communion day, it was the best day of my life.

Playing for the club of Denis O'Sullivan and John Dowling was a supreme honour for a small 'blow-in' from the country. What's more, we would be playing against Austin Stacks. I was absolutely amazed when I saw the crowd at the game; even John Dowling and Denis

O'Sullivan were there. I wouldn't have been surprised by this if I was from Tralee, as then I would have known that John Dowling never missed a game for O'Rahilly's, be it challenge, league or championship, underage or adult. I can't even remember who won the match, although I think we did. Now if I were a true blue, born and reared, I'd say Rahilly's definitely did. But honestly, I can't remember. However, I do remember scoring a goal in the second-half—a pure fluke. I got the ball about 20 yards out, kicked as hard as I could for a point, didn't reach the target and it dropped short into the net. Some knowledgable Tralee folk said I'd 'lobbed' the goalie. I hadn't a clue what they meant. I remember that when we were togging off afterwards, John Dowling came over to us saying, 'Where's that small boy that scored that great goal?' and then he added, 'Any boy that scores a goal against those bloody Stacks so-and-so's deserves an ice cream.' He put his hand in his pocket and pulled out a shilling. Manna from heaven; the seal of approval from god.

I bought the ice cream and devoured it. It reminded me of the very first ice cream I had ever eaten. That had been at the creamery in Kilcummin one day, when my father went in for some farm supplies. Another Kerry footballer, Gerald O'Sullivan, was the creamery manager. Gerald was talking to my father and then said, 'Hold on a minute, I must get something for those two boys.' At that time ice cream was sold in three different sizes: 2d, 4d and 6d. Gerald brought my brother and I two 6d ice creams. I tell you, nothing ever tasted so sweet. Gerald O'Sullivan: a great man and a great footballer.

On this auspicious day, John Dowling had done something similar. I never forgot it. Many years later when I was preparing to marry my wife, Juliette, I said to her, 'I must get the shoes for our wedding in John Dowling's shoe shop in Tralee.' And I did. But the story doesn't end there. When I reminded John why I wanted to buy the shoes in his shop, he said to Juliette, 'When ye are married and have a son, send him in to me because I want to give him his first pair of football boots.' And so it came to pass. Our young Pádraig's first football boots were supplied by John Dowling—again, no charge. What a man!

I often think no man loved the GAA more than John Dowling. He loved Kerry and he loved Kerins Rahilly's. He used to get dreadfully upset when they were beaten. He told me once that anytime Rahilly's were beaten, he would go home and say to his wife, 'Leave me alone, leave me alone, don't say a word, don't come near me,' and then he'd go to his room for hours, until he'd come up with some idea as to how matters could be improved in the future. When Eoin 'Bomber' Liston took O'Rahilly's from being perpetual also-rans to win the County Championship in 2003, the first time in forty-five years, it would have been better than all the gold in the world to the great John Dowling.

Years later, after John had died, we started a Munster Senior Club League. AIB sponsored the competition. Pat Healy of AIB, and also chairman of Strand Road, came to me with the suggestion that the Cup for the new competition be called after John Dowling. I was honoured to agree. No better club man; no better county man; no better man.

It was in Tralee that I began to play handball with a friend of mine, Francis Griffin. I often stayed in his house and discovered the great world of comics—*Roy of the Rovers* and his soccer exploits. I never heard of soccer until *Roy of the Rovers* came along with his brilliant goals. His equal has not been found since and never will; eat your heart out Pelé, Maradona and Best!

A few doors up the street on Strand Road was a boxing club, run by, I think, Ollie Brown. I joined that too and it was a very worthwhile exercise. In the pre-knife and pre-gun era, all disputes were settled with the fist. Ollie's sessions prepared us well for this and I fought a few rounds with boys my own weight, which is a very good system. Years later Jimmy McGee, the celebrated RTÉ commentator, told me an Irishman by the name of Seán Kelly, boxing under the pseudonym Jack Dempsey, won a world boxing title. I can assure you, Jimmy, it wasn't me, but if I had stayed in Tralee much longer, you'd never know where my boxing career might have taken me!

Another boy I became very friendly with at that time was Ger Power. Occasionally I stayed with a Mrs Crowe, who lived next-door to the Powers. I spent a lot of time in Powers' house. Mrs Power and Jackie Power were very kind to me and I became very attached to them. Jackie, who one of the best hurlers of all time, was a great character. Ger and I used to race to school and I still tell him I used to beat him. Imagination is a great thing. Ger usually replies, 'You did, yeah, you Kilcummin All Star.'

At the end of my year in sixth class I sat the entrance exam for the Sem and both Lar and I were accepted. While I was getting on fine academically, I was way too young, too small and too giddy and immature to be mixing with lads much older than me. Moss Keane makes the same point in his book. Now, if a giant like Moss felt it disadvantageous to be in a class with boys older than him, what chance had a pipsqueak like me? Football was the first obvious disadvantage, but as Peig Sayers rightly remarked in her autobiography, 'Is mór an crua ar leanbh bliain' 'A young person matures a lot in a year'. Besides, I liked Tralee. Another year with the Christian Brothers, with the Kerins Rahilly's, with the boxing club and the racing Powers would have done me the world of good. It wasn't to be, however. At that time most boys went into seventh class, and from there to secondary school. I think I was the only boy to go straight into secondary school out of sixth class. It was out of the CBS and into the Sem for me.

St Brendan's College, Killarney

Ever since I can remember, I always wanted to go to St Brendan's College in the town of Killarney. The 'Sem' was equally famous for football and learning. Founded in 1860 as a seminary to prepare young boys for the priesthood, it was primarily a boarding school that was set up, and mostly funded, by the Diocese of Kerry. My grandmother, Maria Kelly, always spoke fondly of it and from the time I was in the womb, there was going to be no other secondary school for me.

At that time priests and brothers were sent out to schools, and indeed homes, to recruit young boys for their religious orders. Thus Pádraig opted to go to Castletown to join the De La Salle order, while a few years later Seamus joined the Presentation Brothers. He subsequently decided he wanted to be a priest, not a Brother, and switched allegiance to the Missionaries of the Sacred Heart. When the orders' representative came to our house, my mother asked me would I like to go. I replied immediately in the negative, saying, 'I'm going to the Sem.'

Of course, wanting to go to the Sem and going there were two different things. There was the little matter of an entrance exam, for starters. Places were limited, especially for boarders. As there was no school transport in those days, and despite the fact that Kilcummin village is only about 4 miles from Killarney town, the plan was that the Kellys would board at the school. Brian, the eldest brother, had been a boarder, Pádraig was at Castletown, so it was now Larry's turn to sit the entrance exam. Even though I was over a year younger than him and a class below, I did the entrance exam as well. We both got accepted and so we were off to the Sem in September 1964, even though I was only twelve years of age.

I quickly realised that not only was I the youngest boy in the Sem, I was also the smallest and the lightest. A few days after arriving we were weighed, measured and examined by the school doctor, Dr Leahy, a lovely, gentle man. The school matron was in charge of operations. She was known as 'Winnie' or, when well out of earshot, as 'Winnie the Pooh'. She was a tiny, thin woman, probably around 4' 4" tall, but she was very elegant and intelligent. She spoke through her nose with a 'grand' accent. 'You are very small,' she said to me, 'only 4' 6" and you are very light, only 6 stone.' I was going to say, 'I am bigger than you anyway', but thought better of it. Over the years we got to know and like her very much and we all developed a soft spot for 'Winnie'. She took good care of us whenever we were sick and had to go to the infirmary, so much so that it wasn't unusual for fellows to swallow a bar of soap or a tube of toothpaste so that they could spend a day or two in the 'infir'. It rarely worked because Winnie was not fooled easily. 'You have no temperature,' she'd say, 'go back to class. Your parents are paying good money to have you educated and you pretending to be sick, you scoundrel.'

Boarding schools were tough institutions in those days. They were certainly no place for over-sensitive souls. Some boys were dreadfully unhappy, some ran away home, while others never returned after the summer holidays. Most of us survived, however, and the Sem made men of us. It's little wonder that many who survived went on to have highly successful careers in the world at large. At one stage, three secretaries of government departments were Sem boys and known in government circles as the Kerry Mafia—Paddy Teahan, Michael Dowling and Tim Dalton. Denis Brosnan, who created Kerry Group, was a Sem boy, as were some of the top surgeons, professors and clerics in the country—not to mention the great footballers it produced.

Eamonn Stack, later Chief Inspector with the Department of Education and Science, was Head Prefect during my second year in St Brendan's. He saved me from expulsion one day. Being 'expelled' was an umbrella term that covered the territories now covered by 'suspension' and 'expulsion'. It was the worst fate that could befall a student. If you were expelled, a stigma was attached to you forever more—or so we thought at the time. Your parents would be ashamed of you. It was not uncommon for parents to keep an expelled son indoors so that the neighbours wouldn't see him for the entire period of suspension— usually a period of two weeks or more, or until the end of term. The errant son wouldn't even be allowed to go to Mass, which was a grave sin in those days.

My own brother, Brian, was expelled once. He committed the cardinal error of leaving the grounds without permission. He went down town to get a football (or so he told us) and got the boot instead. Paudie O'Shea was expelled for good, but he never forgot or forgave. So, Brian, at least you're in good company!

I was nearly expelled for a very different offence. The then President of the school, Fr Moynihan—known to us as 'Johnny Boss', or 'Johnny Birdook' (that's how it was pronounced anyway)—introduced drill to the school. An army man was in charge of this dreaded ritual. What made drill reprehensible altogether was that it took place after school, between 4.00pm and 5.00pm, which was the only free time we had. When we wanted to be out playing football, we had to do blasted drill for an hour, which comprised jogging, running and marching around in never-ending circles. Not surprisingly, fellows started to duck out of it, using a wild variety of concocted excuses. If you weren't legitimately excused, invention took over. There was a row of trees near the monastery side of the grounds. Fellows would duck behind the trees and scoot when the drill-master's back was turned. It worked for a few lads the first day, but as the numbers marching dwindled ever further, the drill man copped on and went straight for the President. Johnny Boss called us all together and lectured us on the value of drill and the competence of the drill-master, and issued a severe warning that any fellow who ducked drill would be expelled on the spot.

Drill day came around again the following Thursday. I asked if I could go play football instead. The reply, 'No', was both answer and explanation. On that day, drill was tougher than ever. As if in punishment, we had to do all sorts of exercises and march like a crowd of 'Hitler youths'. A few brave souls ducked behind the trees and escaped undetected. 'Next time round, I'm going too,' I said to myself as I heard the *thwack* of the leather in the football field. I timed it perfectly, as I thought. We were walking backwards, then the shout went out, 'Forward march', we all marched forward. 'Now jog.' This was the moment of opportunity. I made a dash for the sanctity of the great sycamore, but just at that moment, like a cat sensing a mouse, the captain turned around. He was already in foul humour as some boys had been calling him names and farting from the safety of the back of the group, but he couldn't identify them. I could have told him that Horace, Vin the Grin, Jack Butt and Big Tough Jim were largely responsible, but no one would have told him that.

I was caught red-handed. Drill was abandoned for the day and I was frogmarched up to Johnny Boss' presidential room. In went the captain and out came Johnny, wearing his trademark long, black soutane, his hands clenched firmly together in front of him, his face ashen with anger. He uttered the immortal words, 'You're expelled, Boss.' (He called everyone Boss, so everyone called him the same.) 'Get your belongings and I'll take you home at twenty minutes past five.'

Word spread through the school. Expulsion was like an explosion: everyone heard it almost instantly. So too did the Head Prefect, Eamonn Stack. He said, 'This is ridiculous,' and with great courage went to plead my case with the President. I doubt if anyone else would have had the presence of mind or the courage to face Johnny Boss, but Eamonn did. His pleading didn't fall on deaf ears either, but I wasn't to know that for some time.

The clock showed 5.15pm. All the students went off to study and I was left all alone, waiting at the President's car. At the appointed time of 5.20pm—he was never a second late—Johnny Boss arrived, still dressed all in black, but without the soutane. 'Get in, Boss,' he ordered. My heart sank. How could I face home? What shame would forever more be associated with me and my family? How would my two uncles, who were priests in the diocese, face their confrères again? I thought of the 1916 leaders and how they must have felt as they were led to the execution yard. The difference was that they had died in glory; my fate was to live in shame. Then I thought of Ned Kelly, the great Australian outlaw, and his mother's final words to him as he awaited execution. She told him to be brave and 'die like a Kelly'. But I was no Ned Kelly. I was no Pádraig Pearse. I was a Kelly alright, but not worthy of the name. I was a coward who ducked out of drill and got caught. But it wasn't such a big sin, was it? Perhaps not. People would not remember the cause, no, they would remember the expulsion, the stigma, the shame. I was so upset, I could barely hold back the tears.

When Johnny Boss turned right for the town instead of left for Kilcummin at the top of High Street (it was a two-way street then), I didn't take much notice. When he stopped at Dicko's shop and went in to buy something, I assumed it was a personal matter, probably cigarettes. But when he continued on down Main Street, up the Port Road and back into the Sem, I was perplexed. For a fleeting moment I thought he was going to collect my brother, Lar, and expel him too, to get shut of the Kellys altogether. But then he pulled his car right into his garage, handed me the packet and said, 'Go to study, Boss, and don't miss drill any more.' I was so delighted, shocked and surprised that I could scarcely say 'Thanks'. The packet contained two bars of chocolate. I skeltered up the stairs and into the study hall, to be greeted by an instantaneous burst of applause. They all felt that justice had been done, thanks to a great Head Prefect and a fair-minded President. I didn't have to worry about missing drill again either, because 'Fr Johnny Boss', probably having investigated further, put a stop to it altogether. We gladly returned to what came naturally to us between 4.00pm and 5.00pm: football.

I had learned my lesson, though, and never came close to expulsion again. Even though I was very young and small, I was lucky to escape most of the 'rutting', i.e. slaps of the cane, which was commonly meted out because I was useful academically. Others were not so lucky, and learning by rote reams of information did not come easily to them. I used to feel sorry for some as they got rutted (caned) so often. If you knew the answer to a question and your classmate didn't, you'd try to prompt him. There was a good friend of mine, Noel Kerrisk from Killarney, who was more interested in horses and betting and smoking than he was in study, but he was fierce nice. He sat near me for a year or two and although I was a boarder and he a 'day boy', we got on great and are still good friends. In the morning he'd 'cog' (copy) whatever exercise I had done and in class I'd try to prompt him. Whenever I prompted him correctly and he escaped a few ruts, he'd say 'Thanks, Kell, you're a genius, Kell,' and if he had had a successful gamble the day before, he would produce a few sweets under the desk.

Sometimes the class would be wild and you would get 'rutted', or even thrown out of class for a while. Being thrown out wasn't too bad. It was the possibility of being caught by Johnny Boss that was the danger. I remember being thrown outside the door one day and who should come along the corridor but El Presidento—Johnny Boss. He gave me a right going-over as he wigged the hair just above the ear, and I copped onto myself afterwards, well, for a while anyway.

We did all our subjects through Irish then, and we managed fine. I liked all subjects except French, which had just been introduced to the school. The teacher went much too fast at the beginning of the year, so those of us who were beginning raw lost touch with 'Jacques Méchant'. It told in our exams as well. I remember when the Intermediate (now called the Junior Certificate) results came out. While I did pass French, it was over 100 marks behind my next worst subject. I wanted to give it up for the Leaving Certificate and continue Science, but there was no Honours Science class. I asked Mr Eoin Carra, the Science teacher, could I sit in on the Pass class and do Honours on my own. Being the gentleman that he was he didn't say no, but he advised against it. I stayed with the French, but at the end of fifth year the teacher departed and we were left high and dry. We finished up taking up Applied Maths instead, and doing the course in one year. I loved it—anything but French. We all got on grand with the Applied Maths, despite losing some valuable weeks around Easter due to a teachers' strike.

Many of the problems and fights we had in the Sem centered around grub. It was Spartan and scarce. All 200 of us boarders ate in the refectory—indeed, our lives seemed to be spent in 'orys': dormitory, refectory and oratory. The morning bell went at 7.15am to call us for Mass in the oratory at 7.30am. Sometimes some sleepy-heads would try to go back to bed or would defiantly stay there, causing ructions if they were caught by the priest in charge, who 'rutted' them out of it. There were a lot of priests in the Sem then, and they'd nearly all say Mass in the cathedral. This was before Bishop Eamonn Casey renovated it and removed most of the side-altars. There were several side-altars, so there was a rota for each priest to serve Mass at each altar. Of course, the Mass was in Latin then, so you had to know *Dominus vobiscu* and *et cum spiritu tuo*.

The breakfasts after Mass were predictable and basic. You knew in advance what you were going to get everyday: for breakfast it was cornflakes, tea, white bread and butter. It never changed. Dinners, on the other hand, were a mixed bag. Some you'd like, some not. The ones you did like, you tried to accumulate or trade-off for some other dish. If swapping failed, you tried playing a fellow in handball for Sunday dessert (apple and custard), for Tuesday and Thursday main course (sausages) or for breakfast (a bowl of cornflakes), or for the minced meat on Wednesday, known as 'cowpie'.

There was one lad who, between bartering and handball, was able to accumulate thirty-four sausages on Tuesdays and Thursdays. The trouble was that you had to go around the tables and collect your dues. That meant you had to time your collection so that Johnny Boss, in particular, didn't catch you. The priests supervised mealtimes in rotation, but I don't think they minded too much—not as much as Johnny Boss at any rate. Anyway, the 'sausage boy' went on his rounds one day and collected all thirty-four sausages. He turned for home, when who should he bang into but the same Johnny Boss. Sausages went skittering, gravy splashed all over the President's soutane, and he was not a happy man. Catching the sausage boy by the hair just above the left ear and wigging it furiously, he ordered, 'Pick them up and eat them, Boss!' So he did, all thirty-four of them, despite some being rightly squeezed by the shoes of some delighted and pitiless boys.

A big boy, usually a Prefect, sat at the head of the table of the junior cycle tables. He controlled the table and divided the grub. Most were very fair and each got his just share. One year, however, Lar and I were unlucky to be at the table of a big hungry guy who kept most of the food for himself and two of his pals. The rest of us were being slowly starved. We couldn't do a whole pile about it, though. I even discussed with one boy, Michael Foley from Killorglin, who was big into Science, the possibility of making an incendiary device to blow up our tormentor. Our plan was well past the initial stages when it was rendered redundant, thanks to the great John O'Keeffe, holder of seven All-Ireland medals. He was in our class and, luckily, also at our table— Kelly and O'Keeffe being very close in the alphabet. For all his strength and power, Johno wouldn't have hurt a fly. In fact, in all his years playing football, he never hit anyone a dirty belt and never retaliated. He was the same in school—except for this one day. Our greedy, grumpy gazelle at the top of the table was doing his usual division of the spoils—'one for you and two for me, two for me and none for you'—when we started remonstrating with him. He challenged Johno to have it out in the alleys afterwards. Johno was probably reluctant to fight, but with starvation facing us for the rest of the year, he sprinted into battle. At the appointed time they squared up to one another. In no time Johno had hammered the living daylights out of the gazelle, to immense cheers from the starving masses. Suffice to say we hadn't another bit of bother for the rest of the year. With one belt of his fist, Johno had fed the starving urchins of St Brendan's.

As well as being our saviour at the dining table, Johno was by far and away the best footballer in our year. He was also the best handballer, golfer, swimmer and sprinter. Later he became the first man to captain a Kerry college to win the Hogan Cup when the Sem clinched that sweet victory in 1969. His star-studded adult career began with Kerry. I remember it well. Before the Leaving Cert. results came out he was picked to play for Kerry in a challenge against Westmeath in Killorglin. He never looked back. He and I were together in St Brendan's, together in St Pat's, Drumcondra, together in UCD and together again in St Brendan's as teachers before he went back to Tralee CBS, where he still teaches PE. During all his years as full-time teacher, he has always trained teams outside school hours. Neither victory nor defeat changed his commitment. He trained Kerry and managed Ireland. Yes, without a doubt he is one of Ireland's greatest sportsmen, a football immortal who never used his fist in anger—well, only once. Oh, thank God for that once. Once was enough. Thank God for King Johno.

Two of the best days of the school year were 8 December, the Feast of the Immaculate Conception, and 16 May, St Brendan's Day. Why? Grub again. On those days we got a four-course meal, and plenty of it. We looked forward to those feasts for weeks and they sustained us for months.

St Brendan's Day was also Sports Day, the day when fellows who might not have been great footballers could excel. There were some great performances from the likes of Philip J. McLouglin, Micheál Ó Sé, Barry Hanly, Roibeard Ó Dwyer, Ger O'Keeffe and that man again, King Johno. Moss Keane threw the hammer almost as far as Currow. I won my first medal in the Sem sports; I think I finished third in the mile race. The trophies were presented in the 'refec' after tea and it could have been Olympic gold, such was my delight. They are the days we'll always remember, when the few bad ones are forgotten.

At that time nearly all the teachers in the Sem were priests. There were only a few lay teachers. The most senior of these was Dr Tadhg McCurtain, an uncle of the great Cork hurler, Dermot McCurtain.

Tadhg had no interest in football or hurling, however. He even rang me one night in the middle of the Sunday game, which featured Cork's All-Ireland win that day, in which his nephew was playing. When I went back to the Sem as a teacher and he'd see us heading off to play a football match, Tadhg would say, 'Kelly, I see you are going mud-larking again.'

For all that, though, he had a heart of gold, would ensure your classes were covered and took a keen interest in your affairs. He did tax returns free of charge for me and for many more. He was always giving me good advice and was very anxious that I would marry well. Once, when I brought a good-looking girl from Killarney to the Sem Ball and she wore a low-cut dress, Tadhg took one look at her and said to me, 'Drop her, she's not your type'! Tadhg lived for the Sem, taught Maths and Science and when he retired the school authorities very kindly kept him involved.

Another layman was Noel O'Sullivan, who, like Tadhg, was a Corkman who taught me and taught with me. Sadly he died one morning in the classroom, at the young age of fifty-two. When we were students Noel had started class football leagues, which generated huge interest. Staff and students used to come out to see them. A teacher managed each team. One day I scored two goals in the first half on a tall, gangly boy twice my size. I heard Noel admonishing him at half-time, saying, 'You big fostuk, you, that small squirt has scored two goals on you. One more mistake and you're coming off.' When we were in fifth year, Noel organised for us to go out to *céilís* in Loreto girls' school. We were like young bulls left loose in a paddock full of heifers! It didn't last too long, unfortunately. Apparently the nuns caught a boy and girl kissing in the cloakroom when they should have been doing the Siege of Ennis, and that was the end of the *céilís*. These things have a funny way of coming full circle. Noel's son, Noel Patrick, whom I taught, is now teaching my daughter, Julie, and like his Dad he is great at music, too.

As the years have gone by, more and more lay teachers came on board and now out of over forty staff, there is no priest; the last, An tAthair Seosamh Ó Beaglaoi—*ardfhear eile*—going out to parish duties in 2007, ironically as parish priest of Kilcummin. Many people didn't realise, or certainly didn't realise then, that very few priests went for the priesthood in order to finish up teaching. For many, I'd say it was their worst nightmare. Not alone had they to teach but they had to give up half their wages to run the school and most had to take turns at supervision of refectories, dormitories, etc, which ate into their extra-curricular time. The hardest job of all for the clerics, however, was that of Dean. My own brother Lar did it for over twenty years. Lar is tough, though, and would never complain. He was one of the few who could really handle the job and not let it get him down.

The Dean has to be in constant touch with the students. It isn't a total exaggeration to say that the students' quality of life and happiness are very dependent on the Dean of the day. For my time in Brendan's, I was very lucky that Dr Dermot Clifford, now Archbishop of Cashel and Emly, was Dean. Some got on his wrong side and probably didn't like him because he could be fiery and wasn't afraid to challenge you or administer punishment, if he deemed it necessary. Nevertheless, he was a reforming Dean with a great zest for life, bundles of energy and a brilliant brain. He wasn't tied to the old ways and tried to improve the lot of students. For example, when we were in a football final in first year, the Dean said the footballers should leave his class early to be 'mentally prepared' for the impending encounter. I felt 6ft tall walking out in front of those who weren't playing. I had never heard of 'mentally prepared' before and I hadn't a clue what it meant. I assumed it had something to do with the mental hospital, which was nearby, and that getting mad was good preparation for a game—which it probably is, come to think of it.

Dermot, or Archbishop Clifford as he is now, also organised fantastic day trips for all the boarders. We had splendid days out when we climbed Mangerton Mountain, saw the Devil's Punch Bowl, walked through the magnificent Gap of Dunloe, up through telephone mast-free Black Valley and visited all the other world-famous beauty spots at our doorstep. It's a fair bet to say that only for the Dean, most would never have enjoyed the experience. He also organised day trips to Dublin, where we visited Kilmainham Jail, the National Museum, the Dáil and Croke Park. After night prayer on Sundays in the oratory he would read out a witty poem, composed by himself, satirising in a very humorous way the events of the previous week and the world at large. He put on plays and concerts. I had a part in *Big Maggie* once, which was performed in the Árus Phádraig, but I got sick the week before and lost out on a great career on stage! He also wrote his own novelty acts for school concerts. I had a part in one such. The first line of my piece is one I can never forget: 'Of all the diseases that go about, The worst of all is the foot and mouth.'

'Cliff', as we called him, had a soft spot for me. It was fated then, I suppose, that we finished up together: he as Patron and I as President of the GAA.

The Way of Things

Some interesting customs flourished in the Sem. Boarders were grouped according to their districts or baronies. Those groupings were called 'columns'. As Lar and I were the only boarders from Kilcummin, we didn't know whether we belonged to the Firies (west of Kilcummin) column or to the Rathmore (to the east) column; we were in no-man's-land. 'Columns' protected their own and rallied to their members' cause, especially if a fight broke out. It also provided a very useful method for integrating first years, who were universally called 'plebs', into the school and offering them some sense of security.

There was one custom that no 'pleb' could escape: baptism. This usually involved the bigger lads catching a young lad and putting his head under the tap until he was drowned wet. Some unlucky guys were 'baptised' by having their heads stuck into the toilet bowl and the chain pulled. Whatever the manner of it, no pleb escaped baptism. Accordingly, one day when I was in first year two or three lads tried to put my head down the toilet. A combination of being too small to hold properly and vicious kicking helped me escape—but not for long. I was cornered again in the washroom and this time fully dosed under the tap. It was preferable to the toilet bowl all the same.

Another great, and indeed valuable, custom at that time was known as 'combo'. Combo was a form of twinning, whereby a senior boy would 'adopt' a pleb and take care of him. You could be lucky or unlucky with this because there were no guidelines. I had 'combo' with two Kenmare boys (maybe that's the column for Kilcummin). Mikey Murphy, now a teacher and very good footballer, and John Quinlan, now a priest in the diocese, were my combo boys.

Combo was very handy when it came to TV. A television was set up in the study hall, again thanks to 'Cliff'—one TV for 200 boys. The problem was that the study hall was divided in two, with the supervisor's rostrum in the middle. The junior desks faced one way and the senior ones the other way. It was at the senior end that the TV was erected. (Incidentally, all those desks were made by the school carpenter, Bill Kennedy, who has worked in the Sem for the past fifty-five years. He designed them well: a sloping desk with a big box beneath it for schoolbooks, all numbered in red ink from 1 to 200.) We were allowed watch 'The Riordans' every Sunday night. All the juniors had to go and find a place to sit on the senior side. My combo, John Quinlan, shared his desk with me as we watched the scowls of Tom Riordan, the nosiness of Minnie and the antics of Benjy.

'Walking the grounds' was another habit we got into. If you weren't playing football or handball, snooker, tennis or croquet (yes, we had croquet on the lawns in third term), you were walking the grounds. My best mate, Michael O'Keeffe from Cullem, Co. Cork (you see I always had a soft spot for Cork people), walked miles and miles with me, around the tennis courts, then down around the New Building (Moynihan Building) and the small circle between the New Moynihan Building and the Old Brosnan Building, which resembles a parade ring for horses. Michael O'Keeffe and I would discuss everything. Michael was a great musician and he even tried to teach me the accordion, but I progressed no further than 'Fáinní Geal an Lae'.

Anything that distracted from the routine of school life was most welcome. Muhammad Ali was in his heyday and we all loved him. Trouble was, his fights were on in the middle of the night. Luckily a few fellows had small transistor radios that invariably worked only when placed against a copper pipe. The only vertical pipes in our dormitories were in the toilets. It wasn't unusual for all of us to be gathered in the toilet of the old cubicles at 3.00am, with one boy holding the transistor to the water pipe to the sounds of, 'I am the greatest, I float like a butterfly and sting like a bee'! After Ali was crowned World Champion, it was not unusual for fights to break out amongst us at that unearthly hour as some fellow fancying himself as a future champion of the world would land a haymaker on some other boy, and probably get a bloody nose for his troubles.

By a remarkable coincidence I met Muhammad Ali in July 2006. Pádraig, now a qualified veterinary surgeon, was on a year's internship in Lexington, Kentucky. Juliette and I went out to visit him. By mistake we landed in Louisville and I inquired was there anything in the town in honour of the 'Louisville Lip'. On being told about a Muhammad Ali Centre, we headed straight there, arriving at 5.00pm, which was closing time. However, when she heard we were from Ireland, the receptionist let us in and who should be visiting the Centre for only his second time ever in twelve years, but 'The Greatest' himself. We had our photographs taken with him and he invited me to accompany him down the lift as he departed. I reminded him that Jack Lynch was the first Prime Minister in the world to acknowledge him formally. It is quite obvious that he and his party loved Ireland. On the escalator up to the Centre, 'Welcome' is written in several languages, the first being 'Céad Míle Fáilte', which I wrote out fully in English for the receptionist. We got a Céad Míle Fáilte from 'The Greatest'—the man in the world who I most wanted to meet.

Another great novelty introduced around that time were films. There was a priest called Fr Donagh O'Donovan, or 'Donie' to us, who was very mechanically minded and used to service his own car. He carried with him at all times a load of spanners in his pockets. Some days in class some boys would rattle the radiator and Donie would ask was there something wrong with it. 'I think it's beginning to leak, Father,' would come the reply. 'Em, I better have a look at it,' he'd say and out would come the spanners from his pockets and that ended the lesson for that day. Donie was a kind old soul though. He smoked a pipe and loved films. Once a month he'd order a film from Dublin for the school. There wouldn't be any late study that night. Buddy Meara, the local shopkeeper down the lane, did a roaring trade on film nights as students stacked up with 'goodies'. It was illegal to leave the grounds, but a few students organised a little cartel. They arranged watch-out posts for any prowling priests and then one or two would scurry down the footpath or climb over the wall to go to 'Buddy's'. They charged a small fee to supply the students with their loot. They deserved it because if they had been caught, they would have been expelled. Donal Hickey, now of the Irish Examiner, and his fellow Gneeveguilla student Gerard McAuliffe were expert outpost men and never got caught. Taytos, sweets, biscuits, oranges and fags were the main items they supplied and it all added to a lovely few hours 'at the movies' in the study hall.

To convert the hall into a cinema, big black sheets were put on the huge windows to keep out the light. Donie would sit on a perch, spin the spool, smoke his pipe, arrange everything and the film would begin. Thus we were introduced to the world of Charlie Chaplin,

Groucho Marx and John Wayne. I started noticing some fine women too, especially Audrey Hepburn. It's funny, I could never see much in Liz Taylor, who was reputed to be the most beautiful woman in the world. No, it was Audrey Hepburn for me, and then in later years Brigitte Bardot, Sharon Stone, Meryl Streep and Liz Hurley.

'Donie' himself really loved the films and it wasn't unusual for him to burst out laughing at some event as he puffed his way through the spinning reels. The films must have had a big effect on us, too, as one of my classmates went on to become the most respected film critic in the country, Michael Dwyer of *The Irish Times*. There was always a big pause in the middle of the film when Donie had to change the reel. But looking back, he was some man as the old contraptions he had to work with never broke down and we were able to see all films through to the end, and Donie to the end of his pipe.

My final year in the Sem I was made a Prefect, which was a big honour and carried with it a fair few privileges. Lar wasn't made a prefect, which surprised me because he was always 'steadier' and more mature than me (well, he was a year older). I think they thought I was going to be a priest and this was to encourage me in that direction. I was thinking strongly about it, too, but I reckon a combination of those *céilís* in the Loreto and Audrey Hepburn in the films began to lure me down a different path.

It was customary for the bishop to come to meet all those who had a vocation for the priesthood. Bishop Eamonn Casey was bishop of Kerry when I was in my final year. When he arrived in the college, all those with 'vocations' were asked to go and meet him. A huge number of boys went, about twenty in all. I went along with them, but was toing and froing in my mind about whether or not I wanted to be a priest. When I reached the noticeboard in the old building I hesitated, stopped and said, 'No, deep down I don't want to be a priest.' And that was that. I returned to class and never got to meet the bishop. Lar did make that appointment with the bishop, however, and afterwards went to Maynooth, where he was ordained. He has been serving and working as a priest ever since and is now the Canon in Rathmore.

Teachers

One thing I must say about the Sem is that during all my time there, I never came across any sign of abuse by any of the priests or teachers.

Some 'bad apples' have been exposed nationally and rightly so. But I never, either personally or anecdotally, came across any evidence of this in the Sem. I discussed this once with Paudie O'Shea and he (not a great exponent of the Sem due to being expelled) was of the same view. There were some great teachers amongst them in my time, like Fathers Tom Pierce, James Kissane (Bishop), Diarmuid O'Sullivan, Bill Hickey, James Linnane, Ned Corridon, Michael Manning, Donie O'Donovan, Brendan Harrington, Eoin Mangan, Dermot Clifford, Jimmy Hegarty, Eamonn Prendiville, Patrick Horgan and Denis Costelloe. They were tough, but then, they were of their time.

In fact, the only instances of any abuse I witnessed personally occurred when I was much younger. Once, when I brought the tea my mother had made for a man who was doing some work for my father, the man pulled down my trousers. I objected instinctively, pulled away from him and never brought him tea again. On another day a man on a tractor let me up on the tractor with him and even let me steer the wheel. But as I was steering the tractor, he started touching my genitals. I pushed his hand away and steered well clear of him thereafter. I was too young and innocent to be upset about these incidents, but at the same time I instinctively kept away from those two 'bold men' and never said a word to anybody.

In terms of abuse by adults, by far and away the worst experience I ever had happened in the Sem one night in study hall. The supervising teacher on that evening was normally a pleasant and affable man, but he could be very erratic. Something happened during study period and he got hot and bothered. Naturally, this only encouraged more mischief and boys started hissing and playing up. He got really mad and, turning around, suddenly picked me out. He physically hauled me from my desk and then laid into me with his hands and fists. He was giving me a terrible battering—me, the smallest boy in the place being pummelled by a grown man for a racket in which everybody was involved. The students, especially the seniors, began to shout at him to stop. It must have been a particularly bad beating because senior students would usually take great delight in seeing juniors sorted out. But this was Sonny Liston type of stuff—all one-way traffic.

One senior student roared at the teacher, 'Leave him alone, ye big bollix!' The teacher stopped beating me, tore up to the top of the study hall and shouted, 'Who said that?' He never expected someone would actually own up, but own up the student did. 'I did, Sir,' announced a lad from West Kerry who was known to me as 'Smockers'. 'Come out here, you cheeky pup,' said the teacher. Smockers, cool as Clint Eastwood, slowly closed his copy and book in front of him, put them into his desk, got up, then closed the buttons of his jacket and walked out, clenching his fists, ready to fight the teacher. Everyone waited with bated breath (except me, as I was bent over and crying with pain). But the teacher—probably having cooled down a little and realising that if things went against Smockers, there was a grave danger that the other students would come to his aid and probably beat seven shades out of him—backed away, saying, 'I'm going to see the President,' and with that he left the hall. He didn't go to the President, though—how could he?—and neither did I, even though if it happened today, he'd be fired on the spot. Still, I was grateful to Smockers. What a brave and just young man. Being young and enthusiastic I gradually got over the incident, but I had a black eye for a few days. Even when teachers asked me in class what had happened to my face, I merely replied, 'It was an accident, Father.'

Sport

Football matches provided another great distraction from the daily school grind. It was customary at that time for supporters to go to all matches played by the senior team. We had great trips to neighbouring Cork towns like Mallow, Ballyvourney, Kanturk and Buttevant. Enterprising students went down town to purchase green and gold sheets of light paper. Then, with the aid of staples, stapler and a scissors, they made green-and-gold hats and everybody had to buy them. When it rained, the dye ran and we returned to base with our heads and clothes coloured green and gold. But nobody took much notice. Some senior lads also managed to turn a nice little profit on 'Forecast the Score'. We had many great successes and in 1969 went all the way to capture the Hogan Cup for the first time, under the guidance of coach Fr Linnane. There were some great players on that team, some of whom went on to be part of the great Kerry team of the 1970s, such as John O'Keeffe, Ger O'Keeffe and his brother Tony, Paudie O'Mahony, Paudie Lynch and John Long.

Paudie Lynch was a beautiful footballer and in my book one of the real greats of that Kerry team, even though his quiet nature means he doesn't talk about himself and therefore may not get the acclaim he deserves. John Long was a real stylist, too. He was only a third year when he played midfield on the Hogan Cup team. We were always very good friends and I remember saying to John the night we won the Hogan, 'John, it must be a great feeling.' He replied, as cool as a breeze, 'Yerra, Seán, 'twas hardly ever worth it, too much training.' He was probably exaggerating, but worldly acclaim or popularity would never worry John. When he went out on the field, though, he was class itself and we wouldn't have won without him.

Another great pal of mine on that team was Donal Kissane. Donal was a most intelligent forward from Ballylongford, the home of the Kennellys and McCarthys, all great players too. He looked destined for a distinguished career with Kerry, but while captaining the County under-21 team he suffered a bad injury to his knee. Recuperation followed operation, but to no avail. One night the pair of us decided to have a run-around in St Anne's Park in Raheny. Everything went according to plan for half-an-hour. Then we tried short sprints to the 14-yard line and back. All of a sudden, bang goes the knee and Donal never fully recovered after. A great career was ended on the 14-yard line of St Anne's Park.

Yes, the Sem was the place for football. We played and trained as often as possible. If there were no organised games, we organised ones ourselves. Nearly every Sunday morning we had study until about 11.00am, then we were free until lunch hour. A list would go around the study hall to get thirty players to play a game of football. My name was always on the list and we had some great games in the Big Field. If there was no game on in the afternoon, we'd go for a walk and maybe organise a game between six or eight of us. I was out on the football field every chance I got, especially when Fr Linnane told us one day, 'Ye should practise to kick both left and right. Every second ball should be kicked with left and right.' I was a natural *ciotóg* and had never kicked a ball with my right leg before that. From that day on, until I retired, I kicked every second ball with left and right leg and became fairly accurate off both.

As the cliché says, football was our life, and certainly it was the best part of it to us young students in the Sem. Associating and playing with like-minded fanatics was a tonic and set me up for a life-long love of football and of the GAA. It was as natural for me as eating, talking or walking.

Post-Leaving Cert.

Once I had decided that the priesthood was not for me, I knew I had to start thinking about the other options. Once the Leaving Certificate exams were over, it would be 'make your mind up time' as far as a career was concerned. There weren't many options to choose from: it came down to teaching, doing a B.Comm or joining the bank.

When the Leaving Certificate results came out, I knew I'd get called for an interview for teacher training in St Patrick's College of Education in Dublin, so I forgot about the bank. I was in fact called for interview by both banks—Bank of Ireland and AIB—but I didn't go. I considered joining the army cadets too, and if I had known anybody at all in the Army, I'm quite sure I would have gone for it. There was something about the Army that appealed greatly to me. If I had known then that cadets were able to go to university to do degrees, my instincts would definitely have taken me there. As it was, without such wisdom I settled on becoming a primary schoolteacher. The fact that it took only two years to qualify was probably the decisive factor in my final decision.

Now my big problem was the interview. Two big problems, actually—my voice and the singing exam. My voice had become very hoarse—from singing and roaring at matches, I suspect. At all the Sem matches we used to roar all the way through and sing such fine tunes as, 'Yellow belly, yellow belly, yup, yup, yup. Who is going to win the Munster Cup? B R E N D A N s!' and such like. I firmly believe all the roaring and singing had damaged my voice, and a voice is a teacher's best friend. When I was doing the interview, one of the interviewers, known to me later as Fr Philip Walshe, noticed my hoarse voice and said, 'You are hoarse, is it that way always or have you a cold?' I replied, 'A cold, Father, I have a touch of hay fever. We were drawing in the hay at home yesterday.' It was a neat sidestep that saved me from rejection.

Moss Keane says in his book that he failed the interview for St Pat's because he failed the singing exam. Well now, Moss, singing 'Three Blind Mice' wasn't the most inspirational of songs, was it? I was much better prepared. The late Bishop of Kerry, Diarmuid O'Sullivan, was teaching in Brendan's at the time. He was a brilliant teacher and very helpful. On his own time he prepared all of us—which was about fifteen young men—for the singing section of the interview. My two songs were 'Oró, sé do bheatha abhaile' and 'Roddy McCorley'. I 'sang' with gusto and passed the interview, although I think by that stage if you got high enough marks in the Leaving Certificate, you didn't have to do that well in singing. Either way, I passed the interview, got my call to teacher training and headed for good ould Dublin town.

College life

St Patrick's in Drumcondra was simply a brilliant place to study. The buildings were lovely, the student accommodation wonderful, the food fine and the staff nice. The accommodation was in five separate three-storey buildings, which were arranged in a semicircle opposite the main educational building. The houses were called after famous Irish historical locations: Moville, Clonmacnoise, Lismore, Glendalough and Bangor, in that order, exactly as they are positioned on the map of Ireland. I was in Lismore, room 123. I spent two happy years there, made some wonderful friends and even started to shave!

St Pat's was not the 'doss' some people say, but neither was it the half-crazy, high-pressure environment that some third-level institutions are nowadays. It was just lovely, steady as she goes. At the end of two years we had a good grounding in the basics of teaching and the proof is there for all to see—look at the thousands of fine teachers who graduated from Pat's and have gone on to make such a fantastic contribution to this nation, giving so many young people a love of life and country and helping to produce one of the best-educated populations in the world. To this day, over thirty years later, every time I drive up Drumcondra Road past the high walls of the college I am filled with pride and gratitude. St Pat's College of Education made teachers of students and men of boys.

I am a fan, obviously, but not all, I must admit, found it so idyllic. We weren't long in the college—about a month or so—when word went round that a mass meeting would be held outside the college chapel at 6.00pm. John O'Keeffe, Johnny Walsh and I went over together. Johnny was also an ex-Sem boy who had gone to All-Hallows College for a few weeks to study for the priesthood, but when about a dozen of us Sem boys arrived in Pat's, Johnny suddenly lost his vocation and switched across the road to join us in our endeavours to become teachers. He had purchased a new black suit to go to All-

Hallows and needed to get some wear out of it. He wore it on solemn occasions. This was one such solemn occasion, or so we thought. Not having experienced a mass meeting before, we three Sem boys thought it had something to do with Mass itself, seeing as it was being held on the chapel steps. So Johnny dressed appropriately in his black suit, black tie and white shirt.

We arrived to hear the leaders of the students' union in full cry. When we realised that the meeting had been called to organise a protest over the quality of the food, we were utterly amazed. At first we thought they were joking, but then we realised they were serious ... and we couldn't believe it. After five years in St Brendan's, to us the food in St Pat's was gourmet stuff and what's more, there was plenty of it. Whatever else the Sem boys in St Pat's might go on strike over, it certainly wasn't going to be the grub.

St Pat's broadened our minds, opened us up to the world and helped us to embrace ecumenism. An ecumenical spirit pervaded the place. Even in sport, all games were given equal prominence. They had an admirable system to decide which was the best house for sport. Competitions were held in all sports, points allocated according to the prestige of each competition and the number of participants, then the house with the greatest number of points was declared the winner. It was a great idea. It gave recognition and prestige to minority sports and encouraged us to try different sports as well. That's how I came to play my first hurling game. Lismore house were short a few hurlers. My friend Tom Fitzpatrick, a hurler from Clare, prevailed upon me to play, even though I had never played before. I may have got a few *sliotars*, but I doubt if I succeeded in pucking them. I had never even been at a hurling match before. Seeing hurlers up-close, I was amazed by their skill, dexterity and bravery. It made a huge impression on me, one that has never left me since.

I also played my first ever soccer match in St Pat's, for the college team. Tony Brown from Limerick was a very good soccer player. The college was playing a game in Swords against a team I cannot remember, but our team was stuck and Tony asked me to play. 'Why not!' says I. And what's more, I scored not one but two goals. It was the only officially recognised soccer competition in which I ever took part. Now, who else can boast that they scored two goals in every soccer game they played!

Rugby was one game I didn't go in for. I had once played in a rugby game in the Sem and that put me off for life! During that game, Moss Keane fell on me and nearly killed me. That ended the career of a promising scrum-half before it had even begun.

It was in Pat's that I saw a gymnasium and an auditorium for the first time. Johno quickly mastered the gym and we merely followed him along. Some great plays were put on in the auditorium, produced by the college Speech & Drama professor, Aidan Rogers. One production of *Romeo and Juliet* was quite brilliant, as I remember it. Aidan Rogers quickly spotted the hoarseness in my voice and examined it. He gave me exercises to do to build up the vocal chords, which he said had been damaged, and he took me once a week for therapy. It worked, too, and I had little trouble with my voice until about six years ago when I developed polyps and had to have an operation in the Bons in Tralee.

We had great freedom in St Pat's. Basically once we attended our lectures regularly, we could come and go as we pleased. Many students were regular visitors to the Cat and Cage pub across the road from the college, but as I was a non-drinker at the time, I rarely went there. Besides, money was fairly tight and I needed to spend it on the bare necessities of life, not luxuries like drink. A useful way of supplementing my income whenever I needed to was by paying a visit to my Dublin relations. I visited my Auntie Eileen and my Uncle Seán's houses regularly, where I was well-fed and never went away empty-pocketed.

In fact, the only really bad day I had in St Pat's was, ironically, Sports Day. I was hellbent on winning the mile race and had trained hard for it. It was timed for 4.00pm. It was a warm day, so I decided to conserve my energy by staying in my room until 3.30pm, at which time I headed for the track. When I got there, it was only to find that the race was over. It had been held at 3.00pm. I was devastated, especially when I found out who had a won—a fellow I had often beaten. But such is life, I guess.

Part of the training to be a teacher involved teaching practice in Dublin and also a couple of weeks in one's local school at home. In Dublin I did teaching practice with sixth-class girls in Gardiner Street, and in Finglas. John Fleming, a former Sem boy, was the teacher I was assigned to in Finglas and he took good care of me and gave me solid advice. Mick Gleeson, a Kerry All-Ireland medal-winner, also taught in that school. Summertime brought me back to my first school, Kilcummin National School. I really enjoyed that as I got to know all the neighbours' children again. When the principal, Tom Dalton, was out for a week, I was fully in charge of fifth and sixth classes and you could say I was Acting Principal as I used to open up and lock up each day. Experiences like that always stand to a person.

The female factor

Gradually, women started to feature in my life, as was inevitable. St Pat's students used to be allowed free entry into the Irish Club and we had our own dance in Parnell Square on Friday nights. In time I became a frequent visitor there and began to learn how to dance. I had noticed girls always liked guys who could dance properly. My college mates used often 'shift' women, which involved asking a girl to dance and then, at the end of that dance, asking her, 'would you like to stay on for the next dance, please?' or 'Would you like to go for a drink at the bar?' If she said yes, she was yours for the rest of the night—unless you made a right fool of yourself altogether.

After a while I decided I should have a go. But being very young-looking and not able to dance well, it was a slow process. I persevered though and on this night I got dancing with a very nice, attractive girl. After the dance ended, I asked her to stay on. She replied quickly, 'Stay on with you? Sure I'd be accused of baby-snatching.' Not impressed, I returned to the wall and told one of my mates, Paudie Walsh from Cordal in Kerry, what she'd said to me. 'What age do I look?' I asked him. 'About fourteen,' he said. He was delighted and couldn't stop laughing at me. He told all the other lads, of course, who also thought it was hilarious. I didn't see any funny side to it. The next day I walked into town and bought a razor. I hadn't shaved till then as I didn't really need to. But I started then and that did the trick. Bristle sprouted and so did I. And at last, I started to 'shift'. The first night I walked a woman home from the Irish Club a fellow across the room from me, Frank King, a Dub, started slagging me. 'Kelly shifted a bird tonight,' he said. 'Go on, tell us what she was like.' But never a word says I, and from there on I never looked back and rarely spoke about my women.

Despite shaving, I still looked younger than most my age. A few years later, during my first year teaching in St Brendan's College, I had an embarrassing run-in with a parent. I was dressed in my best suit, looking all grown-up and mature for my first parent–teacher meeting, when a mother of one of the students came into the room and said to me, 'Do you know where I'd find the teacher?' and before I could say, 'It is I, Ma'am', she added, 'Tell me, love, are you doing the Inter. or the Leaving?' I had been shaving for five or six years by that stage! After that, in order to make myself look older and more mature, I grew a beard. I have never shaved since that parent–teacher meeting, although I suppose the wheel will go full circle: one of these days I'll decide to shave again so that I will look younger! Such are the ways of the world.

Like all things, a bit of practice did me no harm and over time I became quite good at chatting-up women. I was a fan of the one date only, or maybe two or three if she was really nice. After that I cut out, especially if a girl said to me, 'Mum and Dad said to invite you over to lunch some day.' That was the kiss of death for me! I was gone like a shot and never did make lunch with any 'Mum or Dad' when I was in Dublin. I had long held the notion that thirty years of age was a good time to be thinking of marriage, so I didn't want to be leading any one on to think otherwise. So short-term contracts were the order of the day! Still, it was good fun and I hope the girls enjoyed the *craic* as much as I did.

One thing I never did do was stand-up a girl. It must have happened to some girls, and guys too, because sometimes a girl would say to me, 'Don't say you'll ring if you don't mean it and don't stand me up.' Well, I never did, but I came very close to it one night. I was due to meet this girl outside the Harp one Saturday night at 8.00pm. My bus came early and on it I met a Garda friend of mine from Coolock Garda Station. He asked me to go for a pint with him and as I was early, I did. The chat was so good that we had one or two more. Before I knew it, it was 9.30pm. I said to myself, she's probably gone by now, but I decided to go to the Harp anyway. Well, it was lucky I did because because there she was, still waiting for me. I apologised and made up some excuse about the bus or somesuch. But I also made up my mind that it would never happen again, and it didn't.

Walking was my favourite method of transportation then. It was a time when Dublin was a safe city, so boys and girls alike felt they could walk around undisturbed. In fact, I had one bad experience of violence, but it was the only time such a thing happened. One Saturday night I was walking down O'Connell Street on the inside of the kerb. It was about 11.00pm and I was heading towards the Crystal Ballroom to meet a girl. All of a sudden this fellow grabbed me and pulled me into a dark corner, where he demanded my money. I had no intention of giving it to him, but as I tried to release myself, I got this unmerciful thud in the forehead. It happened so quickly, I didn't know what had happened. I managed to get free and ran away, with two fellows chasing me. They hadn't a chance, though, as thankfully I was much fitter than them, due to all the football. I made my way to the Crystal, nursing a splitting pain in my head. It was only when I relayed the story to my girlfriend that she told me what had happened. 'You got a head-butt,' she said. 'What's a head-butt?' says I. Well, I may not have known what a head-butt was, but I knew what it felt like. I learned my lesson from that unfortunate incident. Afterwards, whenever I walked up or down streets, I walked well out from the walls. Otherwise, I kept out of trouble and confined my socialising to respectable places with respectable girls.

PART II

University and Teaching, 1971–1975

Cromcastle Green

We completed our two years in St Pat's and in 1971 said goodbye to the good life of the full-time student and faced into the real world. I got a job in Cromcastle Green Boys' National School in Coolock and spent a great few years teaching there, starting with First Class, which involved preparing them for Holy Communion. The classroom was a common area in a pre-fabricated building with four classrooms off it, which meant that if anyone wanted to go into or out of any of the classrooms, they had to come through my classroom. Naturally traffic was heavy. But being young and enthusiastic and knowing no different, we got on with the business of teaching all those kids.

Even though Coolock has a name for being a tough area, I must say I found both pupils and parents to be lovely people. There was only a very small minority of nasty people and it was they who gave the area a bad name. The mothers, in particular, were dotes and did everything they could to bring up their children well, doing all possible to help them. I taught the same class for my first four years there and was quite pleased with the progress they made. There were some really bright sparks in that class—six, at least. I expected them to go on to third-level and do really well. They certainly had the brains to do so. But when I made enquiries some years later, I was disgusted to learn that due either to a lack of direction or insufficient finances, only one went to third-level; many started working while still in secondary school. This is the real challenge if we are to achieve equality of opportunity in education. Fine to say we have equal opportunities for all when those who need it most aren't aware of it, or they haven't enough confidence in themselves to go where no one in their family has gone before. Making kids in areas like Kilmore and Coolock understand just how good they are is a big challenge, and giving them the ambition and the opportunity to recognise and fulfil their potential is a very important part of the education process. It is, unfortunately, often ignored.

My biggest complaint when I first started teaching at Cromcastle was the constant noise from the aeroplanes as they took off from and landed at Dublin Airport. I even suggested one day, in all innocence, that we should try to get the airport moved out further to lessen the noise and the vibrations in the pre-fabs. If only Michael O'Leary had been around then—what a double-act we would have been!

As I said, the parents were very involved in their children's education and welfare. There was one father who used to collect his son an hour before school ended every Friday. 'I like to go to town early on a Friday afternoon for a few gargles,' he used to say to me, adding, 'after a hard week's work, you'se know what I mean, Mr Kelly.' I did, but I don't think he worked at all.

Anyway he would always enquire how the son was getting on. 'I do give him all the help I can,' he'd say. But as the year went by the Maths were getting beyond the Da, so before he'd go to town I'd do some Maths questions with him, to prepare him for the son's homework. He would do a sum on the blackboard and when he got it right, off he'd go for a few 'gargles', whistling as he went, the son, who was a lovely lad, in tow behind him. In this way we all progressed nicely, but then we hit the brick wall that was long division. It was simply beyond him and try as I might, he just couldn't grasp it. This particular Friday, in he comes again at 1.30pm and says to me, 'Do you'se mind doing that long division on the board again, Master Kelly?' I did and he twigged it at last. Then I gave him a sum to do on the board as the whole class watched. He struggled at first, but when he had finished I went up and marked correct (✓) alongside it. The class gave him a big round of applause. Then he turned to me and said, 'Mr Kelly, you'se are a f**king genius.' Turning to the class of ten-year-olds he reiterated with feeling, 'I'm telling yese, Mr Kelly may be a bleedin' culchie, but he is a f**king genius, too, a bleedin' f**kin' genius,' and off he went to renew acquaintance with his good friend, Arthur Guinness, long-division mastered at last.

I really loved teaching at Cromcastle Green. When I started there first, a gentleman called Seán Kennedy was principal. I remember one evening I was last to leave the school because I had taken some boys for football training after school, and Seán was there, waiting for me to lock up. He asked me about St Brendan's and football in Kerry and we took our leave with Seán saying, 'I'll see you in the morning.' Well, he didn't see me in the morning, or any other morning either, as he died suddenly that night at home. Sad, but true.

Some time afterwards Seamus Doyle, a Clare man, took over as principal. He was very conscientious and the school progressed well under him and vice-principal John Connolly. When Seamus retired, another Clare man, Tom Boland, assumed the principalship. He was a very dedicated GAA man and totally passionate about hurling. Himself and Ritchie Rally did marvellous work for hurling, and kids who before that had regarded hurling as a 'bleedin' game for culchies' soon became hooked. There was one guy in Ritchie's class for whom learning and schooling were anathema, but he came to school everyday for hurling. He rarely had a schoolbook on his person, but inside or outside the school the *camán* never left his hand. I was glad for Seamus and Tom when, twenty years later, Clare made the breakthrough under Ger Loughnane. They re-surfaced again in my life when I worked with the GAA and the gentle art of acquiring tickets for Clare's big games began to occupy their minds.

Fr Seán Kitt, uncle of politicians Michael and Tom and of Áine, was parish priest of the Cromcastle area and therefore manager of the school. He too was a GAA devotee and was to be found in Croke Park every Sunday, regardless who was playing. He was a kind of unofficial chaplain to the GAA. With a manager, principal and many teachers, like Mick Lynch and Jimmy O'Grady, all GAA fans, it was a thriving school for sport. Football got a great surge when Heffo's Army burst onto the scene in 1974, and when Bobby Doyle, Gay O'Driscoll, Seán Doherty *et al* visited the school with Sam Maguire, it gave our efforts a massive boost.

One of our biggest problems was the pitch. There was enough room for a reasonable pitch, but there was a big sycamore tree in the middle of the green area. I waged a pitched battle for years with the school authorities to get the tree felled. Fr Kitt used to get a great kick out of it years later when I'd meet him in Croke Park and he'd remind me, with a laugh, about my one-man tree-felling campaign.

From my first year at Cromcastle Green I coached football to the boys. The following year another Kerryman, Jimmy O'Grady, joined me. The nearby Parnells club, especially the late Brendan Quinn (trainer of the 1963 Dublin All-Ireland champions) and Patsy Kiernan, offered us any assistance we required and even donated footballs and jerseys to our team. We used to train near the Oscar Traynor Road, so eventually we threw in our lot with Parnells. We had a lovely team and won the Dublin under-11 league, which was greatly appreciated all round and well celebrated by Parnells.

At that time, I started playing football with Parnells myself. I was afraid I'd be caught and suspended, so the first day I was playing and the secretary asked my name for the referee's list, I replied, 'Feardorcha Ó Ceallaigh.' He paused, 'What's that in English? Frank, is it?' 'Yes,' says I, and for a long time afterwards I was known as 'Frank Kelly' to the 'Nells. To this day some of them probably don't realise that the Frank Kelly who played with them went on to be Seán Kelly, President of the GAA!

Playing with Parnells was a great experience. I often played three games each weekend. On Saturday it would be an under-21 game, under the careful eye of a former Kerry footballer from Knocknagoshel, Jack Murphy, who had a wonderful repertoire of colourful language. He once told us that if we didn't play better the next day, he'd have to 'invent f***ing curses' for us. No better man. We always retired to the Goblet Bar in Artane after the matches, where Jack carried out his 'Après Match' analysis for us. We nearly pulled off the shock of the championship one Saturday afternoon when we were leading UCD by two points with time up, only for my old pal John O'Keeffe to solo fifty yards and crash the ball to the net to give UCD the win.

On Sunday mornings I played with the club junior side, with Malachy Keena in charge of affairs. Getting fellows out of their beds was Malachy's most difficult management task! Then on Sunday evening the Seniors played, with Brendan Quinn and Gerry Brady in charge of operations.

I also took part in a number of seven-a-side competitions, some organised internally and others in general tournaments. They were great fun and any decent forward got great opportunities to score regularly, which made it all the more enjoyable. I think clubs with lots of players should hold many more seven-a-side, nine-a-side and possibly eleven-a-side tournaments. The one thing I have always noticed is that if players are guaranteed a game with regularity, they'll turn up without fail. After all, the GAA is primarily about playing the games, not watching from the sidelines. There's great scope for innovation. If Parnells could do it in the 1970s, imagine what could be achieved in the third millennium!

All in all, Parnells was a great club. A few years later they won the Dublin and Leinster Club Championships, and hopefully some day they'll take the All-Ireland. When I was Uachtarán of the GAA, the club organised a lovely reception for me and my family one night, which was most enjoyable. There's no better company in all the world than the Dubs in full flow and in good voice, and I became one of their own through my involvement with Parnells. 'One of our own?' I can hear them say. 'Go on out of that, you bleedin' culchie!'

University College, Dublin

Based on the results of final exams from St Pat's, students could get exemptions from First Arts in university. Some of my fellow students received exemptions in one or two subjects; to my surprise, I got exempted in all four. It turned out to be a mixed blessing. I was too young to go straight into second year, and I missed the company of my pals, who were all doing first year in university as a night course.

To use my time well, I decided to do some night courses in the technical school in the North Strand. I did Physical Education, where the great Tony Wall of Tipperary was the instructor and Ger Power was in attendance as well. I also did woodwork and woodcarving, which was a bit of a waste of time as I never put it to use afterwards. I cycled from Artane to the school on the North Strand for my classes, but one night my bicycle was stolen and that was the end of that. The one good thing to come out of those extra courses was that I became firm friends with Philip Fitzsimons, now MD of FBD. I spent the winter studying at the Tech, then rejoined my pals in UCD.

I liked UCD very much. The lecturers were good and businesslike and there was a lively buzz about the place. I had no choice but to study some of the subjects I had received exemptions in, namely History, Geography, Irish and English. That's another reason why exemptions were a mixed blessing: you were quite constrained by them. I think I'd have been better off trying my hand at something new, maybe a B.Comm, but the die was cast and I got on with it.

Studying at night in UCD meant teaching during the day, catching the bus into town from Artane, another bus from town to UCD and afterwards, when the three or four lectures were over, doing the same journey in reverse. As lectures started at about 6.30pm and finished at 9.30pm, we always went straight back to digs afterwards because we were teaching at 9.00am every morning. One particular night, though, I was coming in on the bus with Jackie Walsh and I said to him, 'Jackie, today is my twenty-first birthday.' I hadn't told anyone else. 'Are you serious?' he said to me, probably not believing I could be so blasé about it. I convinced him it was so, and he insisted that we mark it. At that time the Kerry players studying or working in Dublin used to eat in a place called Daly's on the Quays, just off O'Connell Street. Brooking no opposition, Jackie brought me there for steak, peas, onion rings, french fries and a pint of milk—the staple diet of 'privileged' Kerry footballers. It was delicious. So that was how I celebrated my twenty-first and it was as good as any party, thanks to Jackie.

I played a lot of football in UCD, too, but they had such a star-studded team it was almost impossible for me to make the first fifteen. Nevertheless, hanging around with Jackie Walsh and John O'Keeffe meant I was able to train with them, which was great. Eugene McGee was in charge of the UCD team and he was some trainer, bringing them all the way to become Sigerson and All-Ireland Club Champions. Later he masterminded Offaly's march to glory, culminating in their smashing of Kerry's five-in-a-row bid in 1982. Sending on Seamus Derby with a few minutes left and telling him to 'hang around the square' was a typical move by the tactical genius, Eugene McGee. His training sessions were brilliant and couldn't go on long enough for me.

I am also fortunate that one of my best pals, then and ever since, was Eamonn O'Donoghue. Eamonn was an exceptional man. He was captain of UCD and player/manager of Kildare at the same time, taking them to a Leinster Final where they came up against Heffo's machine.

Eamonn was very kind and considerate and gave me a game with UCD every chance he got. Years later, as Uachtarán, I invited himself and Cathleen (his wife—a Dub!) to the GAA box in Croke Park and said it was for all the times he had selected me on UCD teams when I didn't deserve it. A week later he wrote to thank me: 'Seánie, you deserved to be on those teams, you had a very cultured left foot.' Like love, friendship can also be blind!

The UCD teams played an inter-faculty competition, the Duke Cup, which was named after the great Cavan footballer, R.J. Duke, who died while still a student in UCD. These were ferociously contested. I am very proud to be able to say that I won a Duke Cup medal playing wing-forward with the Arts faculty team. The quality of the team was such that John O'Keeffe was playing on the other wing. For probably the only time in his life, John was substituted. I played well and scored a couple of points. Afterwards, Jackie Walsh, Gerry Dineen and I gave John a fierce ribbing. He wasn't too amused at first, but being the great sportsman he was, he saw it as an insignificant blip and forgot about it.

At that time, when you studied at night you couldn't take an Honours degree, so we all passed our courses and were quite happy. We had just one more year to go now and that was for the H.Dip. in Education, which would qualify us for secondary-school teaching. That was a very interesting course, in fact, and professors such as John Colohan were superb. Most of those doing the H.Dip. were full-time students; only the national teachers were part-time because we were teaching by day. In total, 520 students sat the H.Dip., but only four achieved first-class honours. When I first looked at the noticeboard, I thought I had failed. I looked at the 'Pass' list and didn't see my name there. Then I looked at the second-class honours list, but it wasn't there either. My heart skipped a beat. Then I dared a glance at the first-class honours list, hoping against hope. I was delighted, absolutely chuffed, to see my name in the top list.

One of the reasons I was so pleased with my results was that I hadn't missed a single match for Kilcummin while studying in UCD. Even when we had exams on a Monday morning, I still went home and played in the Sunday game, returning to Dublin on the late train. I have always believed that not only can sports and study mix, they can complement one another. I had now proved it for myself.

One thing I never did as a student was to attend any conferrings. I didn't fancy the gowns and pomp, but looking back now, I realise that was a mistake. The photographs of those conferrings are very important for posterity and the gown is a bit like an All-Ireland captain with the Sam Maguire. If you work hard to get it, you should enjoy it. I think I've learned that you can partake of a bit of pomp without being pompous!

As I was teaching full-time and studying part-time, I didn't get much opportunity to enjoy the many resources offered by UCD. I think in the three years I was there, I visited the college chapel once, the gym once and the bar once. My one and only visit to the bar was on my final day. A group of footballers arranged to rendezvous there, which we did, staying until closing time. Maybe it was just as well I hadn't discovered it sooner!

My H.Dip. wasn't long past me when I got a telephone call from the President of St Brendan's College, Fr Donagh O'Donovan. (He was the man responsible for showing us the monthly film that I remembered so fondly.) Fr O'Donovan, or Donie as he was universally known, asked me to call in to see him in the college when I was next in Kerry. Kilcummin was playing the following weekend, so I availed of the opportunity to visit Donie. Unexpectedly, he offered me a job in the Sem. I asked him to give me time to think about it. He agreed, but when I was departing asked me, rather strangely, 'By the way, Seán, what [degree] subjects do you have?' I'm sure he must have had a fair idea before he rang me—there wouldn't have been any point taking on a guy with a degree in History if he had a vacancy for a Maths teacher.

Now I had some thinking to do. It is one of the things that everybody has to do occasionally in life: an unexpected opportunity arrives and you haven't much time to make up your mind. Quite frankly, I was enjoying life in Dublin—Cromcastle Green was a lovely school, Parnells was a great club and I had a few very good friends out the Northside with me with whom I used to go socialising and dancing regularly, such as Jimmy O'Grady, Don Kissane, Connie Williams (Glenflesk), Pat O'Neill and James Sheehan (Templenoe). It was a great set-up. On top of that, I had also found lovely digs, staying in the home of a wonderful lady called Veronica Dalton and her husband, Derek, both great Dub supporters. She was the best landlady I ever had, very kind and a great cook. What more could any man want! I shared the digs with a friend of mine from Athenry, Co. Galway, Frank Kennedy, who was a brilliant musician and artist. So life was good in Dublin and it was a dilemma whether to go or stay.

Nonetheless, this was my beloved *alma mater* and I was afraid the opportunity might not come around again. I had never intended staying permanently in Dublin, but neither had I intended moving back quite so quickly. I talked it over with a few pals, including my buddy, Eamonn O'Donoghue, and in the end I decided to accept the offer of a position in the Sem. My reasoning was simple: single pals usually scatter or settle, you can't stay in digs forever and the nightlife in Killarney, while not as varied as Dublin, was probably better than any place else. So I accepted Donie's offer and prepared to move back to Kerry.

With the benefit of hindsight, I now understand that there was a very real drawback to leaving Dublin. I had been accepted to do an M.Ed. in Trinity College, which is what I should have done before returning to Kerry. The M.Ed. degree was an innovation then and Trinity wasn't an easy place to get into. Yet I had been given the opportunity to study in that famous establishment under a Kerry professor called Mr Rice. I think I should have done so. One of the reasons I decided against it was that I believed I could do an M.Ed. in ucc. But when I went back to Kerry and checked this out, the college did not, in fact, have such a course; I was offered a place on the M.A. in History instead. Of course, one never knows how things would have turned out if I had opted for Trinity: would I ever have gone back to Kerry? Would I ever have been Chairman of the County Board? Would I ever have been President of the GAA? There's no telling now.

Return to the Sem
So it was off to the Sem, starting as a wee teacher in 1975 and continuing unbroken service until I took leave of absence upon becoming Uachtarán GLC in 2003. As always, I settled in quickly. Those two words summed up my time in the Sem—teaching and football—and I was happy to be there.

Fr O'Donovan gave me an Honours Leaving Cert. Geography class to teach in my first year there. There was a completely new syllabus and I used to spend two to three hours nightly studying it, preparing notes and correcting copies. The class did quite well, but due to the vagaries of the timetable, the following year someone else was teaching Honours

Geography and I got the Leaving Cert. Irish class instead. After that things settled down and teachers worked classes in two-year cycles.

I trained teams in the Sem from the outset. Sometimes we were lucky, other times not so lucky. My partner in training was Fr Jim Kennelly from Millstreet, Co. Cork, probably the best priest in the world—and that includes the Pope! An absolutely marvellous man, he was, with a ready wit. We had great fun training the teams, enjoyed some great successes and suffered some crunching defeats. St Augustine's, Dungarvan, fair dues to them, caught us two years in a row. In 1978 they came from seven points down, kicking eight fantastic points to pip us at the post. The following year we were flying and were five points ahead with time almost up, when they got two goals and we lost again. Naturally, we blamed the referee!

There were memorable days too, of course, the best of all being the day St Brendan's won the Hogan Cup in 1992. Fr Larry and Fr Jim trained the team and Pat Moynihan and I were selectors (as then Chairman of the County Board, I couldn't be available all the time). Powered on by a young star called Seamus Moynihan, we beat all before us and in the final took no less a scalp than that of the most famous and successful college of all, St Jarlath's of Tuam. We had a wonderful celebration in the Killarney Manor. For me, the day we won the Hogan Cup was one of the best days of my life. It was only the second time the Sem had won it and I was absolutely thrilled for all concerned, especially Fr Larry and Fr Jim. They had given years and years of unstinting dedication to the Sem, paid for everything out of their own pockets, driven players home after training, taken them to doctors and physios and paid for that too and now, at long last, they had received their just reward.

The great thing about winning an All-Ireland is that it can never be taken from you—it's there forever more and gets more important as the years go by. Niall Mangan, a Kilcummin man, was a great captain, but Moynihan was the star of that team. We played him centre-forward at first, then we wondered should we move him to centre-back to bolster the defence. I remember saying to Pat, Jim and Lar that we might as well because he'd probably play the two positions. And that's exactly what he did. He scored as many points from centre-back as he did when playing centre-forward. Moynihan and John O'Driscoll of Coláiste Íosagáin in Cork were the two best college players I ever saw.

Fr Jim and I used to put two players on O'Driscoll, but it was a futile exercise, he was that good.

Coláiste Chríost Rí were the bane of our lives. They were ultra-competitive and we had many a raging battle with them. Kevin Cummins and Brother Denis were like men possessed on the sideline, but they produced some fabulous teams and enjoyed well-deserved success—even if we didn't always think so at the time. A man called Colin Corkery was one of their protégés. I'll never forget the day I first saw him in action. We were playing with the aid of a raging storm in the second-half and had drawn level in the closing minutes. Then Chríost Rí got a free at least 40 yards out. Against that gale, I thought to myself, God himself couldn't score. I hadn't reckoned on Corkery. He managed what looked like the impossible and it was another sucker punch for us, but that's sport.

Brother Denis used sometimes get into bother with referees. I was sitting alongside him once, at a Munster College's meeting, when the Chairman announced that he was being suspended for two or three months. Thinking this would look terrible for a Brother, I whispered a consoling word in his ear. Brother Denis' response? 'To tell you the truth, Seán, I couldn't give two shits about them.' No wonder he was such a great trainer.

Another great man I crossed wits with was Billy Morgan, perhaps the best goalkeeper of all time. The great thing about Billy was that he was just as passionate about an under-15 match as an All-Ireland final. We'd sometimes have a few words on the sideline. One day, a Cork referee was giving my team a hard time, or so it seemed to us. I said to Billy, 'How much did you pay him, Billy?' Well, he nearly hit the roof, but when the game was over we calmed down again, and I must say it was always an honour and an inspiration to be involved with him—whether in opposition or otherwise. There are very few people of his calibre who have given so much on a voluntary basis to club, college and county. Without doubt, Morgan is a superman of the GAA.

One of my final victories as a trainer was when I was Chairman of the Munster Council. Along with another lay teacher, I took the under-14 (Russell Cup) and under-15 (Munster Cup) teams that year. The team wasn't great and after we got a trouncing in the Munster Cup, my training colleague got fed-up and gave up training, saying, 'They'll never win anything.' Still, I said I'd see it out and we trained away. We hadn't won the Russell Cup for a long, long time. I decided to change the team around completely and, lo and behold, we began to improve, beating Dingle and Tralee. We qualified for the final against Killorglin Inter-School, who were enjoying great success at the time. The final was played in Beaufort and after a great game we emerged victorious by two points. It was a great feeling and the principal, Tony Behan, was thrilled. It was especially pleasing for me as my son, Pádraig, was wing-forward on the team. It was the first time I had trained a team with a family member involved and it was a nice way to end what was supposed to be a barren year.

One of the things I could never understand, or accept, was that there were two different bodies involved in organising GAA activities in second-level schools: vocational and college bodies. As a result, for instance, Killarney Vocational School and ourselves would often play challenge games, but we could never play in competition against one another. I saw this as a bit of sporting apartheid and always spoke against it. When I became Uachtarán I appointed a taskforce to bring about an amalgamation of both bodies. George Cartwright (Cavan) and John Prenty (Mayo) acted as Chairman and Secretary, respectively. Delicately and determinedly they moved things forward. There was huge opposition to overcome, but they produced their recommendations and we got them passed.

I then asked Seán Fogarty, a man who had chaired the schools committee in Munster and did a great job of it, to oversee the implementation. He agreed. Things moved along nicely and now it has come to pass. It should make a big difference over time and I look forward to further co-operation and closer ties between all second-level schools. There should be no distinction between schools. Let each play in the grade relevant to their ability and size and give them all due recognition. This can now happen, and I am very grateful to people like George, John and Seán—who aren't involved in the sector at all themselves—for steering the ship of unity forward so successfully.

I was lucky to have great years in sports with second-level schools. I enjoyed it all and I really hope that, as we move forward, we give more and more support to our schools at all levels so that teachers will feel appreciated and thus motivated to continue the great work they have been doing for generations. I hope, too, that through this extra help and encouragement hurling will be given more prominence. If hurling is encouraged and played in the schools, it will thrive. Hopefully Paudie Butler, whom I appointed as first National Hurling Director, will be able to help bring this about. It is absolutely fantastic that pupils now have the opportunity to play Gaelic games and many other sports in schools in Ireland and I look forward to the day when that will occur in every single school in the country.

Teaching and team games certainly prepared me for my later work: there were numerous expectations to fulfil, ambitions ran high and the personalities demanded a lot of diplomacy in the handling! I didn't know it then, but it prepared me well for the next step in my life—into sports administration.

PART III

Chairman of East Kerry, 1975–1987

Family legacy

Women were scarce in the Kelly household. Indeed, until the arrival of my second daughter, Julie, I used to say that I had only one mother, one aunt, one sister, one wife and one daughter—maybe it's best to take women singly! The reason for this was that while there were seven siblings in my family, six were boys. It must have been tough for my sister Mary, but she survived and was always very kind to all of us. Later she married a Donegal man, John McGlinchey from Glenfin, who is a wonderful Irish speaker and scholar. My father came from a family of five boys and my mother had only one sister—our Auntie Eileen. So, not surprisingly in such a male-dominated household, football was the first and the greatest passion.

My grandfather and grandmother, Brian and Maria Kelly, were very interested in sport, which in Kerry meant football. My grandfather, an old War of Independence veteran who, to his credit, took no part in the Civil War, was Chairman of Kilcummin for many years. Years later, when I was President of the GAA, a great GAA man from Spa, Donie O'Leary, said to my father of me, 'Your son, Seán, is a great chairman. I have only seen one better than him, and that was his grandfather, Brian.' *Briseann an dúchas trí shulaibh an chait*, as the old Irish proverb says.

My grandfather had a few very narrow escapes from the Black and Tans. Being the leader of the rebellion in Kilcummin, they were always trying to catch him. Once he received a bullet in the heart—at least, what should have been his heart. As a shopkeeper, he had a habit of carrying coins for change in a box in his breast pocket. The bullet pierced the box of coins, otherwise 'twould have pierced his heart. On another occasion the Tans came early one morning to capture him. But as Kilcummin is about 1,000ft above Killarney, somebody noticed them coming and sent word to the house. Grandfather escaped out the fields and into the woods. The Tans searched the house and finding the bed was warm, demanded of my grandmother the whereabouts of her husband. My grandmother replied that the young child (later Fr Brian) was sick and she had put him in there for comfort.

Years later, the parish priest announced at Mass one Sunday that he was selling a field to make money for the church. When Mass was ended and the people were leaving, my grandfather went outside, jumped up on the ditch and called the people together, saying, 'We must buy that field ourselves as a sportsfield for the parish.' And so it came to pass. That field is still headquarters to Kilcummin GAA.

All my uncles, as well as my father, being sons of the great grandfather Brian, played for Kilcummin. Uncle Seán had an All-Ireland Senior medal—one of only three such heroes in the parish at that time, the other two being Eugene Moriarty and Dee O'Connor.

Dee O'Connor, he of the first Kerry four-in-a-row, died a young man. There was snow on the ground. It was a big occasion in our parish as all the great Kerry footballers, old and new, came to his funeral. We were not allowed outside the door when the funeral was passing—probably in case we made noise—so we all looked out the windows of our house as the Kerry greats passed by on that cold, snowy morning. From a distance I caught a glimpse of some of our childhood heroes, such as Mick O'Connell, Johnny Culloty and Tom Long.

Incidentally, my uncle Seán was the last man from our parish to win an All-Ireland Senior medal until modern-day All-Star Michael McCarthy came along. Mike won three All-Ireland medals, in 2000, 2004 and 2006.

Uncle Seamus had played for Tipperary and for Kerry. Fr Laurence (the quiet brother) was a great goalkeeper and was selected for the Munster College's team—no mean feat. Fr Brian was the Daddy of them all, however: football for breakfast, dinner and supper, football at Mass, football all day long. When Glenbeigh GAA field was being developed, he ensured there was a collection during Mass every Sunday to pay for it. He was a fine footballer during his time at the seminary in Maynooth and he went on to be a great trainer, administrator and tormentor of referees and opposition alike. I was his 'pet' and he carried me everywhere. He trained Glenbeigh, Kilcummin and Allihies to major breakthroughs in their respective championships. He trained Mid-Kerry to their first county championship success in 1967, developing such fine players as Pat Griffin, Teddy Bowler, Gerry Riordan, the Lucey Brothers, Kevin Griffin, Timmy Kelliher and Pat Aherne and many more who wore the county jersey.

Fr Brian was a terror on the sideline, though, and thought nothing of going onto the field to admonish the referee or opposition, complete with black suit, black hat and black umbrella. I once witnessed the former Kerry and John Mitchell's full-back Niall Sheehy give Fr Brian a kick in the rear when he came into the square, and telling him politely to get back to the sideline. These were only skirmishes, though, battles for the moment and any advantage to win the match, but when it was all over and things had cooled down—which to be fair took Fr Brian longer than most—they were all friends again … until the next big championship game.

Fr Brian was also fanatical about the Kerry team. He wanted them to win every All-Ireland, without fail. He would say, 'If we could only win on Sunday, 'twould do us for a long time.' Trouble was, 'a long time' meant about a week to Fr Brian. Every game had to be won. If Kerry lost, the players, selectors, county board officials as well as the referee got a lash of his tongue. They were all 'dopes' or 'donkeys' or 'bloody smart alecks'. If Kerry won, it was, 'Well, thanks be to God now, they were great.' And if it was Cork that was beaten in a Munster Final, he'd add, ''Tis always great to beat them shaggers. Thanks be to God.' When Kerry was playing important matches, Fr Brian would ask his congregation at Mass to stand and 'sing "Faith of Our Fathers" for the lads today'. If Kerry was beaten, the following Sunday's homily would carry a stinging post-mortem. One year Kerry was burdened by a smallish team and a small management team, and they lost. Fr Brian concluded his post-mortem homily by saying, 'How could Kerry win, with a crowd of grasshoppers picked by a useless crowd of midgets? Amen.'

Fr Brian died in 2006 at the age of eighty-six. Ironically, I was in Lansdowne Road, where Ireland were playing the Pacific Islands, their last game before the closure of the venue, when I got the call that Fr Brian had just passed away. Kerry were All-Ireland Champions then, something that made him very happy in his final months. A few months afterwards, on 6 May 2007, Glenbeigh GAA Club asked me to unveil a plaque at their grounds, dedicating the field in his honour: Fr Brian Kelly Park. In my few words, I said that if Fr Brian had a choice of being canonised a saint or having Glenbeigh field called after him, he'd choose the latter.

With that kind of a background, how could I escape football?

Playing the Game

Strangely, there was very little organised under-age football when my brothers and I were growing up in the 1960s. We played a couple of games at under-14 level. Michael Fleming—known to us as Mick Jack Mike—used to pack us all into his car and transport us to wherever a game was taking place. As we were boarding in St Brendan's, we only got to play with the club during the summer holidays.

All that was about to change. It was probably in the early 1970s that things really took off in Kerry. People like Brendan Walsh, Denis Fenton and Fr Linnane became involved on the East Kerry board, while Dr Jim Brosnan, Andy Molyneaux and Gerald McKenna took on matters at County Board level. Bord na nÓg was established and county leagues were started, which guaranteed eleven extra games per year to all club players.

It was perfect timing for me. In 1971 I had finished in St Pat's and qualified as a teacher, so I was now independent for the first time in my life. What's more, I was playing on the Kilcummin senior team, along with my brothers, and the new county leagues and extra competitions meant football, football, football. Even better, Kilcummin was putting a right good team together, which we proved two years later in 1973, when we won the O'Donoghue Cup (East Kerry Senior Championship). It was the first time Kilcummin had won it. The previous major success had been forty-eight years earlier, when Kilcummin won the Senior League. It was a major achievement for us as more than half the team were studying or working away from home during that time. Much of the credit must go to our trainer, Fr Brian, and to his selectors for overcoming this major handicap. Sadly, Kilcummin hasn't won the O'Donoghue Cup since.

In 1973 Rathmore, with the great D.J. Crowley and John Saunders on board, were expected to dispose of us in the quarter-final, but after a great tussle we emerged victorious and went on to meet the great Dr Croke's team in the semi-final. Naturally, a whitewash was expected. They had so many star players that we, despite beating Rathmore, couldn't be expected to triumph. But once again we upped our game and, after a titanic struggle, held on for a magnificent victory. Crokes are always a great team to play: they have their own brand of attractive football and are very sporting. On that day I was on top of the right (corner-forward) and my direct opponent was Greg O'Donoghue, of the famous Killarney sporting family. Kilcummin people were delighted, and probably amazed, with our win. The shouting, roaring and celebrating in the dressing-room afterwards as the whole parish seemed to come in to congratulate us was something I had never seen before. To their credit, the Crokes took defeat like true sportsmen. I remember well their captain, Tom Looney, jumping up onto the bench in our dressing-room to congratulate us and wish us well in the final, saying, 'Ye are a way better team than people thought and ye are good enough to win the final.'

I, along with over half the team, including my five brothers, missed the preparations for the final as I was teaching in Dublin. The game went very well for us, nonetheless. We were leading Glenflesk by six points with ten minutes left to play. Tim Sheahan, who played for Kerry in the 1960s, was playing outside me. I said to Tim, 'in a half-hour's time we will be below in the Fáilte celebrating.' I spoke too soon. Here came Derry Crowley, father of John, who had also played for Kerry. In the space of a few minutes he turned the tide, scoring two goals—the second one a brilliant solo effort—and we were mighty lucky to escape with a draw.

Everybody in Kilcummin was furious: we had blown it. Undeterred, we gathered our forces together and determined that, having escaped once, we wouldn't make the same mistake again. The replay posed a huge dilemma for Lar, however. He partnered our star player, Johnny Doolan, at mid-field, so he was a crucial cog in our machine. But it turned out that the replay clashed with the student retreat in Maynooth, where Lar was studying for the priesthood. Quite simply, there was no way he could the time get off. If he took French leave and got caught, it would mean instant dismissal. We thought about telling Fr Brian, but that would mean making an approach to the authorities, which was almost certain to be refused because an East Kerry final wouldn't mean much to college authorities in Maynooth. After all, at that time clerical students couldn't get out to play inter-county championships, never mind inter-club activity.

So, nothing was said to anybody. Lar came up with a solution himself. In the oratory at Maynooth, each student had his own seat. If you were missing, your absence was spotted straight away. There were two times during the day when every student had to be in his respective place: for morning Mass at 9.00am and for night prayer at 9.00pm. Now, there was a farm around Maynooth and a byroad around the farm. Lar's ingenious plan was for our brother, Brian, to collect him at the byroad after morning Mass and have him back for night prayer. He would leave his gear near the road, slip away around the farm after 9.00am Mass, as if in solitary prayer, collect his gear, into the car and home for the O'Donoghue Cup final, returning for 9.00pm.

And that's exactly what happened. At the appointed time, Brian was waiting at the rendezvous spot when a black-soutaned young man emerged, his soutane bulging from something hidden beneath it—his football gear. They headed straight for the Fitzgerald Stadium in Killarney, played the final and went straight back afterwards, just in time for Lar to take his place at roll call and night prayer. Nobody else knew of this; the secret of all successful missions is just that—secrecy. I'd say most of our team-mates hardly know to this day. Now the cat is out of the bag!

Incidentally, Brian was our captain that year, but unluckily broke his leg early in the year. Rather than handing the captaincy to one of us, his brothers, he handed it to Dan Dwyer—a wise choice. Dan was a great servant of Kilcummin. He had played for the Sem in the Hogan Cup final of 1962 and for the Kerry Minors. As it was, he played a captain's part. With a few minutes left in the match, he latched onto a loose ball and struck it, soccer-style, along the ground for the goal of all goals. Years later, Beckham was to bend it like Dan. Kilcummin triumphed! Tim Sheahan and I did make it to the Fáilte for a celebration, but the first, drawn game had taught me a valuable lesson: it ain't over before it's over. How often do teams make that mistake still? Human nature, I suppose.

Another interesting aspect of that time was how we trained for the replay. I was staying in Artane, in Dublin, and our centre-back, Mícheál Doolan, a great pal of mine, was teaching and living in Kildare. I invited him up for the weekends before the final to train together. We trained in St Anne's Park, Raheny, on Friday evening, three times on Saturday and three times on Sunday. We bought steak and cooked it. We didn't drink a drop of alcohol, and on Saturday night went to a film and straight home. That was in 1973, a full year before Heffo's Army and two years before Dwyer's Babes. And some people think that hard training only started in recent years!

For good measure we then went on to win the County Junior championship and the County League. What a year! Unfortunately, with emigration and perhaps a lack of hunger, we never reached those heights again, even though we did win divisional and county leagues and championships in subsequent years. But 1973 remains, and will remain, the year of all years for all of us.

Our team had:

Four Kellys: Pádraig, who travelled from Belfast, where he was studying in St Mary's College with his De La Salle order; Lar came from Maynooth; Seamus came from Milltown Park; and I travelled from Dublin. (Brian, who was also in Dublin, and Dermot, who was in Cobh, were substitutes.)

Three Doolans: Mícheál, based in Kildare, Johnny and Billy.

Three O'Sullivans: John; Andrew, based in Kildare and who would later become Chairman of the Kildare County Board; and Monty, who was a sub.

Two Healys: Dan, a great cornerback who liked to call himself Tom O'Hare after the great Dawn Star; and Johnny, based locally.

Two O'Connors: Dan, also a Dublin-based student; and his brother Seán, who was a brilliant goalkeeper and later emigrated to Australia.

Two Lynchs: Con and Timmy, who was then a young sub.

The three 'single men' on the team were: Liam Horan, a former Kerry minor and great fullback; Dan Dwyer, our captain and one of the most well-known men in Ireland; and Tim Sheahan, our hero and talisman. Tim was a Garda and it was said he had played championship football in all thirty-two counties. His motto was: 'Have boots, will travel and play anywhere. Call me what ye will.'

We were all bachelors when we won the O'Donoghue Cup, but by the time we took the County Junior Championship shortly afterwards, Billy Doolan was a married man. It was the end—and the beginning— of an era.

The Field

When it was first purchased from the parish priest, the Kilcummin sportsfield was intended for the playing of Gaelic games, but in order to secure a government grant a clause had to be added: 'and other field field sports'. This made no difference at that time because Gaelic football was the only field sport played in the parish. And so it remained until the early 1970s, when a soccer club was founded in the parish. When the soccer people became aware of the addendum 'other sports', they started playing soccer in the sportsfield, claiming it as their right *per* the legal status of the field. Naturally, that did not go down too well with the GAA fraternity, but there was little that could be done about it.

When I became Chairman of Kilcummin in 1976, we discussed development plans for the sportsfield. Improvements were badly needed as it had not been developed since it was originally opened: no dressing-rooms, an uneven field and poor drainage. We still togged out in the furze bushes near the main entrance gate, one half of the field was wet and there was a fair slope in it, too, so if you went over the sideline too quickly on the town side, you descended into a marsh full of rushes. When the ball went into the bushes behind the goals, it took a long time to retrieve it. If it got caught in one of the many blackthorn bushes, it was punctured and useless. We all knew a few renovations were in order.

Modernisation beckoned, but why should the GAA develop the field, at enormous cost, if soccer and possibly other field sports down the line could walk in and play on it without making any contribution? We were in a right dilemma. The committee pondered this, then decided that I should go and get the deeds from the solicitor, old Cono Healy. After a few visits and prolonged searching they were eventually procured. We sought further expert advice. We were scuppered ... or so we thought.

When I read the document, I realised the proviso 'other field sports' had been added to avail of a government grant. I reasoned that if we were to pay back the grant—which was only a few hundred pounds, although that was big money sixty years ago—and if the Minister were then to waive his rights, wouldn't the field revert to the original deed? The solicitor listened to my plan: 'You are onto something there, Seán.'

Fortunately for us, we had the right men in the right place. John O'Leary, a fine Kilcummin footballer and former chairman of the East Kerry board, was our local TD. He spoke to the Minister for Finance and established that he would indeed waive his rights if the grant were paid back in full. The influence of Fr McMahon, our parish priest, was vital in getting the trustees on side. He also arranged for extra ground for us, which we were able to dedicate as a juvenile field. We got to it, work proceeded, money was raised and we were all as proud as punch when our brand new development was opened in time for the GAA's centenary in 1984.

In fairness to the soccer club—many of them were GAA players as well anyway—they accepted the situation. They realised that one field couldn't serve two masters, and now they have developed a good facility of their own in Mastergeeha.

Indeed, the Kilcummin GAA club is now embarking on further development as a growing population, expanded activity and the welcome involvement of ladies means at least one more pitch and extra dressing-rooms are required. My grandfather Brian would be very proud of the tradition he started.

Administrating for the Future

For better or for worse, I always had, and still have, a tendency to look at situations and ask myself: 'Is this all it's cracked up to be? Is your man a bluffer or is he genuine? Can things be improved?' This questioning attitude has landed me in trouble. A lot of people expect individuals, especially chairmen, to come in and keep things going as they always have. This approach to administration can be found from club level right up to Croke Park. Well, I never bought into it and I never will. Indeed, the more experience I get, the more I am convinced that there are an awful lot of people in jobs whose biggest contribution is with their tongue—talking up a good line in self-promotion. To my mind, such people are basically bluffing their way up the ladder as they enjoy the benefits of their position. That is not for me; I don't have much time for bluffers, bullies or dossers.

From the start of my tenure as Chairman of East Kerry Bord na nÓg, I began to make changes. We introduced new competitions to give lower-grade clubs a better chance of winning and, more importantly, of competing at their own level. We also reintroduced primary schools' competitions, which had all but died out in East Kerry. The various competitions culminated in a finals day in Fitzgerald Stadium, Killarney, on a Friday at the end of June. I was greatly encouraged by the response of teachers and parents alike to these innovations. Indeed, some time later, when the pupils went on to St Brendan's, they were asked to write an essay entitled, 'My best day in primary school'. To my delight and amazement a number of boys said the day of the football blitz in Fitzgerald Stadium was their greatest day. I also received a lovely letter from Mrs Lynch, a principal teacher in Clonkeen, Glenflesk, who said how wonderful the revival of football competitions in East Kerry was for the pupils in her school. She was particularly pleased that competitions were graded according to the size of the school—two-teacher, three-teacher, etc.

I continued in that vein when I became Chairman of the East Kerry Senior Board in 1978. The board had made great progress under the direction of my predecessor in office, Brendan Walsh, and secretary Denis Fenton. One of the finest moments was when East Kerry, managed by a wonderful man called Donie Sheahan, won the first ever All-Ireland club title in 1971. I was in Dublin at the time and went to Croke Park for the final. Fortunately—or unfortunately—divisional teams were banned from competing in the Club All-Ireland the following year, so East Kerry went into the history books as the one and only divisional side ever to win the Club All-Ireland. I have to say I agree with the decision of Congress on this matter. Indeed, some would say allowing university clubs to compete is hardly fair either.

When I became Chairman of East Kerry I thought it an opportune time to give more players a chance to play club football. There was a tendency to concentrate solely on the club's senior team and those who didn't make the cut were looked down upon and often forgotten. I disapproved of this attitude, so I looked at ways of giving those who wanted to play football a decent chance to do so. One competition we introduced was a junior league for club 'B' teams only. We said we'd start on the second Tuesday in April and run it through each week until June or July. It proved a great success as players were now getting regular games and they knew in advance exactly when they were going to be played. We agreed that we wouldn't allow any postponements.

In my opinion, irregular games programmes and postponements are two of the biggest faults in the GAA. Too many games are called off for spurious reasons. I made a few enemies in East Kerry for refusing to call off matches. Indeed, calling off matches is all too often the first thing some people think of when something happens or when someone dies. Obviously, there are times when it's the right thing to do, but I often feel a minute's silence before a game might be a more respectful and a more fitting gesture. Certainly, when I die, which won't be for a long time yet, God willing, I don't want any matches called off in my name. In fact, I would much prefer if people put on matches as a mark of respect. When you spend your whole life promoting football and hurling, it doesn't make any sense to call off games as a token mark of respect. Put on games and put on plenty of them, say a prayer and have a minute's silence—that will do fine for me at any rate.

I also endeavoured to present games properly, so we introduced a free programme for all finals, regardless of the division. People were very appreciative of this and it is a practice that has now become fairly commonplace, which is very good to see. I always thought a parade before finals, when bands were available, was important. Unfortunately, there are hardly any bands left in Kerry, so for many finals the norm is to play or sing the national anthem over the loudspeaker.

My taking the chairmanship in East Kerry coincided with Gneeveguilla's emergence as superpowers in East Kerry and Kerry football. Their first victory was the most memorable: the 1979 O'Donoghue Cup. Spa were the kingpins in East Kerry then and with five minutes left to the whistle, they were up five points and Gneeveguilla were reduced to fourteen men—it looked all over. However, a classy veteran called Seamie O'Leary and a young teenager called Ambrose O'Donovan (who later captained Kerry to Sam Maguire glory in 1984) intervened to spark off the greatest celebrations, and certainly the greatest consumption of alcohol, in the history of East Kerry. It marked the beginning of a golden era for the 'Guineas' and brought about a wonderful golden age in East Kerry football.

We also put great emphasis on refereeing and became the first divisional board to purchase full strips of gear for the referees. One of our best moves was to invite wonderful refereeing ambassadors to East Kerry, such as John Moloney, Frank Halbert, Frank Murphy and Tony Jordan, who talked to our referees about the game and professionalism on the field. We finished up with forty-seven qualified senior referees in a board of thirteen clubs—not a bad statistic.

Scór was another area we took very seriously and it grew rapidly as the East Kerry clubs began to clear the boards. Scór was a cultural talent competition first devised by people like Derry Gowan of Fermoy, a former chairman of Cork County Board. He is still to be seen acting as a steward at all Munster and All-Ireland competitions. It takes place during the winter months and is run exactly as the club championships are run: each club enters as many events as it can in the local divisional competitions, then the winners from there go on to represent their division in the county finals. County winners represent their county in the provincial finals, and the four provinces compete at All-Ireland level. Participants compete in figure dancing, set dancing, instrumental music, ballad group, solo singing, recitation and quiz and novelty act.

Scór began in the early 1970s, and when I became Chairman of East Kerry Bord na n-Óg I suggested we organise it in our own area. At that time the senior board used to run a very successful 'Tops of the Parish', but it had run its course by then, so Scór was perfect to fill the vacuum.

I took part in figure dancing, set dancing, quiz and recitation for Kilcummin, even though I was Chairman as well. Through the offices of a good friend of mine, Michael Farrell of Anascaul, Carroll's (God be with the good old days) sponsored Scór in East Kerry and we put in a big effort. It took off like wildfire. When we first started we held our competitions in the Fitzgerald Stadium hall. It soon proved insufficient to accommodate the crowds and we changed to the Arus Phádraig. When that sold out, we changed to the Town Hall. Eventually we finished up in the Gleneagle Hotel.

Scór was great fun and we put in a lot of practice for it. Dermot and I were part of the set in Kilcummin. We had never done Irish dancing before, so we had to be taught from scratch in our twenties. At the time we were both teaching locally, Dermot in Firies and me in the Sem. We had a succession of very good coaches in our chairman, Michael O'Callaghan, his wife Peggy, and especially her sister Patricia, who owned a boutique shop in Killarney. A great dancing teacher called

Paddy Sexton used to come out from the town to fine-tune us for a while, as did Frank Switzer, another man who has given sterling service to Killarney in so many ways. Norrie Sheahan and Marian Sexton had stints at training me as well. It was a great achievement for us when we won our first East Kerry senior title in 1980. Jimmy Brian, an expert in all things from football to singing to Irish dancing, said that we were a 'lovely, balanced set' and we were charmed by the compliment. Sets tend to break up as people move on and the same happened to us, but I am very proud to say I competed in Scór for Kilcummin and equally proud that I helped put Scór on the map in East Kerry, where it has gone from strength to strength, with clubs like Kilcummin, Glenflesk and Spa winning All-Irelands regularly.

I also took part in the Scór quiz, in which I was accompanied by the club secretary, John Dunlea, and a brother-in-law of Nickey Brennan, the late John O'Connor. John and I tried a bit of 'prompting' occasionally, but it rarely paid dividends! Eventually, I gave up the 'quiz' because it was in danger of becoming an unhealthy obsession: everything I saw or read, I was imagining how it might come up in a quiz, and my mind was becoming addled.

I also took part in the figure dancing, where I excelled in the 'Fairy Reel'—or so I tell Juliette. She was competing for Legion and I for Kilcummin; we hadn't met at that stage. As I recollect it, we won. Naturally, her memory of the result is different! Scór was a hugely enjoyable part of life for us all, and I hope it continues that way in GAA communities for a long time to come.

PART IV

Chairman of the Kerry County Board,
1987–1997

Vice-chairman

There is a statistic of which I am particularly proud: I never lost an appeal in the GAA and I never lost an election either. In East Kerry and Kilcummin I was elected to the Chair without a contest. I was twenty-two years old when I became Chairman of Bord na nÓg, twenty-five years old when I was appointed Chairman of East Kerry Senior Board and twenty-nine years old when I was elected Vice-chairman of the Kerry County Board. In the election for vice-chairman I was opposed by two outstanding stalwarts of Kerry and the GAA: Liam Sayers (Blennerville) and Tom McCarthy (Anascaul). In the first count (all Kerry GAA elections are by postal ballot), I received 85 votes, Tom 65 and Liam 58. Following Liam's election, I polled 126 votes to Tom's 76. In his address, Tom said he had been beaten by a better man. I very much doubt that. Tom built up an impressive empire, including the Hillgrove in Dingle and the Kingsley Hotel in Cork, and he has been most generous to the GAA all his life. Liam Sayers has given sterling service at every level of the GAA. Both Tom and Liam have been very helpful and good friends to me ever since.

My years as Vice-chairman of the County Board coincided with Kerry's three-in-a-row between 1984 and 1987. But I was also there when Kerry lost to Offaly in 1982 and to Cork in 1983, on both occasions falling to last-minute goals of sublime execution scored by Seamus Darby (1982) and Tadhg Murphy (1983). When Kerry overcame a fine Tyrone side in 1986, it was generally expected that the team's great run was coming to an end. Thus it proved to be. Kerry was in rapid decline and Cork was in rapid advance. The acquisition of two immense players—Shay Fahy and Larry Tompkins—transformed Cork's fortunes. Many people, especially Kerry people, believe that Cork might never have beaten Kerry only for Fahy and Tompkins.

Fahy was a power-house at mid-field and had great presence, while Tompkins was one of the greatest footballers of his era, and certainly the best 40-yard man I ever saw. His dedication was unbelievable; I'd say very few players broke the pain barrier as frequently as Tompkins did to overcome injury and achieve excellence. He was the lynchpin of a really great Cork team, one that was fully deserving of two All-Irelands, in 1989 and 1990, and probably deserved at least one more.

However, while Cork were undoubtedly better than Kerry during this golden era for the Rebels, many Kerry people just couldn't accept it. They looked for scapegoats. Eventually they found two: the Manager and the Chairman of the County Board. And so another challenge emerged, another contest—and all because the Kerry Seniors weren't winning All-Irelands. I had been watching closely all that had happened in Kerry, its decline. I had come to my own conclusion about it: the well was dry and the county needed to invest in its young players in order to regain its former glory.

Feeling that I had something to offer, in 1987 I decided to run for Chairman. I had been nominated for the past three years in a row, but each time had declined to go forward. This year was different. I decided to contest against then chairman, Frank King. Frank had been chairman for eight years and Kerry had enjoyed unprecedented success during his reign, winning six All-Irelands. Indeed, as reported in *The Kerryman*, on 1 February 1985, Frank had announced at the County Convention the previous Sunday: 'I am now advising Convention that I will not be continuing on as chairman after this year.' But like many a good man, he was prevailed upon to change his mind. I told him that, as Vice-chairman, I wouldn't contest against him, even though I had been nominated to do so. I told him the same in 1986 and decided to hold off for another year. But I understood that he was stepping down in 1987, so I allowed my name to go forward. I remember the day of the Convention. The former County Secretary and Munster Council Treasurer, Tadhg Crowley, a very astute man, said, 'Seán, I expect you'll lose by sixty votes.' When the votes were counted, it was the other way around.

The vote—Seán Kelly 174 votes, Frank King 111. 'A Stunned Silence' was the banner headline in *The Kerryman* the following week in describing the reaction at Convention to the result: 'When outgoing chairman Frank King announced at Sunday's GAA Convention that there was a "new chairman" a stunned silence fell on the crowd of 300 plus delegates at the CYMS hall in Tralee. Then after the lapse of a few minutes the incumbent declared the result of the voting Seán Kelly 174 votes, Frank King 111. The seemingly impossible has happened as the word on everyone's lips was that Frank King would return office with quite a lot on hand.'

For all that, I regret contesting against Frank King. He was a very nice man and he took defeat hard but very graciously. We had worked well together and it was a pity to have to contest against him.

In fact, my election to the Chair took more than Tadhg Crowley by surprise. Even the bookies got it badly wrong, but not being a betting man I made no cash on it. Some officials in Kerry, who may have had their eyes on the Chair themselves, were also taken by surprise. They expected that I would be beaten, but as *The Kerryman* stated, 'the seeming impossible had happened'. Everything now depended on how Kerry got on. If Kerry were beaten, it would be curtains for the young Chairman from Kilcummin. But whatever happened, at least I could always lay claim to being the first man south of Tralee to be elected Chairman of the Kerry County Board since Eugene O'Sullivan managed same in 1903. (By the by, Eugene was an MP in the House of Commons for all of three days!)

I came to the Chair when Tompkins and Fahy came to Cork. Their talent saw Cork take the reins in Munster, with wins in 1987, 1988, 1989 and 1990. When Cork took the All-Ireland in 1989, it was too much for some Kerry people. Mikey Ned O'Sullivan replaced Mick O'Dwyer as Kerry manager (O'Dwyer had decided to call it a day after the Munster Final defeat), and some said it was time to replace me as well. Up stepped two fellow officers to stand against me: Bernie O'Callaghan (Vice-chairman) and Gerald Whyte (Munster Council delegate and former secretary), two mighty stalwarts and great campaigners. Once again it was thought that I was for the high road. But when the postal votes were counted, there was no need for a vote on the floor. I had won the vote, but unfortunately I lost two very experienced and committed officers in Bernie and Gerald.

Under the headline 'Landslide victory for Kelly that few had expected' *The Kerryman* of 19 January 1990 wrote: 'It was the moment of truth in Killarney last Sunday. Seán Kelly, the incumbent, was being challenged for the position by two veteran campaigners, Bernie O'Callaghan and Ger Whyte … The word from the hustings was that Whyte was going to give Kelly the fight of his life … Then at about 3.30 pm the bearded chairman put everyone in the conference hall out of their misery as he announced the result of the postal vote. Gerald Whyte—34 votes, Bernie O'Callaghan—54 votes, Seán Kelly—197 votes. A wave of spontaneous applause greeted the announcement. But quite clearly, few if any delegates had expected that the vote in favour of the incumbent candidate would be of such landslide proportions. The Kerry GAA clubs had, in their wisdom, vigorously endorsed the Kilcummin schoolteacher's stewardship of affairs in the county.'

I continued my work as Chairman, regularly travelling the length and breadth of the county. We put great structures in place: underage improved, colleges improved, hurling improved, development work in Tralee and Killarney took off, extra grounds were purchased, the Kerry ladies were Queens of All-Ireland. However, apart from a Munster title in 1991, Senior success continued to elude us. Unrest stirred once more amongst those who judge success solely by the performances of the Kerry teams, i.e. Kerry Senior footballers. 'Get rid of the Chairman' was the simplistic solution.

Another election and another victory, only this time it was more emphatic: Seán Kelly 217, Gerald Whyte 42. 'Kelly, fair dues to you, you have buried them forever more,' said a good friend of mine from Kilcummin called Gene Moriarty. 'You could stay on as Chairman now for twenty more years and no one would challenge you.' Well, I had no desire to stay on for twenty more years, but I dearly wished to see Kerry restored to glory before I departed, whenever that might be. That would be the icing on the cake—the seal of approval from Kerry football followers.

Eventually it came, in 1997. Páidí Ó Sé and Séamus McGearailt, along with Bernie O'Callaghan, Jack O'Connor and Tom O'Connor, worked the miracle. The 1997 All-Ireland victory is remembered as Kerry's first in eleven years. It is also remembered as Maurice Fitzgerald's greatest hour, although not far behind him was the man at No. 6, Ballydonoghue's Liam Flaherty. It was a great win for Kerry and even greater for me. 'Time to go,' I said as even those who had opposed me in the past, such as Bernie O'Callaghan, asked me to stay on as Chairman. Yes, winning is everything—or at least it feels that way when you are winning. And for good measure Kerry also won the National League in 1997—their first in fourteen years.

The case for hurling

The Vice-chairman of the Kerry County Board is given overall responsibility for hurling in the county, which meant I was the man in the hurling hot seat from my election in January 1982. Many tended to see it as a poisoned chalice, but I relished the prospect of getting to know the hurlers who had kept the flag flying, with little recognition, since Kerry had won its first and only All-Ireland hurling title in 1891.

By 1982 hurling had completely died out in Killarney and was struggling for survival in Tralee, but was still being played with affection in North Kerry and in Kenmare and Kilgarran. Killorglin's efforts had been sporadic, with occasional juvenile teams who were inevitably taken over by football before their adult years. But once the county hurlers were fielding a team and not kicking up too much of a racket, nobody minded too much. That year, 1982, was bang in the middle of the Kerry Senior football team's golden years, so the hurlers were simply not a priority for most people. Nevertheless, I decided to give it my best shot. I think people were surprised that I was enthusiastic about hurling, so much so that when I got married in July 1982, my brother Brian joked at the reception about my 'late vocation': hurling.

Still, I had always liked the game. My uncle, Fr Laurence, gave us our first hurleys as a present for Christmas when we were very young. The first and only time I saw Christy Ring play was also the first time I saw television. The Railway Cup finals were on and the parish priest, Fr Herlihy, had arranged for a TV to be erected in the local parish hall so that people could watch the games. Strangely, the only player I recall from those two finals, the football and the hurling, was Christy Ring.

Every tongue was wagging about the 'Wizard of Cloyne'. The next hurling match I recall is the 1968 All-Ireland, which Wexford won. The name Tony Doran entered my life then and I followed his and Wexford's fortunes with avid interest thereafter. He had a long and glorious career and was without a doubt my favourite hurler—the great strength, the powerful hands, the left-sided swing and the inevitable goal followed by a high jump about 6 inches off the ground, but a grin of satisfaction as wide as the Gap of Dunloe. Yes, Tony Doran. My all-time hurling hero. So now, Brian, it wasn't quite a late vocation after all—more like a dormant one! It's not widely known, but I used to always bunk off to the Aghadoe Heights on a Sunday night to watch 'Sunday Sport', especially if Wexford and Doran were playing. It was a good place for a quiet date.

One of the first things I did when I became Vice-chairman was to carry out a survey of the county players to get their views. God help us, their requests were minimal: sandwiches after training, a good, respected coach and a decent venue for training. That was all they wanted. One, the late Todd Nolan, an outstanding hurler and character, filled up the survey by saying everything was fine, just fine. Todd loved to hurl, never complained and was as cool as they come. One day at a County Championship match in Tralee, Todd stood over a vital 60-yard free for Crotta O'Neills, near the sideline. Hush descended on the crowd and just as Todd was about to strike the *sliotar*, a female admirer shouted out loud, 'Come on, Todd, come on, Todd.' Todd stopped, turned and shouted back, 'I'm a coming baby, I'm a coming,' then coolly bent and struck the ball straight between the sticks. The crowd went wild.

As I was now responsible for hurling in the county, I decided to do something about promoting it in my own area of East Kerry. I got a great response and stars like Ned Power (Waterford, a brilliant coach for children), Justin McCarthy, Eddie Keher and others all came to Killarney on different occasions. Many locals who had played hurling themselves also helped out, such as Johnny and Mikey Culloty, Derry Crowley, Tony Devine, Murt Shea, Colman Dennihy, Pat Glynn and Donie Brosnan. The key man, however, was Pa Doyle: 'Mr Hurling' in Killarney. I didn't know then that Pa had been a driving force in hurling in Killarney years before. So when I spoke about reviving hurling in Killarney, Pa was my most enthusiastic ally. He said to me, 'Seán, we have lost ten years, we must make up for it.' And make up he did. He was a charismatic figure and his appeal was greatly increased by the fact that he was a mortal rogue into the bargain. He gave me great encouragement and help.

When we started juvenile hurling in the Fitzgerald Stadium, I began to puck the ball back from behind the goals, but to my embarrassment I nearly missed the *sliotar* every time. So I decided to go down to the alleys in the Sem and start practicing. Even though I was now thirty years of age, I improved reasonably quickly. Then I suggested to the East Kerry Board that we should try to organise a seven-a-side hurling league, and about eight clubs entered. Like the English captain John Pullin said in 1973: 'We weren't much good, but at least we turned up.' We had great *craic*. I played against Mick Galwey in one of those games—and survived! I remember Mick O'Dwyer allowing me to take Michael McAuliffe, an outstanding footballer, away from Kerry training one night to play seven-a-side hurling. We had already formed a club, St Pat's, East Kerry. Who was chairman? It had to be Pa Doyle. Before long we progressed rapidly and went on to win the Intermediate County Final—a victory that Pa and others celebrated as only hurlers can. St Pat's is still there today. Sadly, Pa has passed on to his eternal reward, but thankfully a great Kilkenny man, Pat Delaney, has filled his shoes admirably and is keeping the black-and-white of Pat's still flying. We celebrated our silver jubilee in 2007 in great style and published the twenty-five-year history of the club, *Kindling St Patrick's Flame*.

I wasn't long in situ when I realised that hurling in Kerry needed the boost and direction of an outside coach—some big name who had done it all. I turned to Cork and to Con Roche. I travelled to Cork City to meet Con in the Market Bar, and he accepted my invitation. His arrival was a massive boost to Kerry hurling. He had been one of the finest wing-backs in the game. The hurlers now felt important and challenged. Con was brilliant and good fun, too. We had some great years with him and some great results. The Kerry hurlers began to train more seriously. We won an All-Ireland 'B' title, which was played in London, for which the County Board gave a few days extra as a holiday for the players. Tom Randles and I nearly walked every step of London during those few extra days, while a gang of the hurlers nearly drank London dry.

Kerry hurlers had a name for indiscipline, especially when it came to drink, and it didn't take long to manifest itself. In my first year as Vice-chairman we had a good minor team, but the selectors warned me that a few had given trouble when playing under-14 and under-16, and would I keep an eye on them. I agreed. We qualified for the All-Ireland 'B' Final and it was fixed for Parnell Park on the morning of Kerry's All-Ireland Semi-Final in Croke Park in 1982. Naturally, the team travelled up the night before. We stayed with the Kerry Senior footballers in the Spa Hotel, Lucan. On the train up the management told me they were afraid some players might cut loose that night. I told the Minor manager and the selectors that we'd have a team meeting at 11.00pm and then send them all to bed. For good measure, I got the great Joe Keohane to speak to them about playing in an All-Ireland and the pride of the green-and-gold. I was well satisfied, having expressed confidence in their co-operation, but added that anyone caught drinking or leaving the hotel would be sent home on the first train the following morning. Well pleased with myself, off I went to bed.

My head was not long on the pillow when a knock at the door awakened me. It was Gerry Whyte and Michael Burkett, telling me that two of the Minor team had been drinking and had taken drink up to their room and given them cheek when challenged. I dressed and went to the room in question with Gerry and Michael. Sure enough, there were a lot of bottles of drink there. Gerry and I took them all, one by one, and poured them down the toilet and told the culprits that they were going to be dropped from the team and would be on the first train home to Kerry on Sunday morning. I went back to bed annoyed with the two lads concerned, especially as I had skipped my parents' 'stations' at home that evening to 'supervise' the Minor team.

The following morning I was up early and would have sent them home on the train only I was reminded, rightly, that if anything happened to them on the way home, it would be our responsibility. One or two of the selectors were now reluctant to drop them, but I insisted. Furthermore, I instructed that the two players couldn't come next or near the dressing-room. On the way into the dressing-room in Croke Park, whatever look I gave behind me I noticed my two boyos in the company of a selector following me into the dressing-room. I turned around and ordered them straight up to the Hogan Stand. So they were dropped and banished from the dressing-room. The final was brilliant and with the last puck, Jerome O'Sullivan pointed a 65 to earn us a draw.

Now for the replay. One the way home on the train some selectors, not unnaturally, wanted to include our two Arthur Guinnesses for the rematch. Again, I insisted 'No'. They should be left off the panel altogether. And they were, but with promising players like Paul O'Donoghue, Paul Doyle, Mike Shea and Jerome O'Sullivan, we won by a point in a thriller. A happy ending. But it had an even better ending. Years later, one of the players involved starred in his club's much celebrated county championship victory. Afterwards, he came up to me and thanked me. When I enquired for what, he replied, 'Only for you dropping me from the All-Ireland Minor Final ten years ago, I would not have been playing today. It taught me an invaluable lesson and I want to say thanks.' What a man, I thought to myself, how brave and forgiving. But that's Kerry hurlers. In fact, that's hurlers. They say hurlers are a different breed and they are, but they are a great breed. No wonder I like them.

The backroom team

During my years on the Kerry County Board—five as Vice-chair and eleven as Chairman—we had some very good and dedicated trainers and managers. Two of the best were Maurice Leahy and John Martin Brick. They have both given their lives to hurling and have occasionally taken terrible criticism for their troubles. They both hurled for many years and Maurice was denied the distinction of taking Kerry to Division I of the National League only by a very fine Laois team inspired by the Cuddys—tough men by any standards! I had great admiration for Maurice and John Martin, who with such stalwarts as Gerry Whyte, Mike Hickey, Michael Burkett and P. J. McIntyre, toiled unceasingly to raise Kerry's hurling profile and fortunes. I always felt it was twice as hard for a native son of Kerry to get support as someone from outside, which is why I turned to Con Roche and others from across the county bounds. Thus over the years we had people like Derry Mannix, Tom Nott, P. J. O'Grady, Ber O'Connor and John Meyler give a helping hand to Kerry's hurling campaigns. They were all excellent men and endured many sacrifices to help the Kingdom's hurling fortunes.

John Meyler of St Finbarr's, Cork and Wexford, was the most successful, however. It was in the Ballygarry Hotel that Tony O'Keeffe (County Secretary) and I 'nabbed' him. Some of Kerry's best years ever followed. We won Division II of the League and played and beat the then All-Ireland champions Clare in the first round of Division I. But our greatest day came in 1992 when we went to Waterford and beat the Deise in a tremendous championship game—our first win in Munster for sixty-seven years. It was greeted with amazement all over the country. Waterford, as always, were magnanimous in defeat, as a letter I received from former referee Noel Dalton exemplified. In congratulating me and Kerry he said: 'In 1957 I stood on the grassy bank of Walsh Park and watched as an unheralded Waterford football team beat the mighty Kingdom in the Munster football championship. Last Sunday (1992) I stood on the same grassy bank and watched in amazement as an unheralded Kerry hurling team reversed the result of 1957 and pulled off a glorious and well-deserved victory.' Yes, it was a great day and 'The Rose of Tralee' got a lusty airing, led by Wexford tenor and our manager, John Meyler.

Looking back at those years in the 1990s, I realise now it wouldn't have taken much more to take the scalp of some of the other counties as well. We ran Cork and Limerick very close in the Munster Championship, and had Tipp on the rack one year, only for the intervention of that great left-handed stickman, Pat 'The Bat' Fox. Tipp got such a fright that Fox was still talking about it in Malawi in 2006. But what we did manage to achieve was still very satisfying and it gave hurling a much-needed boost. And I didn't forget the hurling fraternity when I became Uachtarán in 2003.

Controversies

Anybody involved in administration, especially as Chairman, is going to encounter the occasional controversy. I have had more than my share, most not of my own doing I would hope, but the Chair gets the stick and you've got to be prepared for it and live with it. From the very outset of my involvement some unusual things happened under 'my watch'. At the end of one match in administration as Chairman of Bord na n-Óg, a mentor approached the referee after the game and for once it was the referee who lashed out with his fist and hooked the mentor.

That had to be handled delicately, and it was. I met the referee shortly afterwards. He apologised and said I should have also fined him £200. Could you imagine the headlines: 'Young Board Chairman fines referee who assaulted mentor'!

Once, when I was Chairman of the Senior Board in East Kerry, Joe McCarthy of Gneeveguilla was sent off, rather harshly, six weeks before the O'Donoghue Cup final. Joe wasn't a dirty player, and he was also vital to Gneeveguilla's cause. We heard the case and I suggested that Joe be given six weeks' suspension, which was probably totally unorthodox. Tadhg Sullivan of Spa, the team Gneeveguilla was facing in the final, said, 'That would mean he could play in the final. I think, Mr Chairman, that's only fair.' What a sportsman! It could cost them the final, and it did. Joe McCarthy had an outstanding game and Gneeveguilla took the Cup eastwards again. But to my mind the real winner was Tadhg Sullivan, who put sportsmanship before accolades.

I also had a fair amount of controversy to deal with as Chairman of the County Board. Every now and then some hurler or other would go wild and there'd be an almighty melee. The Board would have to investigate and dish out hefty punishments. It seemed that every time the investigation started, someone would say, 'The media blew it out of all proportion' or 'No one was badly injured' or 'It only lasted two minutes' and other such nonsense. All this was said with a view to getting the culprits off scot-free, or at least off lightly. If you hadn't attended the match in question yourself, it was very difficult to counter-argue, even though you knew that concealment and damage-limitation was in vogue. Once, however, at a hurling championship match between Causeway and Ballyduff, all hell broke loose. I was there that day and from my point of view, one person more than anyone else was the catalyst. When he was charged, the charm offensive started again: he may not have been in line for instant sainthood, but he was assured of very little time in Purgatory, such was his exemplary conduct on the field! Eventually I lost patience and told him and his 'charmers' exactly what I had observed and gave him just punishment: six months' suspension.

A few weeks after that I stopped for chips on the way home from a meeting late at night. It must have been well past midnight. 'The Hurling Saint' was in the chipper. Noticing me, he started remonstrating loudly about the 'great big bollox' I was to suspend him.

I was embarrassed at first, and I suspect so was everybody else. He was very aggressive, just as he had been on the hurling field. Finally I got sick of him and told him, not in a voice as loud as his, that the only mistake I had made was not giving him an even longer suspension. I then turned on my heel and walked out, leaving him ranting and raving. I never did get to eat any chips that night.

I wasn't long in office as Chairman of the Kerry County Board when I approached Kerry Group looking for sponsorship for coaching, a ploy that was unheard of at the time. The Group had never been involved in Kerry GAA before, but Denis Brosnan and Michael Drummy agreed without hesitation and gave me £45,000 for coaching, which was big money then. Kerry Group became Kerry Team Sponsors three years later when county sponsors were sanctioned by Croke Park, and have remained sponsors ever since.

Based on my belief that we had to train up the young boys in order to get Kerry back on track to a winning streak, the Board instigated youth policies from the outset of my chairmanship. Such policies take time to bear fruit, however, and while Kerry supporters are great people, patience isn't a virtue they invest in too often. So it was in the late 1980s and early 1990s. With each passing year the clamour for victories grew. I began to bear more and more of the brunt of the county's frustration. I got some nasty letters, written in vicious language, but the vast majority were able to distinguish between the work of the Chair and the performance of the team. Besides, we were making great strides on other fronts. In 1988 we won our first Minor All-Ireland for many years. We won an All-Ireland under-21 title in 1991. Our hurlers were showing great improvement and we had started to develop Austin Stack Park. We set up Cumann na mBunscoil, a supporters' group in Kerry and in Dublin, established the Friends of Kerry Football, began to write the history of Kerry and had many other fine projects on the go.

In spite of all this hard work, I was heading for choppy waters thanks to that one Kerry truism: when the Kerry team are winning, everyone is happy; when they are not, they ask what's going wrong.

Accordingly, after one Munster Final defeat, no less a person than the Chairman of the County Council, Dan Kiely, called for my head. After another defeat in 1995, I had to spend two-and-a-half hours live on Radio Kerry defending my own position and that of the manager, the selectors and the team. The fans were given the freedom of the airwaves to vent their anger on me as I was live on the phone at the other end. I was persuaded that I'd be on live for only a few minutes, but as it was 'good radio' it was allowed run and run and supporter after supporter vented their anger and frustration on me. Afterwards, the Kerry Executive contemplated taking Radio Kerry to court for the slander perpetrated over the airwaves that day, but we had a meeting with the head of Radio Kerry and decided to leave it lie. It was probably the only really controversial programme on Radio Kerry as, by and large, it's a huge promotional organ for the GAA in Kerry. Indeed, to this day, people compliment me on standing my ground that morning on Radio Kerry, such was the impact on those who heard it.

I also faced a very challenging County Board meeting shortly afterwards. Because Kerry were beaten by Cork, a motion of No Confidence in me was tabled. I remember going to the meeting and fearing the worst. But as I neared Austin Stack Park I said to myself, 'To hell with them. I'll stand my ground, I have done nothing wrong and if I have to stand up to the whole world, I will do so as long as I have nothing to be ashamed of.' I prayed to my late brother Pádraig for courage and wisdom. It turned out to be the toughest meeting I ever had to endure. But I stood up to the delegates and got great support from the Vice-chairman, Liam Cotter. The meeting gradually turned around as we remained calm and gave them fact after fact. So much so, that after about three hours the man who had proposed the motion, Mike Williams (a very good friend ever since, as it happens) wanted to withdraw the motion of No Confidence. But after all that had been said both at the meeting and on Radio Kerry, I insisted that the motion be put to clear the air. Liam Cotter backed me up. 'Put the motion,' he roared. The motion of No Confidence was put to the floor; two delegates supported it; and from thereon never a bother had I.

It had a funny ending, too, as the man who seconded the motion of No Confidence was known as Toots MacGearailt, but when it was reported the following day on Radio Kerry it sounded like 'the motion was seconded by two smart alecks'. All over Killarney they were asking me who the two smart alecks were at the County Board meeting.

They were tough times, but it all came good in 1996 and 1997, and everyone was happy again. We won Munster (1996) and Munster All-Ireland and National League titles in 1997, with Páidí Ó Sé and Seamus

McGearailt on board. The old order had been restored and the people of Kerry were happy again.

It was a huge honour and privilege to serve as Chairman in my native county for eleven years, and to have finished on such a high note made it all the sweeter. All's well that ends well, and it couldn't have ended any better for me thanks to a great team of players and a dedicated management board.

I will always be grateful to all those who supported and backed me, especially the people of Kilcummin. On each occasion I was elected to high office, be it as Kerry Chairman or Uachtarán, receptions were organised, poems written, cavalcades of cars paraded and bonfires blazed in celebration. They were all great occasions, organised by the GAA club with Billy Doolan invariably to the fore. Memories always to be cherished of my band of supporters travelling far and wide in support of 'one of their own' as they enjoyed the *craic* and brought good humour with them wherever they went. *Cill Cuimin go deo.*

PART V

Chairman of the Munster Council,
1997–2000

The Munster Council

I was elected Vice-chairman of the Munster Council in 1995, defeating James Tobin (Waterford) by 36 votes to 15. It seemed a strange coincidence, but each year that I advanced to a new position witnessed the emergence of a powerful force in the games. In 1975, when I became Chairman of East Kerry Bord na nÓg, we watched in awe as the greatest Kerry football team ever rose phoenix-like from the ashes of defeat against Dublin to win a great All-Ireland, and history records all they went on to achieve. Shortly after I took over as East Kerry Senior Chairman, Gneeveguilla won their first ever O'Donoghue Cup and became one of the finest sides Kerry had seen for many years, which was remarkable for a small club. In 1987, when I became Chairman in Kerry, Cork re-emerged in Munster with probably their greatest ever side, which went on to win back-to-back All-Irelands in 1989 and 1990. In 2002 I was elected Uachtarán-Tofa and that same year Armagh won their first All-Ireland and the following year, when I took over as Uachtarán, Tyrone won their first All-Ireland.

Given that trend, it's not surprising that 1995, the year I was elected to the Munster Council, was no different. That year Clare grabbed the headlines, making the great breakthrough both in Munster and at All-Ireland level—a feat I regard as one of the finest ever in the

Association's history. One of the most remarkable things about Clare's success was that it all stemmed from within their own resources. The county team had a disappointing history of setback after setback. They had little or no underage success; indeed, they have yet to win a Munster under-21 hurling title, even though both Limerick and Waterford have won under-21's in football, yes, football! Clare suffered so many frustrations that people began to believe Biddy Early, that much-maligned healer woman, had put a curse on the Clare hurlers.

It was a litany of woes. They had a manager whom they had fired before from that position and would do so again if they got the chance, if the losing streak continued. The manager had never won an All-Ireland and although he had played in over a dozen Munster hurling finals, he had lost them all. That man was Ger Loughnane. He had a mountain to climb with his Clare team, yet he had the courage, the belief, the confidence and perhaps the madness to say to himself, 'To hell with Cork, Tipp and Kilkenny, forget Biddy Early, we're going to win an All-Ireland and we're going to do it fast!' Considering the hammering Clare had suffered in the Munster Final of 1994, I do not know where they got the strength, determination and self-belief to turn it all around in 1995, and to win not only in Munster but at national level, too, by taking their first All-Ireland in eighty-one years. For my money, I regard that as the greatest achievement in hurling's glorious history. It wouldn't have happened save for the extraordinary and complex qualities that make up Ger Loughnane, man and manager. He drove the Clare players to where they hadn't dare go before and then well beyond that. He was also lucky to have had good deputies in Tony Considine and Mike McNamara. Together, those three big men, with big ideas, delivered … big time.

As Vice-chairman of Munster I sat alongside Paddy Hillery, former President of Ireland, at Clare's breakthrough match against Cork in the Gaelic grounds. I said to Paddy, 'Clare should have a good chance today.' He replied, 'Well, we always put up a good show, but we always get caught in the end.' I said, 'Maybe not today.' He wasn't too optimistic at half-time either, but when Seánie McMahon, despite a broken collarbone, made the vital intervention for the line ball that led to Clare's winning goal, Paddy, like all of Clare, and probably nearly all of Ireland, was beside himself with glee. Before he left the grounds that day, he came over to me and he said, 'Seán, will you make sure I am sitting alongside you the next day. You brought us luck today.' I laughed and said, 'Sure, Paddy.' So for all of Clare's great victories that year I enjoyed the company of one of their greatest sons and proudest supporters, Dr Paddy Hillery.

I enjoyed my years working with the Munster Council. Long-time officers such as Donie Nealon, Fr Seamus Gardiner and Declan Moylan were great people to be involved with. Donie was a wonderful secretary and a very strong individual. He worked diligently and while he would be a fierce Tipp man, he also had compassion for the weaker boys. Sometimes an individual or club might write to him looking for assistance—maybe, strictly speaking, they weren't entitled to—and Donie would show me the letter and, sensing if I wasn't too opposed, he'd say, 'Sure the poor ould crathurs, if you saw what they are doing and what they have to endure, sure will we give them a few bob anyway?'

You never saw Donie sitting in the VIP area at matches. He reasoned that a rúnaí should not be going out onto the pitch or into the VIP section, but should be inside in the backroom, making sure everything was going well. He was a great worker who, despite being heavily involved as Secretary of the Munster Council, also found time to serve his local club, Burgess, and his county, as trainer and selector for many teams. His wife, Kitty, was lovely, too, and Juliette and I got on very well with them. Juliette and I were in Croke Park when their daughter, Sinéad, a delightful girl, played on the Tipp camogie team that won their first All-Ireland in 1999.

Fr Gardiner was a wise head and did invaluable work for the Council as PRO and also for the promotion of referees. Fr Seamus, whose father was a former President of the GAA, had a wise and practical approach. He was a great man to say Mass, too—not too slow, a few well-chosen words and out the door with his blessing. He came up with a lot of good ideas as PRO and I think the media, in particular, appreciated his availability at a time when contact was not that easily arranged and communications not always appreciated.

Declan Moylan, our Treasurer, organised all the finances efficiently and with integrity. Like a wise owl, Declan never said too much at meetings, but if the top table was in trouble or some ridiculous suggestions were floating about, he'd be the one to intervene in a calm, logical way, which always commanded people's attention and their respect. It was no wonder J.P. McManus headhunted him for a top job. Declan was the soul of discretion and competence.

I loved working with the Munster Council. During my first three years I served as Vice-chairman under Noel Walsh of Clare and then when I became Chairman, Christy Cooney of Cork took the Vice-chairmanship. I think we made a lot of solid progress over those years. Noel was unstinting in his support for the underdog, but was very articulate and enjoyed standing up to the big boys, which he was well able to do—something that greatly annoyed a few sacred cows. Still, Noel is a truly committed and generous GAA devotee and it was entirely appropriate that in his three years as Chairman, Clare won their two great All-Irelands (1995 and 1997).

I received great co-operation from Council, especially in my final year as Chairman, which was the millennium year. I got the go-ahead for many initiatives to mark that important year in the province. We put up plaques in every major county ground, displaying a brief history of that ground. Each county's involvement in Council was marked by a special banquet to which we invited current and past players, as well as officers and contributors. We also introduced Munster Council Awards to honour the best hurling, camogie, football and ladies' football players of the year, as well as schools, clubs, referees and, of course, the Hall of Fame. These awards are still observed and have grown in stature over the years with the introduction of sponsorship, under Christy Cooney, and teams of the championship, by Seán Fogarty.

Council also agreed to select Teams of the Millennium in hurling and football. The *Irish Examiner* was so impressed by the concept, it agreed to sponsor it and even built the public's involvement into it by allowing readers to select their own teams and submitting them. A panel of experts was appointed to select the teams, with members both from within and without Munster. It was a privilege for me to chair those selection meetings as they were like a brilliant crash course in the history of Munster hurling and football greats. Among those who helped select the teams were Eddie Keher, Len Gaynor, Justin McCarthy, Kevin Heffernan and Jim O'Sullivan.

Hurling:
T. Reddan (Tipp);
John Doyle (do), B. Lohan (Clare), D. Murphy (Cork);

J. Finn (Tipp), J. Keane (Waterford), J. Power (Limerick);
J. Lynch (Cork), P. Grimes (Waterford);
Jimmy Doyle (Tipp), M. Mackey (Limerick), C. Ring (Cork);
J. Smyth (Clare), R. Cummins (Cork), P. Barry (do).

Football:
B. Morgan (Cork);
P. O'Driscoll (do), J. O'Keeffe (Kerry), Donie O'Sullivan (Kerry);
P. Ó Sé (do), B. Casey (do), N. Cahalane (Cork);
M. O'Connell (Kerry), J. O'Shea (do);
Packie Brennan (Tipp), L. Tompkins (Cork), P. Spillane (Kerry);
M. Sheehy (do), E. Liston (do), J. Egan (do).

Council of War

The biggest controversy of my career in the GAA was the Colin Lynch affair in 1998. I regard this as one of the great tragedies of the GAA administrative system and if any good came of it at all, it was my determination to tackle all the procedures by which discipline was administered within the GAA. For a start, it was ridiculous that each provincial council dealt with all disciplinary matters within its jurisdiction as it saw appropriate. I felt, and many others agreed, that one disciplinary body at national level should deal with all disciplinary matters relating to Senior championship games, at least. The year after the Colin Lynch affair, management (of which I was a member) brought through this recommendation. But in 1998 each council dealt with all of its own disciplinary cases. This often led to a situation where councils were either too lenient or too harsh on counties and players. Unfortunately for Colin Lynch, in his case it was the latter.

The Clare hurling team of the 1990s brought hurling to a new high in Munster, and probably in Ireland and beyond as well. They were to hurling what Kerry and Dublin were to football in the 1970s and perhaps a lot more, particularly in the area of controversy. Loughnane and his troops operated on high octane and believed in raising the bar for themselves and for others. Their unorthodox approach, flamboyant behaviour and unexpected success took the Gaelic world by storm. Their initial success was the most popular, but by the time Anthony Daly made his famous speech when I presented him with the Munster Cup in 1998, many people were openly and jealously anti-Clare. Clare were expected to disappear quickly after their major breakthrough in 1995. When they won their third Munster in four years in 1998, it was clear they had no intention of disappearing, either quietly or with fanfare. In the face of this resilience, many enemies gathered at the gates, baying for blood—Clare blood.

When I presented him with the Cup in 1998 Anthony Daly, Clare's outstanding and charismatic captain, said in triumph that 'Clare are no longer the whipping boys of Munster'. His statement went down badly in many traditional quarters. It was seen as arrogance from upstarts. This is something I couldn't understand. Personally, I thought it was a brilliant statement, one every 'whipping boy' should have the pleasure of saying at some point in his career. As I saw it, what the brilliant Daly was saying was: 'We were a soft touch once, for the Tipps and Corks of this world. Not so any longer. When ye come to battle with us in future, you will earn your crust.' The right thing to say, in other words, to bolster your troops and stay primed for battle. Daly also exhibited his intelligence and focus that day: no sooner had he made his speech and accepted the Cup than he whispered in my ear that I should give Brian Lohan, who had been sent off during the game, 'two weeks' suspension'. A great captain—thinking ahead and using his head while most around him were losing theirs in the delirium of victory.

There was nothing that could be done about Lohan's suspension, however, as the referee's report rendered a two-week suspension impossible. This would have been accepted, but when Colin Lynch was charged with striking, despite not being reported for same during the match, conspiracy theories took hold in Clare.

In the Munster Final that year, Waterford, under the management of Cork legend Gerald McCarthy, had nearly pulled off a glorious triumph against Clare. With time up, Waterford got a free 100 yards from the Clare goal. Paul Flynn, one of the really great stickmen of our era, stepped up to take it. I remember watching him strike it and it seemed destined for its target, only for the wind to pull it just wide at the last moment. Replay.

That replay set off the most controversial and bizarre off-the-field shenanigans perhaps in the history of the GAA. A packed Thurles, waiting for the whistle to blow on the replay, was just about to witness referee Willie Barrett throwing in the *sliotar* for the start of the game when he was called over to the sideline to deal with the Clare backroom team, who were refusing to go into their dugout. (Only the team manager is officially entitled to patrol the sideline, a practice that was more honoured in the breach than in the observance!)

While Willie was away on dugout duties, the players were left on the field on their own, hyped up, ready to go ... and frustrated. Such occasions are always tense and can result in mayhem. There was some wild pulling between Colin Lynch and Tony Browne, in particular, and Jamesy O'Connor, Clare's best forward and possibly Ireland's best at that time, had his hurley smashed in two. And this was before the off! Eventually the game got underway, after some more wild pulling between Lynch and Browne. Most spectators felt Lynch was the main culprit, therefore when Clare won the match, the clamour for action began to get louder and louder.

I received some aggrieved phone calls, as did other Council officers. It was suggested to me that we had no choice but to deal with Lynch. I replied that that was fine, but why hadn't we called in a Limerick hurler who was clearly seen to attack an opponent at the end of their championship game. The answer, which in retrospect was very lame, was that Limerick were now out of the Championship and so suspension was meaningless; Clare were still in with a chance.

Looking back now, I feel Clare's success was greeted with jealousy, and indeed dismay, by some people in the traditionally successful counties and that there was a general bitter sentiment that the sooner the Clare upstarts were brought to their knees, the better. While the whole country was delighted with Clare's unexpected success in 1995, by the time they had won their second in 1997, many had changed their attitude towards them. So by the time 1998 came around, Clare's new-found confidence and swagger had got up the noses of many used to success themselves. Clare simply wouldn't go away as they were expected to, and Loughnane kept raising the bar as he put it up to all and sundry. That said, it would be wrong to underestimate the genuine sense of outrage many felt, including Uachtarán Joe McDonagh, at the image presented by the ferocity of the exchanges before the throw-in at the Munster Hurling Final replay in 1998.

The Munster Council decided to launch an investigation, which gradually became the most controversial, bizarre and bitter episode I ever witnessed in all my years with the GAA. It grew in intensity with each passing day and ended with Clare refusing to start their domestic championship until Colin Lynch's suspension had expired. I must say at the outset that during all those months, Colin Lynch was the epitome of dignity and grace. He made no statements, didn't try to influence anybody, served out his suspension quietly and got on with playing. The more I got to know Lynch, the more I admired him. I think most fair-minded people would say that while he played hard, maybe sometimes overstepping the mark, he was one of the great servants of Clare and hurling for well over a decade. My father never in his life commented on any suspensions ever handed down in which I was involved, but in August 1998 he said to me, 'Ye blackguarded Colin Lynch,' and he would never have been at a Clare match, not to mind being biased. I knew he was right, though: three months' suspension was very harsh, especially when compared to other cases.

The problem was 'the charge', and this is where I slipped up very badly. It was my first year as Chairman in Munster and I innocently thought we could do as we nearly always did in Kerry when investigations took place after match brawls. We had our own way of doing things in Kerry: we called in the perpetrators, decided on their guilt and gave them the appropriate suspensions. The suspension was meted out according to rules for striking, dangerous play, etc. It always worked, but at provincial level things had to be far more exact. When Loughnane said that Robert Frost had heard three priests in the Hogan Stand say that Colin Lynch was going to get three months' suspension, he was right about the suspension. But it had nothing to do with the priests. Once Lynch was charged with striking with the hurley, the die was cast. It was going to be three months because that is the minimum suspension under rule. That is where I erred and I take the blame for it. I was too naïve, too innocent. If Lynch had been charged with dangerous play, he would have received a lesser suspension, which would have meant he would have been back before the All-Ireland concluded. I think Clare would have accepted it under protest—and my father might have, too.

I fully hoped that, on investigation, having listened to Lynch's and Clare's case, we would reduce the charge. The delegates would be anxious not to over-handicap our own representatives at All-Ireland level and we could get by without too much acrimony. On reflection, there was no hope of that. Some genuinely felt he deserved three months and nothing less; others, I feel, couldn't wait to bring down Clare and teach the new kids on the block a lesson.

Unfortunately, Clare didn't help their cause either. They chose to go to the courts to get an interlocutory injunction to prevent the Munster Council from hearing the case, which wasn't a wise move. When they lost, they had nowhere to turn but to the GAA for leniency: some chance after going to court first. If they had sought an interlocutory injunction *after* the Munster Council had dealt with the case rather than before and had appealed to management, the chances are they could have got it. As we have seen in the recent past, several interlocutory injunctions have been granted to players in the courts, and I would say Colin Lynch could have put a better case than any of them.

Clare also erred in not having or not allowing, whichever is correct, Colin Lynch appear in person at the hearing. I had expected Colin to come in suitably contrite, but also setting his side of the argument, and that Council might be persuaded take a lenient view and to give a lesser penalty. That's what I hoped. I can't say it would have happened if Colin had appeared in person, but certainly it had no hope when he didn't show. Having lost the High Court injunction, Clare might have been more prudent to cut their losses and at least pretend to play ball. When the case began to be heard, Clare insisted that three people would have to be present when the rule stipulated only two. I asked to be allowed to go outside to have a private word with Robert Frost, who was an experienced official with whom I had always gotten on very well. I explained to him the gravity of their stance and told him I'd give them a few minutes to consider, but they were resolute and the meeting re-adjourned.

Colin Lynch was handed down a three-month suspension. Clare went ballistic. However, such was their determination and resolve that in the All-Ireland Semi-Final the following Saturday, despite Lynch and Lohan's absence, they raised their game and looked to have the measure of Offaly when the referee blew the whistle a few minutes early, with Clare leading by 1-16 to 2-10. In all probability Clare would have won, but the referee was rushed off the field. It would have been far better had the officials alerted him to his mistake and announced that the game was not over, order could have been restored and the match concluded properly. It was a genuine error by referee Jimmy Cooney, but it was incompetence on the part of the officials that they didn't react quickly and instruct him to finish the game.

I was surprised that Clare, sportingly—maybe too sportingly—agreed to replay the match. It was rumoured that they were told that if they agreed to a replay, Colin Lynch would win his appeal against the Munster Council and be eligible to play. In any event, Clare lost the appeal and draw with Offaly in the replay, and even though they put up a most gallant effort in the second replay in Thurles, they were just too depleted and exhausted from all the shenanigans and Offaly just got over the line and went on to win the All-Ireland.

Colin Lynch's appeal meeting was chaired by Phelim Murphy because Uachtarán Joe McDonagh was in France. Clare made a strong case to the effect that the Munster Council had been unnecessarily harsh on Colin Lynch. When I, as Chairman, had to defend the Council, I said that many people outside of Munster were unhappy and that even the President had called me to express his views. If Joe had been chairing the meeting, there wouldn't have been any need to say that as he would have told management himself, but I felt management should know that. Clare seemed greatly surprised by this revelation and I know that when Joe heard of it he wasn't too pleased with me. But when you are defending a case you have to put your cards on the table, and that's what Donie Nealon and I did.

To be honest, I wouldn't have been upset if Clare had won the appeal, but in all my years I never lost a single appeal I have defended. The Colin Lynch case was one I'd have been quite happy to lose.

At this stage people were saying the Munster Council might re-hear the case and give a more lenient sentence. Even though I was on holidays at the time, I'd have been willing to come back to hear it. I asked Christy Cooney, the Vice-chairman, to check out if there was any appetite for leniency in the Council, but when he told me he felt there was no hope, it was decided there was no point calling a meeting. It would only make sense to call a meeting if the sentence was going to be reduced. Otherwise, one would only be incensing Clare even more. A statement was issued saying no meeting could be held as the Chairman was on holidays. The fact that I was on holidays had nothing to do with it, though. I was on holidays in Wexford and went to Dublin for the appeal. There was no reason I couldn't go to Thurles for a meeting if it was going to be helpful.

So Colin Lynch served out his suspension, Clare retired the number 8 jersey and lost their All-Ireland crown. What part I played in it I'll never fully know, but it was an unfortunate episode that, if handled more astutely all round, might have worked out differently. One thing that is ironic is that in almost all cases that have arisen since, the accepted position is that where the referee sees an incident and deals with it on the spot, a disciplinary body could not alter the referee's decision. Did not Willie Barrett see and deal with the Colin Lynch incident?

Finally, I must say that to Clare's great credit they put it behind them. They even took the unprecedented decision to invite all the officers of the Munster Council to their victory banquet to celebrate their Munster Final victory in 1998. We went, and they made us feel most welcome and we had a great night. Furthermore, in the books written since, such as Ger Loughnane's and Davy Fitzgerald's, they have been more than fair to me. I scarcely deserved it. The Chairman must take the blame and as I believed Colin Lynch's suspension was too harsh, I should have done more about it. It was an acrimonious time, but Clare have risen above it and moved on. Colin Lynch came back and became a true giant of the game and Clare's popularity and equilibrium have been restored once more. May the great Banner County continue to win many more All-Irelands.

PART VI

Uachtarán of the GAA, 2003-2006

The challenge

I had one more election to fight, but this time for the highest honour in sport in Ireland, a position no Kerryman had ever held before, an office that traditionally you had to contest at least twice before you had a chance of success: Uachtarán of the GAA. The runner-up the previous time, Albert Fallon of Longford, was in the field and tradition would favour him. He also boasted a very good track record as Chairman in Longford and Chairman of Leinster. Séamus Aldridge, Kildare's long-serving Secretary and Chairman of the Leinster Council, was also in the field, as was P. J. McGrath, who had held numerous positions in the GAA in Mayo, as well as being Chairman of Connacht Council and Trustee of the Association. McGrath and Aldridge had also been very successful inter-county referees for many years, refereeing right up to All-Ireland final level. It was a formidable field and once again, the result surprised everybody—including myself.

To get elected in the first count in a four-horse race was an immensely satisfying performance. It was said that it was the highest margin of victory ever. In fact, I polled 195 votes, which was 143 votes more than the second highest candidate, Seamus Aldridge (52), and 66 votes more than the combined total of the other candidates,

Albert Fallon (44) and P. J. McGrath (33). More importantly, it gave me the confidence to go and do the job as I thought it should be done, and by God I needed all that confidence as I went through my three stormy years in office. I would like to thank all those who put their trust in me. Some were probably disappointed, hopefully not too many. *Buíochas, a lucht vótála.*

Hurling

During my tenure in Kerry and on the Munster Council, I had promoted hurling, in particular. On the national front there had been sporadic efforts to promote the game, but nothing consistent. I was determined that if I ever became Uachtarán, I would do what I could for the game. So when I was elected to that great position, I quoted a request from one of the finest ambassadors hurling has ever had, Liam Griffin (Wexford Manager, 1996). In his unique and loquacious style he had said to me, 'Don't forget the small ball.' And I didn't—at least, I hope not.

In my inaugural address as Uachtarán, I outlined my plans to lobby the government for special funding for hurling, it being our native game, a very expensive game and a game in which it was difficult to master the skills. I wasn't long in office when the Minister for Sport, John O'Donoghue, indicated his willingness to help—begod, two Kerrymen coming to the rescue of hurling! But that's the way it panned out. John asked me for a submission and he donated €1.5 million in extra funding to promote the game. This was a major breakthrough and will pay rich dividends in the years ahead. He subsequently renewed and greatly increased that initial funding. Eyebrows were also raised when I announced the composition of my hurling development committee: Liam Griffin, Ger Loughnane, Nicky English, Cyril Farrell, P. J. O'Grady, Jimmy O'Reilly, with Willie Ring (Christy's nephew) as Secretary and Pat Dunny (dual Railway Cup star and Kildare's Central Council delegate) as Chairman and Pat Daly (Croke Park Head of Games) as Servicing Officer.

I believed in keeping committees small. Accordingly, the Hurling Development Committee (HDC) was small, but it had some big hitters. For a start, they were all 'doers', in other words to a man they were confident and dedicated. Indeed, they proved to be an outstanding committee and got through magnificent work for hurling. They drafted proposals for League and Championship reform. The introduction of the Christy Ring and Nicky Rackard Cups was an inspirational move—so radical, it is a miracle we got them through Congress. But people listened to the views of this committee. I told them that if they wanted their suggestions passed at Congress, they would have to go to the counties to 'sell' them. This they did and such was their influence and powers of persuasion that, despite opposition from such strong counties as Cork and Kilkenny, Offaly and Antrim, they sailed through and over 100 years of tradition was consigned to history. Now all inter-county hurlers could aspire to All-Ireland success and could play at least three or four championship games during the summer. Before this, they were all nearly gone after one game in early summer.

Once the HDC had done its work in getting the new system accepted, I felt it was up to me to ensure it worked as well as possible. For a start, I wanted both the Christy Ring and the Nicky Rackard Cup finals played in Croke Park as curtain-raisers to the All-Ireland Senior semi-finals (the Liam McCarthy Cup). Now this is where it got tricky. The curtain-raisers had always been the Minor Hurling semi-finals. And who normally contested these? The strong counties, of course. I was told: 'You are throwing out the Minors, the stars of the future.' But I retorted that as the successful Minor teams invariably came from the strong counties, they were going to get plenty of opportunities as Seniors to play in Croke Park. It was the weaker counties, either Minors or Seniors, that never got a chance to play there and surely should be allowed to play their final in Croke Park. Besides, the All-Ireland Minor Final was still going to be played ahead of the Senior Final, therefore only two Minor teams—the defeated semi-finalists—would be denied the honour. The proposal went to Central Council and after strong debate, my recommendation was carried. I had also included the Tommy Murphy Cup in football to be a curtain-raiser to one of the All-Ireland football semi-finals.

Some suggested that we could play three games on the programme in Croke Park, but I discussed this with the experts and it was agreed by Central Council that we stick to a two-game programme for the following reasons: (1) the pitch was new and three games would lead to compaction (especially if there were games on Saturday and again on Sunday), (2) employment legislation meant that security, gardaí, etc., could work only so many hours in succession, so three matches would greatly increase costs on that score and officially they would be off-duty for part of the games—an impossible position, (3) voluntary stewards, who travelled from all over the country, would have an awfully long day on a three-match programme, and (4) the first game on a three-match programme would likely be played before an empty stadium.

These views were accepted as policy by Central Council, even though the practice was different in 2006, when three-game programmes were put on.

So now we had the major carrot of the Christy Ring and Nicky Rackard Cup finals being played in Croke Park, but we decided to add a few more incentives. No player from the Christy Ring or Nicky Rackard Cups was likely to be selected on the All-Stars teams. Did the best players deserve recognition? Of course they did. So we introduced a Team of the Championship for both, with the added proviso that no more than two players be included from any one county. It worked like a dream and many, including Brian Coady and Liam Griffin, said the inaugural night of the Christy Ring and Nicky Rackard Cup 'All-Stars' was the most pleasant GAA function they had ever attended. For good measure, those selected on the teams would represent Ireland in the annual Shinty Series and the winners of the Christy Ring Cup would travel to the USA to play a team over there. So now, hurling had been given a right shot in the arm and all commentators agreed that it was a move in the right direction.

Our first Cup winners in 2005 were Westmeath and they headed across the Atlantic, where Séamus Qualter and his boys played a good game and enjoyed a mighty weekend in New York. The status of the competition was really recognised in 2006 when Antrim opted out of the Liam McCarthy Cup in order to contest, and win, the Christy Ring Cup. They went on to play New York, which doubled as the Ulster Hurling Final in a great weekend's sport in Boston. Meanwhile, London won the inaugural Nicky Rackard Cup, and it was wonderful to see our exiles play and win in the great Croke Park stadium. Derry enjoyed success in 2006. Just two years after introducing them, it is clear that the Ring and Rackard Cups were a master-stroke, thanks to the HDC.

One other innovation that helped hurling as well as football was the introduction of the All-Ireland Junior and Intermediate Club Championships. Mícheál Ó Muircheartaigh, who is more in touch with the GAA grassroots than most, described this as my best and most appreciated innovation; I can see his thinking. Now all players, be they club or inter-county, can aspire to winning divisional, county, provincial and All-Ireland medals each year. Again, the icing on the cake is that these finals are played in Croke Park. I had wanted the finals in Croke Park in 2005, but it couldn't be done because the pitch was being scarified and re-sown, but I made sure they came back to Croke Park in 2006. Thus on 12 February history was made when the All-Ireland Junior and Intermediate Club hurling finals lined out in the Park. It was a memorable day as many people from the grassroots came to the stadium for the first time to support their own village team, for Fr O'Neill's (Cork and Erin's Own (Carlow)) in the Junior Hurling Final and Dicksboro (Kilkenny) versus Ballinhassig (Cork) in the Intermediate. Dicksboro and O'Neill's emerged victorious in the end. On the day, I just couldn't believe the atmosphere in Croke Park. Even though there were only 6,000 people present (Finance wouldn't like my philanthropy), the fact that the crowd was all together in the Hogan Stand created a great atmosphere and you'd really need to have been there to understand just what it meant to these fans of the game. It was the real GAA in action in the GAA's greatest stadium. So, for those who criticise us for opening Croke Park to soccer and rugby, well, we opened it to our own as well and (loss of) money wasn't a factor.

In the football equivalent, also played in Croke Park, Ardfert from Kerry defeated Loughrea of Galway in the Junior Final, and Inniskeen from 'the stony grey soil' of Paddy Kavanagh's Monaghan had a fantastic win over Caherlistrane.

Amazingly, Ardfert were back in Croke Park the following year, having moved up a grade to Intermediate, and they made it two All-Irelands in a row by defeating Eoghan Rua, while another Kerry club, Duagh, took the Junior title by overcoming Greencastle. Those games were played under floodlights and in the hurling finals Robert Emmets beat Killmordally in the Intermediate and Domesfort beat Clooney Gaels in the Junior.

Back in January 2005, Liam Mulvihill, Seán Fogarty and I had travelled to Glasgow to meet John McKenzie, President of the Shinty Association, and his colleagues. John is a really lovely man and was reputed to have been the Christy Ring of Shinty in his day. I was anxious that we should tie down a long-term arrangement with Shinty.

We agreed a ten-year annual schedule that guaranteed a senior, under-21 and ladies international. I told them about our upcoming Junior and Intermediate Club All-Irelands and said that we'd be prepared to send the winners to play their corresponding winners at club level in Scotland. That was agreed and so in 2005 Kildangan and Galway travelled to Scotland and in 2006 Fr O'Neill's and Dicksboro flew the flag there. I am not sure about the quality of the hurling/shinty, but by all accounts the quality of socialising was first class as the bonnie boys from Scotland mixed in glorious fashion with their Celtic cousins from the Emerald Isle. I believe it took Fr O'Neill's four days to get home!

The final piece of the hurling puzzle was the adoption of plans to promote hurling utilising the €1.5 million granted by John O'Donoghue and €1 million committed from our own resources. The HDC debated long and hard on which plans to back in the pursuit of promoting hurling. Eventually a national plan was agreed through clear-cut, definable projects under the supervision of the provincial councils. After many meetings agreement was reached and we were ready to appoint hurling officers and coaches around the country to grow the game. The HDC was most anxious to appoint a National Hurling Director to oversee the whole plan as the members surmised, perhaps rightly, that the whole thing could fall flat after they and I had stepped down. A National Hurling Supremo was needed to steer and oversee the plans and also to show that hurling was being taken seriously at the highest levels. A dedicated executive, with no responsibility other than hurling, was pinpointed as the best way to secure the future of the game.

It proved problematic in the beginning because it wasn't easy to define the role and it was essential to get the right man. It was suggested by some that I should do the job myself, but while I'd love to do it and would no doubt enjoy promoting the game, how could I give the job to myself? The position would be undermined straight away. No, I couldn't do that and I wasn't prepared to wait until after I had stepped down. Out of respect to those special men on the HDC, it had to be filled before I left office.

After exhaustive interviews we finally got the right man, who hailed from the home of hurling—Paudie Butler. The Tipperary man was a great choice; his background, knowledge and attitude made him perfect for the job—far better than I could ever be. I was pleased, the

On my First Communion day, I bought my first football with my communion money—the best investment I ever made.

East Kerry Scór champions in set dancing 1979. (*Front row*): Mé Féin, Peggy Doolan, Cathleen Doolan, Michael O'Riordan. (*Back row*): John Lenihan, Mary O'Riordan, Dermot Kelly, Sile Lenihan.

Juliette and I on our wedding day, 16 July 1982.

East Kerry Board were the first board to introduce a special strip for referees. Included are referees John Somers (Currow), Ritchie Williams (Fossa), Mé Féin (Chairman), Weeshie Fogarty (Legion), Martin Hayes (Kilcummin), Teddy Counihan (Secretary). Teddy is grandson of legendary Gael, Small Jer O'Leary, who was involved in the purchase of Croke Park from Frank Dineen.

Ardán Ciosóg
Roinn 5   Lower Deck
Suíochán
Nº   0844

All~Ireland
Football
Finals
19-9-1982

MIONÚIR = 1·30
SINSIR = 3·15

LUACH £6.50

This portion admits to Stand after entry at Stiles via James' Avenue

location map at back

éi RE

Ardán Ciosóg
Roinn 5   Lower Deck
Suíochán
Nº   0844

This portion admits at STILES only.

19-9-1982

Riam Ó ... SJ
Ard-Stiúrthóir

No wonder Kerry lost to Offaly in 1982! A few days after the match I discovered this unused ticket in my pocket. Note price of ticket! Now they cost €70.

My late uncle, Fr Brian Kelly, and Jimmy Coffey (Killorglin), long-time treasurer of Kerry County Board.

Kilcummin's greatest day: O'Donoghue Cup Champions 1973.
(*Front row*): Seán O'Connor, Dan O'Connor, Diarmuid Moynihan, Dan 'Tom O'Hare' Healy, Timmy Lynch, Andrew O'Sullivan (later Kildare County Board Chairman), Mé Féin, Dan Dwyer (captain), Brother Pádraig Kelly (RIP), Michael Doolan, Patie Dunlea (RIP).
(*Back row*): John Dunlea (selector), Jerry Coffey, Liam Doran (RIP), Dermot Kelly, John O'Sullivan, Fr Seamus Kelly, Monty O'Sullivan, Billy Doolan, Johnny Doolan, Gene Moriarty (with hat), Dan O'Connor, Fr Larry Kelly, Liam Horan, Tim Sheehan, Fr Brian Kelly (RIP), Mike O'Connor, Joe Lenihan (selector).

Juliette finished the exams for her degree on 5 June 1983 in UCC. She came home but we went straight back up again—to the Bon Secours Hospital, as Pádraig timed his arrival into the world perfectly, arriving the following day. Here he is with us at Juliette's graduation.

Baby Pádraig with proud parents.

The Sem team that won the Russell Cup 1996, after years in waiting. Included are (*seated*) Haulie Clifford, Tony Behan (Principal), Mé Féin, my brother Fr Larry (Dean); and (*back row*) PE teachers, Ed O'Neill (now Principal) and Seamus Greally. My son Pádraig is third from end (*seated*) of the second row, and my nephew Darragh is third from left on the front row.

The four young Kellys on Laurence's First Communion day, 1996: Laurence, Julie, Muiread and Pádraig.

All-Ireland glory 1997, after eleven years of famine. I stepped down as Chairman of the Kerry County Board shortly afterwards.

When I was in Perth in October 2005, the Prime Minister gave me a book about the Irish patriot, John Boyle O'Reilly. Ironically, I was going on to Boston, where O'Reilly went after escaping from Fremantle. I enlisted the aid of Micheál Ó Muircheartaigh to locate the impressive memorial to O'Reilly in Fenway, Boston.

Vodafone All-Stars 2005: Seán Óg Ó Halpín receives the trophy from Helen Marks.

My parents and I (May 2006) at a luncheon in Killarney organised by National Cumann na mBunscol, in honour of my presidency.

The Vodafone function to honour my family and me in the Westbury Hotel, March 2006. (*Left to right*): Laurence, Theresa Elder (CEO, Vodafone), Muiread, Julie, Juliette, Mé Féin, An Taoiseach (who flew in specially from London), Pádraig.

All-Stars in Hong Kong: Eugene Mulligan (Tyrone), Alan Milton (journalist, footballer and administrator), Mé Féin, Jim O'Sullivan (*Irish Examiner*), Liam Mulvihill (Ard-Stiúrthóir).

An aerial view of the rebuilt Croke Park, looking north.

With President Mary McAleese, prior to the All-Ireland Football Final of 2004. (*Sportsfile*)

The great D.J. Carey lifts the Liam McCarthy Cup after the All-Ireland Hurling Final of 2003. (*Sportsfile*)

The cortege of Seán Purcell, the Master, moving through the streets of Tuam, 31 August 2005. (*Ray Ryan*)

Celebrating with Páidi Ó Sé in Croke Park in 1997. (*Sportsfile*)

With the Taoiseach, Bertie Ahern, at the All-Ireland Senior Hurling qualifier between Dublin and Offaly in Croke Park in 2003. (*Sportsfile*)

Taking part in a warm-up with Cormac McAnallen during a training session, in preparation for the International Rules game between Australia and Ireland in 2003. In a tragedy that shocked the nation, Cormac died of a viral infection of the heart a few months later. (*Sportsfile*)

Most delegates gave me a standing ovation after my speech at the 2004 Congress in Killarney, but some past presidents were less enthusiastic. (*Eamonn Keogh/macmonagle.com*)

At Congress, 2005. (*Inpho*)

An historic day: Croke Park provided a magnificent background for the first Rugby International ever played there, when Ireland hosted France on 11 February 2007. (*Irish Examiner*)

Handing over. Pinning the presidential badge on the lapel of my successor, Nickey Brennan. (*Sportsfile*)

HDC was pleased, the hurling fraternity at large was pleased: it was a good choice all round. I look forward to the expansion of the game under Paudie's leadership and, of course, the government will continue to provide funding for Ireland's national treasure—the fastest and most skilful field game in the world. Yes, Liam Griffin, I didn't 'forget the small ball', nor will I ever. Here's to hurling's legendary heroes, from strong counties and weak counties, from big clubs and small clubs, alive and dead and those not yet born. As Des O'Malley said at the graveside of the great Jack Lynch: 'As long as hurling is played, your name will be revered, and may that be forever.' Forever and ever. Amen!

The Guinness sponsorship debate
Another matter related to hurling that received a fair amount of media coverage was Guinness' sponsorship of the GAA. The Association had been reluctant to accept sponsorship from a drinks company due to growing concerns about the effects of alcohol on young people, which was completely at odds with the philosophy and aims of sports promotion. In 1994 the proposal to accept an offer from Guinness to sponsor the All-Ireland Senior Championship was defeated by one vote at Central Council. The offer was renewed the following year and this time was accepted by a large majority. Thus Guinness became the first sponsors of the Hurling Championship and the Guinness Hurling Championship was born in 1995.

It was a controversial decision from the start and some felt very uncomfortable about it. One such individual was former president, the highly respected Dr Mick Loftus of Mayo. He vowed that he wouldn't go to any more hurling All-Irelands as long as a drinks company was sponsoring the championship. I didn't agree with Dr Mick, but I admired his courage and his integrity.

Guinness proved to be marvellous sponsors, bringing a whole new profile and marketing expertise to the hurling championship. Aware of the sensitivities surrounding their advertising, it was planned carefully and was brilliant in its execution: their campaigns for the championships captured the imagination of the public. More and more people either went to the games or watched them on TV, and of course with Clare winning the All-Irelands in 1995 and 1997 and Wexford in 1996, hurling got an exceptional boost as the Irish people were delighted with these popular victories.

Now, with hindsight, there can be no doubt that Guinness has been good for hurling. They were also dream sponsors from an administrator's point of view. People like Michael Whelan, Brian Duffy, Clive Brownlee, Michael Locomeides and Rory Sheridan were highly competent and very easy to deal with. Nevertheless, the rumblings of discontent continued, especially as all the evidence showed that binge-drinking and alcohol abuse was on the increase in Ireland, especially amongst the young. Some blamed the Guinness sponsorship to the exclusion of all other drink-sponsored competitions and events.

Indeed, I wasn't long in office when no less a person than the Minister for Health, Mícheál Martin, singled out the GAA for criticism, without any reference to the multiplicity of other drink-related sponsorships. In fairness to Mícheál, this particular comment was picked up by the media and highlighted; he probably didn't want to emphasise it that much. (Ironically, he explained all this to me afterwards, over a pint of Guinness!) Nonetheless, his comments were reported widely on TV, radio and in the print media. I was asked for a response. I pointed out that all the other drink sponsorships were being ignored and the Guinness Hurling Championship and the GAA were constantly being picked out for criticism, as if the termination of Guinness' sponsorship would solve the alcohol problems of Ireland. Then I added that for too long the GAA had been a soft target for criticism, but that I wasn't going to tolerate this. I added that from now on, anyone who was 'going to kick the GAA in the arse would get two kicks back'. The media highlighted this sound-bite, realising, I think, that I wasn't going to lie down for anyone. I received a lot of letters of support from ordinary GAA followers, who were delighted that I had said we were fed-up with selective criticism and that I was going to give two kicks back for every kick in the arse received. In fairness, when I met Mícheál Martin afterwards, we had a good chat about it and I also mentioned to him that I would be endeavouring to do something practical to help alleviate the scourge of alcohol and substance abuse in Ireland.

I told him that I was establishing a taskforce, under the able leadership of the man who had led the hurlers of Galway to All-Ireland glory in 1981 and had given the best acceptance speech in the history of the Association—Joe Connolly. The taskforce would examine all aspects of the problem, including the Guinness sponsorship, and would report its findings. I promised I'd come back to him at that point. He was very understanding and was pleased with the news. Joe and his committee wasted no time and produced a detailed report, which made many telling recommendations. Membership of the committee included John Lonergan (Mountjoy Prison Director), Colin Jordan (Union of Students of Ireland), D.J. Carey, Trevor Giles, Michael Whelan, Tommy Maher, Noreen Doherty and Dermot Power.

Among those recommendations were that Cups should not be filled with alcohol by the winning team, that youth meetings and functions should not be held in licensed premises, that sponsorships by bars and drinks companies should be phased out and that we should undertake a national campaign in our clubs nationwide to help educate young people about the dangers of alcohol and substance abuse. In order to roll out this campaign effectively, it was proposed that each county and each club appoint an officer specifically to help implement the national programme as envisaged by the taskforce. And, finally, an officer should be appointed at national level to help roll out and implement the programme from the top, down. The taskforce's report was well received overall, although some did say that we should get rid of the Guinness sponsorship as well. I believe there was a strong debate within the taskforce on this very point before they eventually settled on a maximum two-year term for renewal.

When the taskforce report was published and adopted, Liam Mulvihill, D. Power and I asked to meet Minister for Health, Mícheál Martin, to see where we could co-operate on the programme, especially in identifying someone with the expertise and skill to undertake what would be a very challenging job. The Minister was most courteous and appreciative of our efforts and agreed to help source a likely candidate. We were well pleased with the meeting, but unfortunately, when I awoke the following morning, I heard Mícheál Martin had been transferred to the Department of Enterprise and Trade in a government reshuffle. Tánaiste Mary Harney (as she was then) was the new Minister for Health. So we had to start from scratch again. We met Seán Power, the Junior Minister, and then when things had settled down we had a meeting with Mary Harney. Having listened to our case, she immediately and understandably asked me, 'What about the Guinness sponsorship?' Her point was that we would be leaving ourselves open for more criticism by rolling out a campaign to curb alcohol abuse while still continuing to take the money from Guinness. I told her I fully understood her point, but that we were going to put funding from the Guinness sponsorship towards rolling out our campaign and that it was recommended that all drinks sponsorships would be phased out over a period of time. She agreed to help and her secretary, Shay McGovern, lost no time in getting to work.

Eventually, Brendan Murphy of Mayo was identified as a suitable candidate and following various negotiations he was unveiled as the National Co-ordinator for the GAA's programme. He had a wealth of knowledge and experience and got down to work straight away, visiting clubs, county boards and schools. Clubs and county boards began to appoint relevant alcohol and substance abuse officers and we are now, I believe, beginning to have an impact where we are best and where it matters most—at grassroots level.

Brendan is operating to a three-year plan, which essentially involves putting into action the recommendations of Joe Connolly's committee. He called the plan the ASAP programme: Alcohol and Substance Abuse Prevention programme. Brendan produced a club manual, which was launched in early 2007, that outlines the aims and strategies to be undertaken in clubs nationwide over the next three years. The manual is divided into five sections, each detailing a different prong of the attack:

(1) How to develop a club drug and alcohol policy.
(2) How to talk to someone about their drug or alcohol abuse.
(3) Where to get help.
(4) Alcohol.
(5) Drugs and their effects.

In his first year as National Co-ordinator, Brendan visited twenty-four county boards and many clubs, spreading the gospel. The provincial, county and club officers are all now coming on stream, and Brendan's first task will be to train them in the proper implementation of the ASAP programme.

It is also intended to develop a telemetric-based system of communicating with young people, i.e. SMS text, video messaging and the internet. It is proposed to use Senior inter-county players to send this vital and powerful message to young people. I think most people would be surprised by the number of GAA stars who either don't drink at all or drink very little. I remember when we were in Australia in 2003 with the International Rules team, I was amazed that six members of the Irish team never drank alcohol. It would be a very interesting exercise to survey all of the inter-county players. You might hear about the odd guy who goes 'on the tear', but you'll never hear of the likes of Stephen O'Neill, D. J. Carey, Declan Browne, Eamonn O'Hara, Seán Marty Lockhart, Mike Frank Russell, Dessie Dolan or James Sherry being 'on the tear'. Truth is, like many more, they don't touch alcohol at all.

Our players can influence young people in a way parents, teachers, gardaí and nurses might never be able to do. Therefore, by utilising players, SMS messaging, dedicated website and training for ASAP officers, we can make a huge difference in changing one of the worst records Ireland has achieved over the past decade: European Champions at Binge-drinking. Brendan also intends to commission a study of drug and alcohol use within the GAA *vis-à-vis* the rest of society, which will act as a benchmark for the effectiveness of the ASAP programme. Bar staff will be trained in the Responsible Serving of Alcohol programme and indeed it is planned that alcohol- /drug-free café-style venues for young people will be developed in GAA premises. Close co-operation with other bodies under the umbrella of the HSE will ensure a co-ordinated approach to rolling out the ASAP programme, and I am confident that we can help kick (or give two kicks in the arse to) the twin evils of drug and alcohol abuse in our society today.

Of course, it would have been easier and more media-friendly to have ended the Guinness sponsorship a couple of years ago. Instead, the GAA has used the sponsorship money to create a programme that will restrain a galloping cancer. Now that we are doing all that we are able and have the means to do it, we can, by mutual agreement and over time, end direct drinks company sponsorship of our teams and competitions, as recommended in Joe Connolly's report. Only time will tell how effective the ASAP programme will be, but credit must be given to the GAA for making such a big and sustained effort. I am proud to have had that chat with Joe Connolly a few years ago—only good can come from it—and in a year or two I hope to see my good friend and Iar-Uachtarán, Dr Mick Loftus, back in Croke Park for the All-Ireland hurling finals.

The GPA

There has always been, and probably always will be, a certain amount of friction between players and officialdom. Players play and draw the crowds and without them there would be no games, no crowds and no money. But then, the same could be said for referees—you can't have a game without one and officials are vital, too. Most of them serve because they want to give something back and they just love to see their club or county competing.

For years the players had no say in anything and, in truth, most didn't want a say. They just wanted to train and play and let someone else worry about providing pitches, transport, accommodation, a schedule of games and referees. Players really only became active and vociferous when they felt a sense of grievance, whether individual or collective. Their only form of protest was verbal persuasion or abuse, or failing that withdrawal of service. In the history of the GAA the latter rarely happened, although it did occasionally—as far back as the 1930s the great Kerry fullback Joe Keohane refused to play for Kerry one year because of a dispute about expenses. There are other examples, but they were exceptional incidents. By and large, for years and years, the players looked for little and got little.

As the GAA became more affluent, however, and the players became more educated, some felt the need for a stronger players' voice to ensure players were taken care of properly. Education brought knowledge of the outside world; players compared notes, read the financial statements, counted the attendances at matches and began to say, 'Isn't there something wrong here? We are the ones bursting our guts training, yet our lot hasn't improved much despite a burgeoning organisation.'

This kind of thinking began to be articulated in the media, where 'guest' players were beginning to write columns, and after a while the idea of a players' representative group began to emerge. As usual in such 'breakaway' attempts, there were a few cul de sacs before a better-thought-out and better-structured body was created. People like Donal O'Neill, of that great GAA family in Co. Down, did a lot of research and thinking before coming to the table with the Gaelic Players Association (GPA).

The GPA caused massive ripples amongst traditional GAA officials. The initial responses were predictable: 'Who do they think they are?' 'Ignore them and they'll die a death.' 'We'll drop anyone that joins the

GPA,' etc. Nonetheless the GPA was set up, during Joe McDonagh's presidency. As a former All-Ireland-winning hurler himself, Joe would have been seen to be pretty close to players. In fact, he had set up a players' committee, under the chairmanship of Noel Lane, to make recommendations on player welfare issues. They undertook probably the first ever professionally commissioned survey of players' issues at national level. I was on management at the time and when they came with the results of the survey, I remarked to them that the findings were very interesting, 'but why didn't ye put meat on them by way of recommendations?' I am not sure whether they saw this as their remit or not, but they said they would do it and duly went away and came back with some very novel and much-needed, forward-thinking recommendations.

Trouble was, while all this surveying and recommending was in the planning, Donal O'Neill, Dessie Farrell, etc. had stolen a march on them and launched the GPA. The launch of the GPA took the GAA by surprise, so naturally the first reaction was not to engage with it. This was a widespread view at the time. Joe McDonagh, reflecting this view, refused to engage with the GPA, and I dare say regardless of who was president at the time, he would have followed the same course of action. Joe was understandably annoyed, especially as his players' committee was so close to producing key recommendations. No matter what they now proposed, it would be seen as a direct result of the forming of the GPA. I felt at the time that if Noel Lane's committee could have brought in their recommendations based on the national survey six months or a year earlier, the GPA might never have been formed or, if formed, would not have got off the ground. As it was, the GPA grabbed the high moral ground and couldn't lose. If the GAA introduced player welfare measures, the GPA could claim credit for them; if they didn't introduce measures, the GPA could claim acres and acres of column inches outlining why they should have done so.

This effort at establishing a players' representative group differed from previous attempts by virtue of bringing on board from the outset high-profile players, such as D. J. Carey, Kieran McGeeney, Séamus Moynihan, Donal Óg Cusack, Peter Canavan, Brian Whelehan—the biggest names in the GAA. They couldn't be ignored and, furthermore, the GPA had acquired sponsorship: the seal of approval from the commercial world.

I found the emergence of the GPA exciting and a vital development, too, based on my own observations down the years of the attitude of many officials to players. As I was now eyeing the presidency and was unsure as to the direction the GPA might take, I said little on the matter but became a keen student of their *modus operandi* and progress.

Seán McCague took over as President from Joe McDonagh. He had watched the way things had progressed and played it very cleverly by going to a meeting with the GPA, thereby giving them some form of recognition. But at the same time he set up his own players' body in Croke Park. His appointment of Jarlath Burns as Chairman was a master-stroke; essentially, Jarlath kept the lid on the GPA for Seán's three-year term in office.

Jarlath Burns had just retired from playing, having captained Armagh to Ulster Final glory in 1999 (although just missing out on All-Ireland success in 2002). Burns was an able dealer, a fluent Irish speaker, a great club man, a great Scór man, a total GAA man and, most importantly, a players' man, but not a GPA man. He did a brilliant job in the Chair and was mentioned regularly as 'one to watch' as a future President of the Association, something that might well happen sooner rather than later. Burns is strong, articulate and streetwise. As a result, he became a thorn in the side of the GPA and introduced some valuable recommendations on the whole issue of the proper treatment of players. He occasionally laid into the GPA in his weekly column in the *Irish News,* but while they often 'took him on', they rarely got the better of him.

For all that, by the end of his term as Chairman, Burns had come up with some suggestions the GAA simply could not countenance because they were ahead of their time. Basically, the Association felt it had gone far enough for now. McCague, steady as always, had kept one step ahead of the GPA. He and Liam Mulvihill attended occasional meetings with the GPA, but these were going nowhere—and probably weren't intended to either. Nevertheless, when I was elected Uachtarán-Tofa (President Elect) in 2002 and the GPA was voicing concerns over gear for players, etc., Seán McCague asked me to chair a taskforce that would decide exactly what players should get each year by way of boots, jerseys, training gear, leisure gear, etc. It was a pleasant exercise and one that was welcomed by the players, the GPA and the counties—especially as we recommended that the weaker counties should get help in providing same. It was probably the first real player welfare decision taken at national level to benefit all inter-county players. They now knew how many pairs of boots, trainers, runners, training tops, all-weather gear, etc. they were entitled to and when they would receive them. I think the majority of counties accepted these proposals—indeed, some were doing this already anyway—but of course there were some who were either unable or unwilling to deliver to their players. What did the players in these counties do? They went straight to the GPA, of course.

In November 2002 I received an invitation to a GPA banquet in City West. They would have invited Liam and Seán, and probably more too, but they were unlikely to attend. I told Juliette that I was thinking of going and she said, 'Will you get into trouble over going? Be careful.' I decided to go nonetheless—not many GAA officials would elect to turn up at a GPA banquet. I asked the GPA not to make a big deal out of my attendance on the night and, in fairness to Dessie and Donal, they appreciated my position. Dessie merely welcomed me in the course of his address and left it at that; the Taoiseach also mentioned me in his speech. I must say I was treated with great courtesy and made to feel most welcome. Several players thanked me for having the guts to come and I remember at the end of the night my old travelling colleague from Kerry, the maestro Mick O'Dwyer, came over to me and said, 'Seán, you were bloody well right to come. Sure the rest should be here as well, if they had any sense,' and off he went with his usual laugh, wink and right thumb up.

At this stage, Seán and Liam's meetings with the GPA were getting fractious and I was asked to go along to the next meeting, as a kind of a stalking horse, I'd say. At the meeting the GPA, having despaired of any more progress under Seán and Jarlath, wanted to know what I was planning to do regarding Jarlath's committee. I told them that as they had claimed that Jarlath's committee wasn't representative because the members had all been appointed by Seán, I was thinking of giving all players an opportunity to elect a players' committee at national level to sit on the GAA panel. Donal and Dessie took a good gulp of air and it was agreed that we would consider the matter again at the next meeting. When we did, they came back saying the proposal wasn't to their liking. The reason was obvious: where would the GPA stand if there was an officially elected players' committee in Croke Park and not all players were members of the GPA, which would mean, in theory at least, that the players might elect anti-GPA players' representatives?

In response, I said I'd mull it over. I was coming to a certain conclusion when I read an article in the *Irish Independent* by Eugene McGee that concurred with my own thoughts. McGee observed that Kelly, being a cute Kerryman, would give the players an opportunity to elect a committee and if they didn't avail of that, he'd have no players' committee in Croke Park at all. And that's exactly what happened. It suited me. I gave the players an opportunity to elect a committee. They may not have liked the GPA, but they didn't want to oppose them either, so I accepted that. That left the GPA *de facto* the only players' representative group, which was fine by me. It also got me off the hook with the sizeable and vociferous group of officials who wanted a separate committee from the GPA. I was now able to say that we had given the players an opportunity to elect a committee and that they had declined.

My acceptance of that decision essentially constituted recognition for the GPA. They were now the only show in town: they knew it, I knew it, everyone knew it. That fact was far more important to them than official recognition, which might come in time. Although Donal O'Neill, among others, often wondered if 'official recognition' would benefit them at all—would they be controlled from within? Would they lose their independence? Time would have to tell on that one.

One of the first things I did when I took over as President was to arrange a meeting, one-to-one, with Dessie Farrell. I had found the atmosphere in the two formal meetings I had attended as President Elect to be suspicious and cautious. It's hard to do business in an atmosphere like that, so I asked Dessie to meet me in the Burlington Hotel. We had a very good discussion, open and frank. I liked Dessie, knew he was a dedicated GAA man and knew that we could make good progress by taking small steps. And that's what happened. I told Dessie that the player welfare taskforce set up by Seán McCague, which included Liam, Seán, Jarlath, Kevin Heffernan, Seán Donlon, Joe O'Toole, Tim Dalton agus mé féin, had examined all the issues and would be putting forward major proposals for improvement at my first Central Council meeting as Uachtarán, in May.

The most relevant proposal for the players was a recommendation that the mileage rate be increased from 35c to 40c per mile in that year

(2003), rising to 50c a mile in 2004. We also covered a raft of medical, training, endorsement and sponsorship issues, which were a priority at that time. When endorsements had first been approved, a player was expected to give a certain percentage of money earned to the team pool. This sounded grand in theory, but was unworkable in practice. At any rate, in a relatively small country, only a small minority of GAA players would be 'marketable' to any lucrative degree. If players, or managers for that matter, made a few bob, it made sense that they should keep it. The situation evolved that way pretty quickly.

I continued to meet Dessie on a regular basis and was constantly smoothing the way ahead, even though there was still major opposition to, and indeed widespread dislike and disdain for, the GPA in official circles. In my address to Congress in 2004, I began to prepare the way ahead for reconciliation and realism:

> Remarkable progress was made during the past twelve months in the area of player welfare. Players in particular appreciate these improvements. We must continue to be vigilant and responsive to the needs of our players and even issues such as burnout, training and match schedules, facilities, etc., have to be constantly monitored and assessed . . . I am also somewhat disappointed that while players are much happier now with their lot and feel much more respected, little progress has been made in the area of formal representation. An opportunity to elect a players committee at national level didn't find favour for one reason or another. Nevertheless, official representation is desirable. The GPA have come but not gone as many predicted and probably hoped. Is it the monster that was feared? Is the gap between the GPA and the GAA narrower or wider than it was four years ago? As realism sets in I feel the gap narrows.

The following day the GPA issued a statement welcoming my comments, Gradually, we were progressing, and I was trying to bring the Association along with me. Occasionally, however, there were stand-offs. One issue that sparked a fairly difficult stand-off was the production of a PlayStation game for football. The GAA announced a deal with Sony to produce a PlayStation. The GPA said it was also working on similar lines and during discussions with our marketing people stated that it would either take preference or enter into a joint venture.

As it was, the GAA went ahead with the Sony PlayStation game and no players' names were used. The game sold well, but didn't create the impact we had been promised. Indeed, I have to say that without real players and real teams, it was very stilted and most children lost interest in it very quickly. If a PlayStation game or other such development is produced for hurling, I hope real teams and real players' names and actions are included. Otherwise, it won't be worth the effort, at least as a promotional tool anyway. It might sell well because there is a big GAA market, but that shouldn't be its primary aim.

When we had overcome the PlayStation stand-off, I began to move things forward again. In my address to Congress on 16 April 2005, I made the following observations:

> Player welfare issues have been positively addressed in most counties and clubs. This is only right. But we mustn't take things for granted and wait for the next threatened revolution before moving forward. I am pleased that we are building benefits for players into our sponsorship deals, because players deserve it and also the higher the profile players have, the higher the profile of the GAA . . . We can now sit down with the GPA and either decide to ignore them, tolerate them or recognise them. I am not 100 per cent sure that we know or that they themselves know, what their focus is, but it is quite clear that while they may or may not represent all players, players do not want anyone else to represent them either.

This latter point was well received by the GPA because it meant it had now been stated officially that they were the only show in town. Formal representation was merely a formality now, but it would take some time yet to prepare the Association for it. One ongoing problem I had, however, was that the players had no representative on Central Council. I discussed this with the GPA and it was agreed that if I could get Central Council to agree, they would co-operate in the election of a players' representative to Central Council. Despite opposition, I convinced Central Council that by having an election in which all inter-county players had a vote, whether or not they were members of the GPA, we would find the official representative of *all* inter-county players. I knew that Dessie was prepared to stand for election, but I didn't say this to anyone because if I had, the whole idea would have been rejected. An election process was worked out and put in train. As it transpired, Dessie was elected and made history by, in theory at least, being the first person to sit on Central Council who was elected by all the players. It was a major step forward. Dessie now wore more than the GPA hat at Central Council and represented the interests of all players. Those who claimed that the GPA had no real support amongst players were forced to change their opinion. Dessie could not be ignored anymore. He was now an officially elected member on the most powerful committee in the Association. The GPA had secured official recognition in all but name. When he joined Central Council, Dessie received a frosty reception from some delegates, but gradually that thawed and the way was paved for further progress under my successor, Nickey Brennan.

Another difficult stand-off occurred during the League in 2006. The GPA had been lobbying hard for years for either tax credits or government grants for inter-county players. On a few occasions they nearly had it over the line, only to be tripped at the last fence by some stumbling block. Indeed, at one Central Council meeting we got Council to agree with the idea in principle and to state that if the government was willing to fund a scheme, the GAA wouldn't stand in the way—even though many saw this type of scheme as being a form of 'pay for play' and therefore discriminatory towards other players in the Association.

As my term was coming to a close, Dessie approached me and asked me to join a delegation to the Minister on this issue. I didn't see why not as it would only be exploratory anyway. I suggested to Liam that he might write to the Department to arrange a meeting. When it came up at management level, I was surprised when Nickey Brennan, then President Elect, asked that nothing should happen until he had had a chance to meet with the GPA. I was asked not to attend any meeting with the government until the President Elect had conducted such a meeting.

The meeting with the Minister took place, but only the GPA was represented at it. They were annoyed and called a meeting, which threatened strike action the following week. When I contacted Dessie

Farrell, he told me that as I was leaving office shortly, they wanted to send a message to the incoming regime. I asked him not to press the nuclear option of strike, but instead to spell out the player welfare issues on which they wanted action and to re-state emphatically that they were not looking for 'pay for play'.

Dessie delivered once again. While they did make a token protest of delaying the start of the League games the following Sunday, they also spelt out their player welfare priorities. As in November 2002, when I went to the GPA banquet, they reiterated that they weren't about pay for play.

By 2006, when my time as President ended, we had moved things along so well that the GPA was no longer seen as a group of dangerous troublemakers; it was now accepted as a respectable, well-run players' association. No other players' group had emerged during my three-year tenure, so there was going to be no turning back of the clock now. The GPA was here to stay, was recognised as such and therefore it was only a matter of time before they would get official recognition—if they wanted it, that is. In reality, official recognition isn't going to make a great difference, but it might in the future, especially if areas of conflict emerge.

Even though I had doubts in the beginning about the GPA, I came to believe that it is a necessary voice for the players. Look what the Cork hurlers GPA strike, for example, did for the welfare of players in Cork. That wouldn't have happened without the GPA. The players' voices must be heard. They have a lot to offer and as the GAA becomes bigger and wealthier, it's only right that the players share in that wealth. Without the GPA, they might not get their fair share. As I said at the outset, there will always be a certain amount of friction between players and officials. The players will always need a strong voice to articulate their views and claim their just rewards on their behalf. If that happens, both the GPA and the GAA can continue to prosper.

The Question of Discipline

Hurling and football are high velocity contact sports, which means physical contact and conflict will always be part of them. The oxygen for the survival of the sports is local rivalry, both club and county. When you have those two in the mix, explosions are bound to occur. The miracle is not that there are outbreaks of violence in GAA games, but that there aren't more—especially in this modern world where violence has become endemic in everyday life. So, before the GAA, and indeed other team sports like soccer and rugby, are criticised for outbreaks of indiscipline, much credit must go to all the participants for ensuring that the vast majority of games pass off sportingly.

Nevertheless, only a fool would suggest that there is an acceptable level of violence in sport. It may happen. We can understand why it happens. But indiscipline must be condemned at all times. The GAA's problem has not been in failing to condemn violence but in not doing enough to stamp it out. Almost every year during his long period in office, Liam Ó Maolmhichíl has been drawing attention to this issue in the Association. And every year the media highlight this aspect of Liam's report and rightly praise him for commenting on it. It often struck me, however, that in highlighting the issues raised by Liam, the media never seemed to ask the question: 'What are you going to do about it?' or, more pertinently, 'What is the GAA going to do about it?'

I was very conscious of this when I took office as President. I had come to the conclusion that the system of discipline, the rules of discipline and the whole implementation of the rules needed reform. The rule book had been growing piecemeal Congress after Congress. The same committee system had been in place for years. By this stage, the rule book had become so complicated that there were very few experts in it. Accordingly, in my inaugural address I said:

> I am also establishing a task force to take a long hard look at our gospel "An Treoraí Oifigiúil". Is it unnecessarily complicated? Are there ten people in the Association who could be regarded as experts in the rules? Are there rules that need changing? These matters will be examined by some of our own legal experts and legal experts who have volunteered their services. Hopefully, we can come up with a modern user-friendly Treoraí Oifigiúil at the end of the exercise.

I decided to establish a committee to look at the disciplinary system and the entire rule book with a view to making it more relevant and more functional. I appointed Frank Murphy as Chairman and Liam Ó Maolmhichíl as Servicing Officer. (Liam and Frank are probably the foremost authorities on the rule book of the GAA.) I also added Declan

Hallissey of Dublin and Dan McCartan of Down, who both had a great interest in that whole area, and I brought in legal expertise in the guise of two Kerrymen and a Meath man. The two Kerrymen were former Supreme Court Judge Hugh O'Flaherty and Mícheál O'Connell, a lawyer who happened to be the son of my football hero, the greatest of all, Mick O'Connell. I had met Mícheál a few times prior to that and had been greatly impressed by his logic, calmness and astuteness. The third legal expert was Liam Keane. I had never met him, but Pat O'Neill, Meath's Central Council delegate, rang me one day and recommended two very good people to me, namely Liam Keane and Brendan Dempsey. I knew Pat would only want what was good for the GAA and would never recommend a candidate he didn't back fully. So without ever meeting Liam or Brendan, I rang them up and asked Liam to join the committee, inviting Brendan Dempsey to chair the Insurance workgroup. They turned out to be two valuable appointments. Liam is now Secretary of the Disputes Resolution Authority and has done sterling work for the GAA, while Brendan is Chairman of the Meath County Board.

It is important to remind people that all work done by committees in Croke Park is on a voluntary basis. In other words, we got all this legal expertise free of charge. When I think what we would have paid consultants, such as Genesis, to do some of the work for us, the mind boggles.

Before the committee began its work, I outlined a number of changes I felt needed to be made as soon as possible. First, I felt that the Games Administration Committee (GAC) had too much responsibility and was overburdened, especially for a voluntary committee. The GAC had been established under rule and its members were elected, except the Chair. Therefore it was a very hit-and-miss affair whether you got a good committee or not. In that kind of a system there will always be a lot of internal politics. This committee had enormous power because it was responsible for fixtures and discipline: having a voice on that committee made a big difference to your chances of getting your way in the date, venue and referees of matches and on whether you were penalised in disciplinary matters. I concluded that it was in fact too big, too powerful, too unwieldy and too onerous.

When I suggested that the GAC be split into two committees, one for fixtures and one for discipline, I met with huge resistance. So much resistance, in fact, that when my suggestion came before Congress in Killarney in 2004, it got so little support that Pat Hamilton (Louth), who had proposed the motion for me, withdrew it in favour of a compromise that it be assessed further. I had no choice but to agree— I was just pushing things too quickly for the Association—but it meant that for two of my three years in office I had an activities committee responsible for fixtures and discipline with whose constitution and responsibilities I disagreed. Still, I had no notion of giving up. I looked into it further and was better prepared for Congress 2005, when agreement was reached on the suggestion to divide the GAC and, what's more, the element of elections was taken out of it, which was essential for independence, competence and general confidence. Subsequently, it was tweaked further as the Rules Revision taskforce got down to business.

The other area on which I had strong views was the whole appeal system within the Association. Quite frankly, there was no appeal system: a player could only get off on a technicality. In order to win a reprieve, you had to prove that the committee that had handed down the sentence had 'misapplied a rule'. If you had an expert in the rules on your side, such as Frank Murphy, you could do that fairly easily. If not, you hadn't a hope. Many people were unhappy with this situation and I discussed it with the Rules taskforce. We were also much alarmed by the growing frequency of 'interlocutory injunctions', which arose particularly when players were suspended coming up to a big match. Even though there was a rule in the official guide stating that there could be no appeal to a court of law by any GAA member arising out of dissatisfaction with the application of GAA rules, it was honoured neither in breach or observance; the rule wasn't worth the paper on which it was written. Every person in every organisation is subject to the laws of the land, therefore on the grounds of natural justice denied, anyone could take his or her case to the courts. The crux of the matter for the GAA was that in taking their case to the courts, the aggrieved merely sought temporary relief or an interlocutary injunction. Judges seemed very amenable to grant these on the logical grounds—logical from a legal point of view, at any rate—that there might be a case to answer. Thus an interlocutory injunction or temporary relief would be granted, allowing a player to play perhaps the most important game of his life the following Sunday.

This situation had occurred on a number of occasions, the most high profile being the Rory O'Connell and Paul Barden cases. One couldn't blame the players, but it made a mockery of the rule book and the suspension system. I was determined to do something about it. I spoke to our legal advisers, Reddy, Charleton and McKnight, and asked them to take one of the cases—the one with the best chance of winning—all the way to a full hearing in the High Court. The one they chose was the Paul Barden case. They prepared the papers and readied themselves for action. If we took and won a case in the courts, it would make players, or more accurately their 'backers', think twice about seeking injunctions. The GAA wouldn't be seen as a 'soft touch' and the expenses of a full court case would cost them dearly. It might stop, or at least put the brakes on, a worrying and embarrassing trend.

There was, however, a better and more lasting solution. In discussing this topic with Pat Daly (Director of Games in Croke Park) in Australia in 2003, Pat said to me, 'You should arrange to meet Brian Collis QC, who is in charge of discipline in the AFL.' Pat duly arranged a meeting with Mr Collis for 8.00am two mornings later, and it was one of the most eye-opening and productive meetings I ever had. Put simply, Australia had a system that was far quicker, far more efficient and far more effective than ours, which by comparison was grossly unwieldy and overly democratic (i.e. too many people elected to disciplinary bodies). Brian gave me the 'tome' on AFL disciplinary rules and I brought it back with me and gave it to the Rules Revision taskforce. Being legal experts, naturally they were able to assimilate it quicker than me. Using a combination of the AFL rule book, plus their own expertise and, I'm quite sure, looking at other systems globally, they came back with a revolutionary disciplinary system that will probably require a little tweaking for a few years, but as a package is light years ahead of the previous system and is fairer to players and units of the Association.

One of the key outcomes of the report was the setting up of the Disputes Resolution Authority (DRA), which overnight ended the embarrassing and costly practice of recourse to the courts. The DRA is basically an independent court within the GAA. Its membership is comprised of a large panel of legal experts (solicitors and barristers) and GAA rules experts of high standing. A secretary (now Liam Keane, whom Pat O'Neill first recommended to me in 2002) calls together a small number from the panel to deal with each case and deliver a judgment quickly. Their decision is final and while some, especially provincial councils, have occasionally taken issue with them, I regard the emergence of the DRA as one of the most important innovations of my presidency. It will get better as the years go by and 'case law' is established, setting precedents that people can understand and respect.

In 2007 the Rules Revision taskforce further reformed the system so that there are no conflicts of interest, perceived or real, from the fixing of games until all appeal processes have been exhausted at DRA level. One major improvement that has been introduced is that if an individual or unit wins a case on appeal on a technicality, it does not mean they get off scot-free as a result. It means the case can be sent back to the Hearings Committee to correct their technical breach and apply the penalty properly. When this hits home a few times it will put a stop to the 'find a loophole' syndrome. You might find a loophole, but it doesn't mean you will get off. That's why I referred to the 'Tyrone/Dublin Battle of Omagh' as the 'Last Great Escape'. If such a situation were to arise from here on, the players wouldn't have their suspensions lifted, instead the case would be sent back for suspensions to be imposed properly.

The Rules Revision taskforce is continuing the good work I asked them to do and when finished, in 2008, I think that, for the first time ever, we will have an efficient, transparent and equitable system of justice, which is a far cry from the bungling, intractable system of old. The setting up of the taskforce might yet prove to be my most enlightened contribution to the GAA; time alone will tell.

Going to 'The Office': working in Croke Park

Most people see the Uachtarán's role as that of chairing Management and Central Council meetings, greeting various delegations, meeting government departments and various others as well. And, of course, there is the very demanding social side, which involves visits to schools, clubs, overseas units, presenting Cups and medals, opening fields, taking part in debates, making 'guest speaker' appearances, etc. I also took on the extra responsibility of chairing two sub-committees: the Dublin Strategic Review Implementation Committee, which has helped put a great structure in place in Dublin to increase the GAA's market share, and the Integration Committee, of which I am still Chair, which works to bring all our sister organisations closer together.

When I took over as President in 2003 the Cusack (1995), Canal (Davin) and Hogan Stands (2002) had been completed, but the Nally Stand and Hill 16 were untouched. One of the reasons for this was money. The GAA was up to its neck in debt and the estimated cost of completing the Northern End was €30 million, which would push the debt to over €100 million. The general feeling was that this was unsustainable.

Another major factor in delaying the completion of the redevelopment was a manner of thinking in vogue at the time that terraces would not be allowed. Hill 16—called after the 1916 Rising because the rubble from the destruction of Sackville Place was used in its construction—was hugely sentimental for GAA supporters, none more so than the magnificent Boys in Blue, the Dubs, who made it their home whenever Dublin were playing. People stood on the Hill, could go in their thousands and it was often the preferred option for the Dubs, even when they could have procured tickets for the stands. For instance, Maurice Ahern TD, a brother of Taoiseach Bertie Ahern, told me that he always stood on the Hill when Dublin were playing, even though he could get stand tickets whenever he wished. Like many more Dubs, this was a vital ritual; Hill 16 is to Dubs what Mecca is to Muslims. Because it was standing only, tickets were half the price of stand tickets, which was an important consideration for many, especially students and younger folk. Also, its capacity was much greater than that of a stand. For these reasons the preferred option was to keep it as a terrace.

This required another trip to the planning offices, of course. One of the arguments was that with the limited space on that side of the ground, a stand would be very costly in relation to the capacity it would accommodate. The railway runs directly behind Hill 16's outer wall and as there are houses in close proximity, the option of moving the railway—as we did with the canal on the other side—wasn't possible. A high stand built either over the railway or inside it was also unlikely to receive planning permission because it would block sunlight to the houses nearby almost entirely. For all these reasons it was decided that Hill 16 plus the Nally Stand should be built as one unit and all terraced. Securing the planning permission was going to be difficult, however. As always there would be objections—some very genuine, some spurious. But once again luck was on our side. A few years previously there had been no hope at all of getting planning permission for a terrace-like construction. After the Heysel Stadium disaster, terraces had been virtually outlawed as a health and safety threat. Gradually things had begun to change, especially on the Continent. Germany, in particular, had many terraced grounds and these had proven to be very safe. We used their experience when looking for planning permission for the Hill 16/Northern End and it worked: the Dublin corporation planning authorities saw the sense in what we were proposing and granted permission.

Could we afford to do it? Were we prepared to go €100 million in the red? These were big questions to be answered. I, for one, was in favour, but I also believed that if we played our cards right, we could get the outstanding €38 million from the government. Liam Mulvihill didn't agree with me and at Coiste Bainistí insisted, 'I'm telling ye, it won't be built.' I spoke to Peter Quinn, who had played such a pivotal role in the reconstruction of the stadium, and he agreed that now was the time to do it. He also assured me that by invoking proper controls, we could get it done for well below the budgeted figure of €30 million. I asked him to chair the re-development committee and he agreed. I also asked him to come to the next meeting of Coiste Bainistí and Ard-Chomhairle and to make a presentation, with Peter McKenna, to the committee. I asked him to speak last because after he spoke, I would put it to a vote.

And so the case was argued, pointing out that the stadium had to be finished some time, that interest rates were never lower and might rise, that the sooner the stadium was finished, the sooner it would generate income and that the quicker we got the ground up to its maximum capacity, the better it would be for ticket-hungry supporters. Delegates to AC were naturally concerned, like Liam, about the debt and were also afraid that ticket prices would go through the roof, or that the counties would be levied. We assuaged their fears on both counts. When Peter had finished speaking, I immediately put it to a vote. Happily, the committee gave its approval: green light! The plan was to start after the All-Ireland in 2003 and have it finished for the All-Irelands in 2004, with a partial competition for the Leinster finals and All-Ireland semis that year. The design team and Sisks construction company got down to work. The Nally Stand had to come down first, and clubs and county boards were invited to express interest in getting it. I thought Mayo would want it, given that it is named after their lauded patriot, but with distance and cost that did not materialise. Instead, the great Gaels of the North once again left the southern boys behind as the great Carrickmore Club, chaired by Arthur McCallan, brought the Nally to their magnificent grounds in Tyrone and re-erected it there, thus preserving the historic stand. I had the pleasure of being one of the guests of honour at the re-opening of the Nally Stand in Carrickmore.

Hill 16 had to be demolished next. Peter McKenna came up with the inspired idea of making souvenirs from the rock from Hill 16, which were sold to fans. The first three were presented to an tUachtarán na nÉireann Mary McAleese, An Taoiseach Bertie Ahern and mé féin as Uachtarán GLC. It was particularly fitting that the Taoiseach should be presented with a memento of Hill 16 as he had spent many a summer's afternoon there, shouting for his beloved 'boys in blue'. I'd say, given a choice between his prime Taoiseach's seat on the Hogan Stand or 6 inches of standing room on Hill 16, he would opt for the latter any day.

So, the work continued apace and with Peter Quinn in control, things were well monitored and no corners were cut. We used to meet at 8.00am on Tuesday mornings to review progress and plan the work ahead, and it was a great experience and adventure for me. I learned more than I contributed, but it was great to work with such professionals.

Even though it was now all one terrace to look at, we decided to call the place where the Nally Stand had stood the Nally End, and the rest was christened the Hill 16 End; Nally/Hill 16 Terrace in combined form. Names mean an awful lot in the GAA and as we were discussing how we'd name the new Northern End, I suggested that other great people should also be honoured. Maurice Davin, our first president, and Frank Dineen, who purchased Croke Park for the GAA and was the only man to serve as both President and General Secretary of the Association, certainly deserved to be remembered. Before I left office in April 2006 we had a lovely ceremony to unveil plaques associating parts of the stadium with historic names: Nally End and Hill 16/Dineen End (Dineen had died in 1916 and I felt it was appropriate to have his name associated with Hill 16 for posterity), Davin Stand (previously known as the Canal End), Luke O'Toole room, Seán Ó Siocháin room, Pádraig

Ó Caoimh room, while the new media room was dedicated to the golden voice of Gaelic games, the magnificent Michael O'Hehir. I was amazed to learn what this gesture meant to the respective families, as evidenced by their words of gratitude on the day and letters of thanks received subsequently.

The Hill 16/Dineen End development went ahead as planned and people were surprised at how well it looked and how it fitted into the overall ambience of the ground. Just as important was the fact that the project came in at €21 million, thus saving a huge amount of money for the GAA. I am quite sure that if anyone other than Peter Quinn was Chairman, it wouldn't have been possible. So when Minister for Sport John O'Donoghue granted us the €40 million, we were almost laughing all the way to the bank. The improving financial climate in the country and the growing reputation of Croke Park as a world-renowned venue meant we had no trouble renewing the sale of corporate boxes and premium tickets, something we had been worried about prior to that.

Another major asset for Croke Park as a venue for matches, concerts and conferences was the decision to build a hotel across the road from the Hogan Stand. It was originally planned to link it directly with Croke Park by an overhead footbridge, but objections scuppered that plan. The architects, led by former Tyrone footballer, the efficient and likeable Des McMahon, weren't too perturbed: they came up with an alternative design to build a piazza that would visually link the hotel with the Park. By availing of the generous business expansion schemes in vogue at the time and getting a hotel consortium to build and run the hotel for thirty years, it cost the GAA nothing but is a great asset, especially as it was Jury's that won the tender. It is now proving its worth and is adding hugely to the popularity of the stadium as a venue for parties, meetings, workshops, examinations, shows, etc. By so doing, it is fulfilling a dream I have long held that Croke Park would be a cash cow for the Association. It is now, and will be even more so in the future.

Much of the credit for this must go to the Stadium Executive, under the direction of Peter McKenna and chaired originally by Dave Mackey and now by Hugh Cawley. The notion to form a separate company to run the stadium was a master-stroke and has proven its worth over and over again. But it wasn't a smooth passage, nor did they get an easy ride. Prior to this, the Croke Park staff, under the guidance of the Ard-

Stiúrthóir, were responsible for everything. Initially this worked out well and, in fairness, some very astute purchases were made. Over a long period of years a number of houses and buildings around Croke Park were bought by the GAA. Indeed, without those purchases we wouldn't have had the property on which to develop the hotel. However, buying property was one thing, managing it was quite another. Whatever happened, the management of these houses was inefficient to say the least. Rent often wasn't collected, a number fell into disrepair and squatters took over others. Even the handball centre was managed very loosely and it was a big job to turn it all around. Thus the necessity of a separate body to run the stadium and its various properties was a practical and brave move, driven by people like Peter Quinn and Joe McDonagh.

It was a move that caused bitter resentment among many long-serving staff members. My arrival on management coincided with this development. Meeting after meeting, there were continuous references to the 'awful stadium committee', with Peter McKenna painted as a dangerous upstart. Outside of meetings, when one spoke to the senior staff, in particular, it was the same message. Many of us, myself included, wondered about the wisdom of having such a man about the place, and the notion that the Stadium Executive should be abolished was floated at management meetings and, of course, encouraged.

The problem was that nobody from the stadium staff sat on management, so we were getting only one side of the picture. I decided that before I made up my mind and embarked on a course of action, I would do a bit of investigating myself. I did a broad canvass of key people, such as ex-presidents, former members of management and staff on both sides. As they say in Irish, *Bíonn dhá insint ar gach scéal*: there are two sides to every story. And there was. Nobody could deny that Dave Mackey and his committee had done great work. Besides, like most of the Stadium Executive, Dave was a voluntary official, albeit from a very successful professional background. Dave was a highly successful businessman, as were his fellow Executive members, Hugh Cawley (AIB), Brendan Waters (Mazars), Paddy Wright (RTÉ) and Peter Quinn. They didn't stand to gain much by serving voluntarily on a national GAA committee. Therefore, when Peter and his staff were coming in for criticism in my first three years on management, I reserved judgment and wondered about the veracity of the reports.

Later, when I became Uachtarán, and especially in the year I was Uachtarán-Tofa, I was fed a steady diet of anti-McKennaisms. The hope was that everything would be put back under the control of the Ard-Stiúrthóir, which from a governance viewpoint might even be seen as logical and proper. My practical instincts and my observations told me otherwise, however. I began to admire the efficiency, single-mindedness and integrity of McKenna and his staff. I certainly wasn't going to join the anti-McKenna brigade, which seemed to comprise most, if not all, of the senior staff members in Croke Park. I think they gradually realised that I wasn't to be manipulated, hoodwinked or convinced into downing or curtailing the Executive's powers. This came to a head one day when Peter McKenna was being verbally decimated and I wasn't 'biting'. Eventually, one senior member of staff said to me, 'Who's f**king side are you on anyway, them or us?'

Well, enough was enough. It was bedtime for diplomacy. I responded, 'Well, I am on nobody's f**king side because where I am concerned there are no f**king sides, no them, no us. I am only on one side—the side of the GAA. That's the only f**king side I see and you'd better look at it that way from now on.' That finished that conversation, but it also upset some senior staff members because they now knew that I, for one, wasn't going to be leading a return to central control. In fact, shortly afterwards we handed over the control of the management and sale of the boxes and premium tickets to the stadium. It made sense: how could they manage the stadium if they weren't in control of key marketing areas?

There were a few more covert attempts to pull everything back centrally, but at that stage I was well ahead of the game and cut them off at the incubation stage. Now the Executive, currently under the chairmanship of Hugh Cawley, is well in control and doing a brilliant job—as the financial returns show. I also think the traditional staff have accepted the inevitable, that a bit of a thaw has set in and that, as new staff join, the old attitudes and resentments will be a thing of the past. Eventually, there will be no 'f**king sides', just the side of the GAA, as it should be.

Before I became Uachtarán, the whole area of staff administration wasn't one to which I had given much thought, but it occupied a good deal of my time. The Croke Park staff could trace their origins back almost as far as the founding of the GAA and had been growing, piecemeal, over the intervening decades. As such, traditional practices had retained a tight hold and 'that's how it's always been done' was seen as a valid argument against change. Successive presidents had grappled with this conundrum. I remember Peter Quinn, Jack Boothman, Joe McDonagh and Seán McCague all making efforts to streamline the situation and to eliminate some outmoded practices that had become almost endemic. During my first stint on management, Joe McDonagh devoted great time and energy in trying to resolve an unedifying pension situation that had been allowed to develop. It took enormous courage and ability on Joe's part to sort it out and while his efforts made him no friends in the corridors of power in Croke Park, he deserves huge gratitude from the GAA for seeing it through. He also tried to modernise the staffing structures within Croke Park, but either time ran out for him or a consensus couldn't be reached as to the best way forward. When Seán McCague took over, he continued in the same vein and made some more strategic improvements. Once Seán had finished, it was my turn and like all new roles it took time to learn the ropes.

A consultancy group called PCS had been operating on behalf of the GAA for some time. It drew up contracts, defined roles, spoke to staff individually and made recommendations. Liam and I used to attend regular meetings with PCS and I had to sign off on many changes. After a while I began to ask myself, is this the role of the Uachtarán? In my opinion, staff management issues, decisions on individual salaries, wage rises and Christmas bonuses ought to have been handled in a different way.

I had absolutely no problem with the vast majority of the staff, especially the female staff, who were to a woman very diligent, obliging, pleasant and conscientious. Indeed, one of the things I did was to insist that for all future tours abroad, two or three of the female staff should be invited in rotation, as up until then it was nearly always the same men who went on every trip. That change has been instigated and hopefully will continue as the women deserve the same privileges as the men.

Almost all of the key positions were held by men and in my book some of them had become too complacent. They needed to be shaken up a bit. Some were already disappointed with me because I hadn't been hoodwinked into 'spancelling' Peter McKenna and his Executive.

But the more I thought about the staffing situation, the more I realised that a bit of surgery here and there wasn't going to achieve much—it would just be papering over cracks. In a private meeting I had with PCS I relayed my thoughts to them and they agreed that my judgment was spot on. It was time for change.

At Congress 2005 I suggested that now that we had introduced a five-year term for all county officers, we should also have a time limit for full-time officials. In my address I said:

> Is it good practice to have all voluntary officials confined to a three to five year term and have full-time officials in the same key decision-making positions for ten, twenty or possibly thirty years? Many state bodies and companies now confine their key decision-making personnel to a term of seven years or so. Should we consider doing likewise? Also, as a voluntary body, we have no effective system in place either to support or monitor the staff we employ. We need to have consistent practices right across the board with proper accountability and proper support to encourage upskilling of staff and effective human resource management . . . Heretofore, and as of now, Coiste Bainistí, or more specifically, the Uachtarán is really the only elected official who is in a position to assess and support and monitor staff at central level.

In general terms this was well received, and I remember meeting people outside of the GAA, like John Treacy, Olympic silver medallist and CEO of the Sports Council, who agreed fully with my views. But how do you think those who had occupied key positions for ten, twenty or possibly thirty years were feeling? Was I flavour of the month with them? Well, nothing negative or critical was said to me personally, but before I left office Vodafone organised a lovely 'thank you' dinner for me and my family. The Taoiseach flew over specially from London to attend and gave what many said was his finest ever speech. It was a most exquisite occasion. But how many in key positions in Croke Park turned up? Yes, you guessed it—none. Peter McKenna and members of the Stadium Executive were there, Moira Graham and some of the girls were there and one staff member, Michael Donnellan, but he had been in office only ten months at that stage. When speaking I referred to the absence of the management staff from Croke Park, just to draw attention to it, and also to thank those who went to the trouble of turning up at the Westbury Hotel, especially An Taoiseach, who came specially from London.

Quite frankly, the same would probably happen in any organisation where longevity is a primary factor. If there was a limit in managerial office of seven to ten years, things would improve dramatically. It would also disperse cliques, which are inevitable in the current situation. The GAA also needs to reform the accountability issue. It sounds fine for the staff to be reporting to the Ard-Stiúrthóir and he to the Coiste Bainistí, but Coiste Bainistí is made up largely of elected officials who have to travel from all over the country for meetings. Usually there are so many items of immediate priority cropping up, there is little or no time to monitor staff. Besides, the Ard-Stiúrthóir makes out the agenda and very rarely would staffing matters appear on it—especially those critical of the inner sanctum, naturally enough. There is therefore a need for a proper steering or monitoring committee, which would act as a watch dog and a support for staff. Questions of salaries and finance, which by their nature should be kept tight, should be dealt with by this steering committee—questions such as who gets credit cards and who doesn't, who goes on trips, who vets future All-Star venues (couldn't one or two voluntary people do it just as well), how long should they be away doing that 'chore', who goes to funerals, matches, etc., what salary increases and bonuses should operate, what reporting structures should operate, how are managers assessed and how is the Ard-Stiúrthóir assessed? There is, as you can see, a litany of issues remaining to be addressed.

I think that a committee made up of three or four ex-presidents, because they are the only ones with real knowledge, plus a few independent experts (NDOS) would make a huge difference and contribute to putting in place proper controls and supports. I genuinely fear that unless some system like this is established, the situation will get out of hand, especially as more and more staff are employed. For instance, in the first year after I left office, five or six new positions were created in Croke Park. That's a wage increase of about half-a-million euro. It may well be a wise decision and a wise investment, but don't look to Coiste Bainistí to make that judgment. They simply couldn't have either the knowledge or the expertise to do so. Outside professional expertise, working with past presidents and ideally two or three future presidents, would greatly improve that situation.

While we're on the subject, a similar system needs to be incorporated at provincial and county level as well, where there are full-time employees. Otherwise I fear that our obsession with ensuring that players don't get paid runs the risk of putting in place a fully paid, professional bureaucracy that could strangle the Association. It has now become almost a mantra for officials to boast about employing professional staff while at the same time warning that 'we must never go down the road of "pay for play". I agree with those sentiments, but a proudly voluntary organisation cannot continue forever saying, 'We need more and more full-time people, but the players must never be paid.' That is a dangerous tactic and possibly unsustainable, but hopefully not. A major rethink and proper corporate governance is needed to preserve the amateur ethos of the Association, to reward the players appropriately, to monitor and support the full-time staff and to foster the voluntary effort at all levels.

Finally, I want to make it clear that I wouldn't want my observations about the arcane system operating in Croke Park to be seen as a direct personal criticism of those operating it. After all, it is the Association as a whole that has allowed it to happen. Liam Mulvihill has been Ard-Stiúrthóir for almost thirty years and I would never question his dedication to the task. He comes in early, is very conscientious, has a good brain and is often there late at night, serving on the committees in which he is involved. He has been a safe and reliable pair of hands and rarely loses his head. In fact, when I finished my term as president, he made a speech at our famous social function in Dunboyne in which he said that in my three years at the helm, no cross words had ever passed between us. That was true. We might have had different opinions on things, but we handled them in a professional manner. Liam has served and survived ten presidents and is on speaking terms with them all—probably a commendation in itself.

Welcoming Committee

One of the privileges and responsibilities in being Uachtarán is that of hosting various dignitaries and guests who come to visit Croke Park. Every visitor likes to meet the Uachtarán. The most frequent and easiest dignitary to engage with during my tenure was undoubtedly An Taoiseach, Bertie Ahern. He loves all sport, especially the GAA. We used to have good conversations and good banter as we discussed anything from Berlusconi of Italy, Bush of America, Paisley of Northern Ireland, Tommy Lyons of Dublin or the surface of Sneem GAA club. Bertie is a gentleman. Sometimes, especially when Dublin were playing, his daughters Georgina and Cecilia would join him. Georgina is very much like her Dad. The first day she sat alongside me in Croke Park (Bertie was on the other side), the lads in Larkin's Pub in Milltown, who were watching it on TV, were saying, 'Christ, boy, who is the fine bird alongside Kelly today?' Nicky Byrne has nothing to worry about, however!

It was always a privilege to have the Aherns, and indeed Bertie's detectives, in Croke Park. He knows as much about the game as anyone I know, particularly the Dublin team. I might ask him about a particular sub, and Bertie would know all about his club career and his prospects. 'Jesus, 'twould be great if he could make it,' he'd say, 'we could do with a few good forwards if we are to beat yous bleedin' lot.'

The All-Ireland finals were always graced by the presence of her excellency, Mary McAleese, President of Ireland, and her husband, Martin. There's another down-to-earth person and I loved the way she made no bones about declaring her loyalties. If President McAleese wanted a team to win, especially an Ulster team, she cheered them on. I suppose that is one of the great things about the Irish and about the GAA: we have no worries about being passionate. Indeed, it is admirable when one declares one's loyalties, as President McAleese does. Occasionally she even had one or two interesting and apt observations on the referee! Her love for all things Irish is evident and she was the first President of Ireland to attend provincial finals. The first one she attended was the Munster Final, when I was Chairman of the Council.

Ambassadors sometimes came to matches in Croke Park. The year of the Beslan school tragedy in Russia, I invited the Russian ambassador, Mikhail Timoshkin, his wife and children to the All-Ireland Final and we observed a minute's silence in respect of the poor children who were killed so brutally. The Ambassador wrote a lovely letter of thanks afterwards. More impressively, earlier this year I was at a function at which he was also in attendance and when he heard I was present, he made a point of coming over to thank me again: a much-appreciated gesture.

Two of the ambassadors we saw in Croke Park most frequently were the British Ambassador, Stewart Eldon, and the American Ambassador, James Kenny. Both had a passion for Gaelic games and were diplomats *par excellence*. One day Ambassador Kenny and his family were in the 'GAA box' for a game. His young daughter, Kate Ann, and her friend went walkabout and the Ambassador came over to me to apologise. I replied, 'Ambassador, do not apologise, children are children, let them look around, they aren't doing any harm to anybody and they are safe out here.' I think he was greatly relieved because I suppose in other places protocol dictates 'no children allowed'. Not in Croke Park, not now, not ever. Indeed, by the time I left Croke Park as Uachtarán, my ten-year-old daughter Julie knew every nook and cranny in the place. Croke Park might be one of the biggest stadia in the world, but I hope it is also one of the most welcoming and safe, especially for children. In 2006 Ambassadors Eldon and Kenny left Ireland to take up new positions, but it was a pleasure to have them in Croke Park so often.

Hosting the President of Ireland and the Taoiseach, along with other dignitaries, means a lot of organisational work because there are protocols that must be observed. One of the considerations is the seating arrangements: who sits where on All-Ireland days. In my first year as Uachtarán I was amazed that when it came to the All-Ireland Final, sponsors' representatives weren't even sitting in the front row. At that time the Ard-Chomhairle section was narrower and longer, which meant the front row was so far down that when it rained, the primary dignitaries got soaked, as happened once or twice. I wasn't comfortable with that, but when I saw the sponsors relegated to the second row I said that if the sponsors weren't sitting in the front row the following year, neither would I as Uachtarán.

And so we decided to change the layout. The Ard-Chomhairle section was widened, which gave more than ample room for visiting dignitaries, special guests, sponsors and GAA dignitaries to be accommodated as they should be. We also put in a proper podium for the presentation of the trophy. Prior to this there was just a table; I told them it reminded me of a table that would be used for killing pigs. Now we had a proper presentation area. It was also decided that a better, more accessible lounge area was needed for the players. Originally they had to go all the way up to the fourth floor and the area was often so packed, there was scarcely standing room. Indeed, sometimes the players had to stay in the wide corridors, which was neither comfortable or fair. A classy players' lounge was installed just opposite the dressing-rooms, which was much easier and better for players.

We also looked at the possibility of erecting new dugouts, firstly in the Cusack side, but the advent of pitchside scrolling advertising rendered that plan redundant. Then we looked at putting them in the Hogan side. While that's still an option, we decided to make the place where the substitutes are accommodated on the Hogan Stand more amenable. They are, after all, the best seats in the house and by upgrading them, ensuring no entry for spectators and providing plenty of suitable clothing, the substitutes should be well catered for during the majority of matches there. On behalf of management, Liam Martin of Westmeath and I looked at all the options and that was the conclusion we came to, but if players find it doesn't suit them the plans are available to accommodate them in state-of-the-art dugouts in the Hogan Stand.

The hotel opposite the Hogan Stand was opened officially in November 2005, and in my address I announced that we would shortly be applying to Dublin Corporation for planning permission to install floodlights. The plan at that stage was to have them in situ for the International Rules game in October 2006, but while planning permission was granted in time for that to happen, objections and appeals by two or three people rendered the schedule impossible. As in most cases, however, objections delay developments, but they do not terminate them. So when the planning process was completed it was decided that the first game under lights at Croke Park should be the opening round of the Allianz National League of 2006, between Tyrone and Dublin. It took place on 3 February and it was fitting that both counties had the privilege because the Dubs are a unique bunch of supporters and vital to the GAA's presence in the capital, while Tyrone are probably the best organised county—at club, school and county level— in the GAA and their first All-Ireland win ever, in 2003, and their second, in 2005, mark them as one of the great success stories of our times.

The first game under floodlights was a gala occasion in front of a sell-out crowd, with Tyrone coming back strongly in the second half to outshoot the Dubs by 11 points. It got great publicity, and deservedly so. It was a triumph for all those who had conceived the redevelopment of Croke Park from the outset, and for the grassroots of the Association as well. For people like Liam Mulvihill and Peter McKenna, it was a marvellous moment. Liam had been involved from the start of the redevelopment and Peter had overseen everything in a most professional manner.

Pitch perfect

Everything about Croke Park was positive as review after review praised its origin, design and appearance. It was always nice to hear. There appeared to be only one black spot and that was the most important consideration of all—the pitch. Like a leak in a pipe in the attic, the problem became apparent gradually.

The first warning sign to us was that players seemed to slip more there than in other grounds. Initially, not much notice was taken of this as it was suggested that it was part of a bedding-in process and that perhaps players were wearing the wrong boots. But as more and more complaints began to roll in, people began to wonder and observe more closely. As always happens in these situations, the first port of call was denial: 'the pitch was grand.' But like many others, I wasn't convinced.

I asked Peter McKenna to contact John Hewitt, the man who had won the contract for the pitch, and invite him over from England for a meeting. The concerns of management and managers were relayed to him. I took the bull by the horns and spoke up, having let others do the talking until that point. I said, 'John, I can see the problem with my own two eyes. Fellas are slipping and sliding much more here than in other grounds and the ball is bouncing and gliding off the surface more than other pitches as well.' I think he got a bit of a fright and eventually it was agreed that compact analysis studies would be undertaken on a number of pitches in Ireland and England. That was agreed and that was done.

The result was that an algae was discovered to have grown on the surface. The solution was to install artificial lighting to compensate for lack of sunlight, to scarify the pitch and re-sow the grass. If this were done, we were told, things should be alright. It was done, in February 2005, which unfortunately meant that the inaugural Intermediate and Junior Club finals could not be played in Croke Park, something I had dearly wished to see happening. Anyway, the job was done and the pitch played well in 2005.

In 2006, however, the problems seemed to return, albeit not as bad as previously, but not good enough for what should be the best pitch in the world. And when they did recur, the lessons learned in 2004 were applied. Independent analysis was commissioned and their recommendations were implemented. The deco style didn't work as well in Croke Park as elsewhere. If the problems recur in the future, the pitch may have to be completely dug up and a new surface laid down. Or, perhaps like Gaelic Park, New York, we will make it an all-weather synthetic surface!

Innovations

One notion that is often mooted for the future of Croke Park is the installation of a mobile roof, such as at the Millennium Stadium in Cardiff. The design is such that it would be possible—indeed, the Hill 16/Dineen End is cantilevered so that it can be roofed, providing the opportunity to install an extra few thousand seats above the terrace. Whether this will ever happen is debatable and weather-dependent. The cost will probably be prohibitive for a long time. As for the weather, during my three years as Uachtarán we had only two wet days and only one really bad one. So that roof is very much in the lap of the gods, and in the hands of future administrators.

As I mentioned earlier, the running of the handball centre left a lot to be desired and we had to bite the bullet after years of huffing and puffing. The handball facility was taking up valuable space on the Cusack Stand side. Nevertheless, handball is one of our native games and we couldn't just dump them, although that said, they really must shoulder some blame for the way things turned out.

In conjunction with the Stadium Executive and Coiste Bainistí, we drew up full plans to erect a brand new, world-class handball facility adjacent to Croke Park. Incorporated into it would be ample office space for a burgeoning staff and apartment-style accommodation, which could be rented or used by the Association. I announced this at the handball convention in Arklow in 2005 and Tony Hayes, then Handball President, and Lorcan Ó Ruairc, Handball Ard-Stiúrthóir, were very pleased to hear it. It will happen, but it will take a few years. But it is the least handball deserves and hopefully it will spark off a whole new era for the ancient game—the one truly international game under the GAA banner.

Around the same time we took the decision to make Croke Park a smoke-free stadium. This came hot on the heels of the brave initiative of Health Minister Mícheál Martin to introduce a smoking ban in pubs, restaurants and public buildings across the country. He met with a lot of opposition, but he deserves great credit for sticking to his guns. It is telling that other countries are now looking towards Ireland with a view to imitating Martin's far-seeing policy. So we decided that we should do the same in Croke Park. Naturally, people objected—many smokers found a puff during matches was a good way to deal with nerves. My main worry was that dedicated GAA supporters, like Kevin Heffernan, who puffed the cigarettes with gusto would stop coming to matches or would come but not enjoy them as much. However, Heffo had been given the freedom of Dublin City shortly before, so I told him that a Freeman of Dublin was free to do what he liked in the city. He laughed, but thankfully he has adapted to the new regulation. I think the vast majority of supporters welcomed our decision and it has worked out well overall.

The presentation of games in Croke Park was another area that I felt needed to be jazzed up. I established a Presentation and PR workgroup under the chairmanship of Gerry Grogan and with the assistance of a good committee, which included Donal Keenan, came up with many good suggestions during my term in office. I told them initially that there was more to presentation of games than having the Artane Band marching around the field. The Artane Boys Band, as it was then known, was synonymous with the GAA, but I felt it was overdone and with a little imagination and initiative our games could be livened up quite a lot. While making some suggestions of my own, I more or less gave them a free hand. On a couple of occasions I was expecting some new presentation piece and when it didn't happen, I enquired what had happened. The word came back that instructions came from 'on high' and the proposed initiative was blocked.

This sounded a bit petty to me, so I told them to go ahead in future once I gave the okay and if any noses were out of joint, they could come to me for surgery! Thus the introduction of teams was changed, with each player being introduced individually backed up by footage from the big screen to the accompaniment of modern music. The big screen was used more and more to communicate with the crowd. New groups, such as The Bridies, the McCrohan Brothers and Liam O'Connor, were given an opportunity to entertain the crowd and, of course, we introduced noted Irish performers like Gillian O'Sullivan, David Gillick, Cian O'Connor (before the awful news of the horse doping result), the Ryder Cup and young whistlers (referees) to the crowds, as well as continuing to facilitate Cumann na mBunscoil's demonstration games. I also asked the workgroup to look at the format and layout of the programmes as these were a little stilted. I started a practice myself—which I had already done at Kerry and Munster level—of making my *Teachtaireacht an Uachtaráin* (programme notes) more relevant and readable. I used them to communicate key messages to the public, a practice I have noted that Nickey Brennan, Seán Fogarty, Jimmy O'Gorman and Liam O'Neill, in particular, have continued. Before this, there was normally a set format of welcome in all the *Teachtaireachtaí*. I bucked the trend and it's good that Nickey Brennan and others are following suit.

My notes, including 'hop balls', were usually well received and I got much positive feedback from the general public. After the classic Galway v Kilkenny hurling semi-final in 2005—the best hurling game I ever saw—I put in my notes that I was so excited by the game, I gave the Taoiseach a few digs in the ribs during it, adding that he too was equally thrilled so 'I had better check my own ribs'. It isn't every politician you could have *craic* with like that. On one occasion, though, my 'hop balls' got me into bother. The All-Ireland replay between Dublin and Tyrone in 2005 was a sell-out match, and the minor semi-final between Down and Offaly was the obvious curtain-raiser. However, Helen O'Rourke and Geraldine Giles asked me if there was any chance that the All-Ireland ladies' semi-final between Dublin and Tyrone could be accommodated. Central Council had already made a decision that only two games should be played in Croke Park on any given day. The easy option was to put on a three-match programme with the ladies' game on first, as some suggested. But if you did that one

Sunday, you'd have to do it every Sunday. Besides, the first game in a three-match programme is always played before an empty stadium. I abided by Central Council's policy and asked the GAC to accommodate the ladies. It wasn't an easy decision because some obviously wanted the Minor game in the supporting role. I spoke to GAC chairman, Tony O'Keeffe, and at the meeting it was decided to give the ladies the slot. This was the first time such an opportunity was afforded to ladies to play before 82,500 people, and I was very pleased.

Naturally, on my programme notes I welcomed the ladies' game to Croke Park and then went on to compliment all the women who were now coming to Croke Park for games in huge numbers. I referred to their fashion sense and complimented them for the imaginative way they dressed up in their county colours. I then jokingly (as I intended) suggested we should have a fashion contest in Croke Park and that the winners could march around the field after the band and be presented with their prizes. Actually, when I wrote that I drew a line through it, but not strong enough, as the typist included it. I feared someone might take offence, and that's what happened.

The game was held on Saturday afternoon and 82,500 people read the programme. But it was only the following Thursday that the 'furore' broke. You'd wonder was someone digging really deep to cause mischief. Anyway, Helen O'Rourke was quoted in an evening newspaper condemning the suggestions and adding that I 'must have been watching too much of the Rose of Tralee'. I was in America when the news broke and Helen rang me a few times in tears, saying she had been misquoted and taken out of context. She asked me to meet her when I came home. I met her and she explained the situation and apologised and I told her that was the end of the matter as far as I was concerned. Thankfully, our friendship continued and we work closely together now on the Integration Committee.

One or two journalists weren't so understanding. They referred to me as a 'moron' and still avert to it at every opportunity, but thankfully the vast majority of women didn't take the slightest offence. Indeed, Michaela Harte, the beautiful Ulster Rose of Tralee in 2005, thought it was a good suggestion, and Michaela is a lady of good taste. A number of women said that if I gave them an opportunity to march around Croke Park on a big match day, they'd do so willingly, adding a few witty suggestions that are best left to the imagination. Nevertheless, I have to accept some blame as I wrote it and I should have erased it completely when I drew the line through it, particularly when I had an inkling that it might not be perceived as I intended. The most important thing, though, was that the ladies got to play before 82,500 people for the first time ever and if I didn't want that to happen, it wouldn't have. Those that matter know that.

The museum is another very exciting development in Croke Park and is a highlight of the stadium tour, which includes a guided trip around the stadium and to the dressing-rooms and is a most enjoyable way to spend a few hours. It was decided to add an educational aspect to the museum by way of public lectures, one of the first being a commemoration of Bloody Sunday 1920, which was most informative and drew people from all over the country—something that really amazed me and the organisers. The museum staff rarely get plaudits from anyone, but they have done a fantastic job and now publish a calendar of events three times a year, which includes lectures, history lessons, art workshops, guided tours and special events for children, and has brought the museum to life in a very unique way.

While competitive matches and Cumann na mBunscoil exhibition games at half-time were normally the only games played in Croke Park, two experiments we introduced were an exhibition game for rounders and an exhibition game for recreational football. Rounders is certainly the forgotten game of the GAA. In fact, I was Chairman of the Munster Council before I even saw a game of rounders and that was in the millennium year when I decided that we should do something, no matter how small, for every facet of the GAA. Thus we asked the rounders organisation to put on an exhibition game prior to a Munster Championship. That day in Thurles was probably the first time that a game of rounders was ever played before a large crowd. They were well pleased and the Council treated them well.

Not surprisingly, when I became Uachtarán the hard-working National Secretary of the Rounders Association, Peadar Ó Tuathnáin, got in touch to ask was there any chance I would do the same for them in Croke Park. Why not? An exhibition game was played on the hallowed ground. I didn't see any big deal about it. After all, it is a GAA game, but again the usual quarters frowned upon it. I would like to see rounders becoming an annual fixture, as I noted schools, in particular, were very taken by it and it provides an opportunity for both males and females to get involved in sport, especially those who might not be suitable or willing to play the other traditional Gaelic games. Rounders is a good game, and if cricket can grow in popularity, it can too. In an age of sport for all, lifelong games and gender equality, rounders has a lot to offer and could grow considerably in popularity with a little help. In this regard, the Ulster Council is way ahead of all the rest. Their Integration Committee has a vision to help promote all GAA sports, including rounders. It is a model that could be followed in other provinces, as well as at national level.

While some officers of the Ulster Council might have disagreed vehemently with me on the opening of Croke Park, leading them to be painted as 'backwoodsmen' by a small section of the media, any fair critic would have to admit that in many areas they are the market leaders. Many of their visionary initiatives, especially in the areas of refereeing and coaching, were 'imitated' at national level. There's nothing wrong with that, except that the Ulster Council was rarely given credit and they felt justifiably aggrieved about this. Dr Eugene Young, an employee of the Ulster Council, and his fellow personnel in Ulster have been pioneering spirits in their special fields, but very few are aware of it. They deserve wider and more generous recognition as the results of their pioneering work is clearly to be seen in the rise and rise of the GAA across the nine counties in Ulster.

Another exhibition game we put on in Croke Park that wasn't greeted with great enthusiasm from within was a mixed recreational game. I had put together a group I called the Social and Recreational Games Committee to explore, develop and draw up rules for social and recreational GAA games. I had seen the explosive popularity of tag rugby and five-a-side soccer, but in the area of recreational games we hadn't even entered the station, not to mind leaving on the train. Inspiration came to me one evening in Naomh Mearnóg grounds in Portmarnock. I was there in my capacity as Chairman of the Overseas Committee and we were planning the organisation and hosting of an international competition for representative teams, both male and female, from all over the Gaelic world. It was a great experience and much appreciated by the overseas units. The competitions lasted the full week.

One evening, as our day's programme was drawing to a close, I was intrigued to see a game of football being played at a leisurely pace between two teams of mixed gender and varying ages, from fifteen to sixty. On enquiring, I was told that this occurred two evenings a week and was the brainchild of former Dublin All-Ireland winner, Mick Kissane. Mick also doubled as the local teacher and groundsman. What a man! With great foresight, he had decided that people shouldn't have to retire at thirty or forty, didn't have to be greatly skilled to play Gaelic games and didn't have to be wonderfully fit to enjoy a good game of football or hurling—the game could be adapted to embrace all. And that's what he did.

I was greatly impressed and when I was elected Uachtarán, I asked Mick to serve on a committee to formalise his unique idea. I also became aware that a good friend of mine, Tommy Maher, had been involved in setting up Wheelchair Hurling and that a great Down man called Joe McGrath, now living in Cork, had been developing and advising manufacturers on the development of hurleys, *sliotars* and footballs suitable for indoor games for all ages, especially the school-going population. I invited them both to sit on a committee and draw up rules for these games. That was done with Tony Dempsey, TD and former Wexford hurling manager, in the Chair, and Fergal McGill of Croke Park doing much of the back-up and organising.

I suggested to them that they should put on an exhibition game in Croke Park, which they did. Some insiders who didn't fully realise what the concept was described it as 'dreadful', but that was hardly the point. The following year, as part of the Kilmacud Sevens, an exhibition game involving TDs, senators and ex-GAA stars was played. Nickey Brennan played in goal and I played outfield—and scored two goals—but it was only exhibition stuff and so it wasn't about being good or bad, but enjoying it. Ask Jimmy Magee—he will tell you all about it.

I would like to see much more being done in this area. Looking back now, it would have been far more effective if we had given the committee a good budget and if more people had bought into the concept. In this day and age, given the problems society faces in terms of obesity and sedentary lifestyles, the ideas of Mick Kissane, Joe McGrath and Timmy Maher have much to offer. We often hear GAA people talk about competition from other sports, but when it comes to the recreational side of it, we need to get proactive. A dedicated resource driving these concepts could reap rich dividends. One of these days now someone in Croke Park will wake up and realise that recreational GAA games are a must for the Association. It will be presented as a brand new concept, never thought of before, as if Mick Kissane, Joe McGrath and Tommy Maher never existed.

The Irish language is also part of our heritage and is embraced in the GAA's charter. For that reason, I always encouraged Scór and, of course, enjoy the competitions greatly. But I wanted to do something tangible to promote the language itself. The committee, under former Armagh captain and possible future presidential candidate, Jarlath Burns, did a lot of hard work in organising and encouraging Scór and promoting *úsáid na Gaeilge*. Conradh na Gaeilge organises *Seachtain na Gaeilge* each year and I felt we should become part of this week of celebration, especially as it fits in perfectly with our club finals on St Patrick's Day. Jarlath, Moira Graham and the committee ran with this idea. Each year a Tráth na gCeist Bord (table quiz) is held throughout the country and the finals are held in Croke Park on St Patrick's Day. We introduced the winners to the crowd on the Croke Park pitch and presented them with their medals. It was very pleasant for me when my neighbours from Rathmore, under the brilliant direction of Donal 'Jinks' O'Leary, won the All-Ireland Tráth na gCeist Bord and I had the privilege of presenting them with their medals on the Croke Park pitch in 2006. As I shook his hand, Donal said, 'Haven't we come a long way since we were involved in East Kerry thirty years ago?' He was now an All-Ireland champion and had the medal to prove it.

One of the features of the new qualifier system in hurling and football is the 'live' draw on RTÉ to determine who is going to play in the next round. Now it is a 'live' draw in every sense of the word, but when I became Uachtarán the practice was to do the draw earlier in the day and then present it as 'live' to the viewers some hours later. It was a good safety-valve because if anything went wrong, it could be ironed out and covered up before 'live' transmission. Human nature being what it is, however, people in the know passed on the word, and news could spread very quickly. There was an agreement that the draw would be given to journalists on the QT because by the time the 'live' draw took place after 'The Sunday Game', their printing deadlines had passed. I felt the whole arrangement was messy and didn't like being part of it. The night of the U2 concert in Croke Park, I had to go over to RTÉ to do the pre-recorded draw. Dublin were in the draw that night. When I arrived at the studio, there were people present and I wondered why they were there. I was unhappy and told RTÉ that 'if the draw leaks out tonight, I won't be taking part in this farce anymore.' Marty Morrissey said it was the only time he saw me angry during my term in office. The draw was made and, sure enough, it turned out to be the farce I had feared. When I went back to Croke Park, one of the stewards could tell me the draw! It spread like wildfire and shortly afterwards Jason Sherlock was on stage at Croke Park, exhorting all fans to come and support Dublin against Armagh the following Sunday.

In fairness, Jason wouldn't have known that it hadn't yet gone out 'live' on television. An hour afterwards the draw took place 'live' on 'The Sunday Game' and, lo and behold, all the 'rumours' were right— Dublin were playing Armagh—and of course everyone in the RTÉ studio that night swore they had never said a word to a soul. Well, thankfully that put an end to the pre-recorded draw. From then on it was properly live and besides, RTÉ now moved around the country, to whatever venue the President was at, to make the live draw. It nearly went wrong live on air once or twice, but experts like Michael Lester and Marty Morrissey were able to draw on their experience and steer the draws through successfully. Young lads, in particular, loved watching the draw and I used to collect the bits of paper for Jarlath Burns' young lads and they would simulate the draw in their playtime at home. When the draws were first made a viewer drew my attention to the fact that the names of the counties were in English and he asked why they weren't in Irish. He was quite right and to this day the county names are called out in Irish as well as in English. *Tacaíocht beag eile don Ghaeilge.*

PSNI

At a Special Congress in 2001 the GAA abolished Rule 21, which prohibited the security forces of the Crown from playing Gaelic games. The PSNI were pleased as many nationalists had now joined the Police Service of Northern Ireland as a result of the Patten Report. They had a Gaelic football club that could now look forward to playing football. But while Rule 21 was excised in theory, little or nothing changed in practice. Nobody would play the PSNI team, apart from the Gardaí, and in frustration, Gerry Murray, Damien Tucker and Paul Leighton got on to me about it. I promised I'd do something and, with unfailing co-operation from the Ulster Council, we devised a strategy. We would get the team into the inter-firms competition and the Sigerson Cup. This took a bit of manoeuvring as there was very strong opposition. Fortunately, Martin Meagher, President of the Third-Level GAA body, agreed to do as I requested and a decision was taken at that level to allow the PSNI College into the Sigerson. A week later I received a call from Brian Mullins, Head of Sport in UCD, telling me that UCD would play the PSNI. And they did. Ironically, my son Pádraig and nephew Darragh played in that game, they being veterinary students in the College. After that the opposition to the PSNI slowly evaporated and now career choice is not a barrier to participation. It was another important step to bring about peace and reconciliation in Northern Ireland. I was pleased to be of assistance and if ever I get pulled over for a driving offence in the North, I expect to get off!

Ever since Ron Barassi brought his super-fit Australian high-fielder to Killarney in 1968 I have been a fan of International Rules, and I enjoyed my time involved with three great managers: Brian McEniff, John O'Keeffe and Pete McGrath. There have been disciplinary difficulties, but these can be worked out and with strict refereeing the games can continue. It's a great honour to represent one's country and, by and large, the games have been immensely attractive to the public. I got on very well with the Aussies and I used to have great banter with Andrew Demetriou (AFL CEO). 'Soccer, soccer,' he used to say to me, 'you'd let *soccer* into Croke Park, never Seán.' I found the Aussies most welcoming and friendly. I didn't see the need to suspend the tour in 2007, and I look forward to a speedy renewal.

The same can't be said, I'm afraid, for the Inter-Provincials, which Noel Walsh, Liam Mulvihill, Martin Donnelly and I oversaw during my presidency, carrying the finals to Rome, Paris and Boston. That has stopped now and it is a pity because players get few rewards. Those that went on those 'final' trips enjoyed them and we were also promoting our games. Others see it differently, however, and when you are gone, you are gone. But I hope the Inter-Provincials and International Rules aren't guillotined out of existence. That would be both a pity and a mistake. Lord, hear our prayer.

The Social Scene

As President of the GAA, almost every day has a different highlight as the huge organisation rolls along on its merry way. The social role of the President is very important, especially for clubs. That is why I, like all my predecessors, never spared myself when it came to club functions at home or abroad. Having an Uachtarán attend a function, field opening or club launch is a huge boost to clubs. Clubs often told me that when it was confirmed that the Uachtarán would be attending a club function, ticket sales would increase rapidly. I found this 'celebrity' business uncomfortable in the beginning, but after a while realised it went with the job and learned to take it in my stride. Anyway, I knew full well it wasn't Seán Kelly who was the 'star attraction', it was the President of the GAA, who just happened to be me for three years.

As Uachtarán I would have been entitled to a driver. Many couldn't understand why I didn't have one. Bertie Ahern would say to me, 'Seán, are you still driving yourself around the country like mad?' But I was very clear on that. I felt that, as leader of a voluntary organisation, it would not be appropriate to be chauffeur-driven around in a swanky car, so I said, 'No thanks, I'll drive myself everywhere'. Most of the time I was on my own, but it was great when Juliette and young Julie could accompany me. I didn't mind being on my own, but living in Kerry meant that you learned very quickly, as the Kerryman said on the ghost train to Croke Park long ago, that 'don't some people live very far away.'

Yes, indeed, having people living very far away meant I was constantly on the road. I covered between 50,000 and 60,000 miles a year in the car and when you throw in flights and train journeys, it came to a multiplicity of that distance. But it was worthwhile and I am delighted I got through it. When I was travelling I rarely stopped to eat. In the beginning I did a few times, but I quickly found that when you asked a waitress how long your meal would take, 'ten minutes' meant half-an-hour or more, so I cut out stopping to eat and stuck to the schedule. Anyway, I usually took in as much as possible when I went to an area. Moira Graham, my PA in Croke Park, was very good at organising the diary in that way and with a pleasant smile could make a proposed heavy schedule, with tight deadlines, sound like child's play. So, off I went, stopping only for a bottle of Lucozade, a couple of bars of chocolate and a pear or an apple. During Lent I always give up the chocolate and alcohol, which made my tummy rumble a bit more on these trips. I often drove six or seven hours without stopping (not to be recommended), depending on schedules.

One day I left Killarney for Ballycastle, in Antrim, drove all the way without stopping and arrived for a function at 7.00pm. I got to bed at 2.30am and was on the road to Dublin at 6.30am for a meeting in Croke Park, then drove to Wexford before returning to Dublin via Carlow and Roscrea. On another occasion I drove to the Glenties in Donegal, went to bed around 2.00am, set out early for lovely Doonbeg for a function, then drove to Dublin afterwards, arriving in the Burlington Hotel at 3.00am and was in Croke Park at 9.30am the following day for business as usual. I was lucky in that I didn't mind driving, and I had lots of energy—thanks to Lucozade and Cadbury's. Indeed, they should have been sponsoring me! But I suppose when you like your job it makes it easier. I found every club and every school wonderful and refreshing. I got a great snapshot of the good people of Ireland, the vast majority of whom take great pride in their communities and are willing to work hard for their betterment. The warm atmosphere everywhere always made me feel so proud of the GAA's foot-soldiers.

The young children were always lovely and as a teacher I think I was able to relate to them by talking their language—at least, I hope so. They can be great fun and sometimes, to break the ice, I'd ask one of them to kick the ball to me or to 'fight'. If I kicked it well off left and right, or took a penalty and scored against them, they'd say, 'Did you play for Kerry?' to which I'd reply, 'Not yet'. We'd have a laugh then. If they were playing hurling I might join in and say, 'I'll show ye how to play hurling the right way. I come from Kerry.' Try saying that to a lad from Tipp, Kilkenny or Cork—their shyness evaporates quickly! 'Kerry! Sure ye know nothing about hurling down there,' they'd reply.

When I was elected President, both the Fossa and Kilcummin clubs put up huge banners which read: 'Congratulations to Seán Kelly, President GAA 2003–2006'. In 2004 a group of Dublin children came down to our club for a few challenge games and a social weekend. When they saw the sign, one young Dub said to our club chairman, Timmy Ryan, 'Is Seán Kelly from this club?' When he was told I was, he looked up at the banner and asked, 'How did youse know when he was going to die?' The chairman laughed, but might have said there were some who'd like to see the back of me sooner. As Mícheál Greenan said (hopefully jokingly) to some members of management when word came through that Saddam Hussein had been hanged: 'And that c**t Kelly is still alive'.

On another occasion I was visiting Cork schools as part of Féile with

Mary O'Connor, that wonderful player and Camogie Development Officer from Cork. The Cork ladies were playing an important game the following Sunday, so the teacher suggested to the pupils that they might send Mary a text message in support. We asked for suggestions. 'Come on Cork', 'Up Cork', 'Best wishes Mary' were mentioned, and then a young lad, about seven years old, put up his hand and when I asked him what his message would be he said, 'Go on, you sexy thing'. The teacher was mortified, but nobody minded. I didn't notice any signs of disapproval in Mary's face either.

Such are the joys of being Uachtarán. I liked being open, frank and accessible to people. As a result, my mobile-phone number was widely known and I had no caller ID, indeed, I have the same number still. But that had its disadvantages, of course, especially at All-Ireland time when call after call came in looking for tickets. All I can say is I did my best for people, but such was the confusion that sometimes you wouldn't return the call or answer the letter. But after the first year, guided by Moira Graham, I got a better hang of the situation and became more organised. Still, All-Ireland time is very demanding, especially if your own county is involved. Most people would pay for their tickets, but others would either forget or not bother, and other times cheques would be out of date by the time they'd been assimilated. It is one part of the job I won't be sorry to leave behind. As an ex-President, I won't have any dealings with tickets anymore—so no more calls for tickets to me, please.

The other big disadvantage to having an open phone is that you can be contacted anywhere, at any time, by anybody. You can be taken very much unawares at times and you have to think on your feet, or on your seat as you drive along. Two occasions that I remember well occurred in relation to ambush marketing. The first was when Paddy Power decided to give a few hurlers, like Paul Codd of Wexford, a few bob to carry his logo on their hurleys. I was on my way to Louth when I got a call about it. Naturally I condemned it out of hand, called it cheap publicity and exploitation of players and threatened to throw Mr Power out of his box in Croke Park. I would have done, too, but our legal advisers said it would constitute a breach of contract and couldn't be done. The controversy raged for a few days, but I stood firm, feeling if I didn't, it would escalate. I was on my way home at 10.30pm a few nights later and had just passed the Red Cow Inn when Damien Lalor (a journalist and a gentleman, now with the *Sunday Independent*) rang to inform me that Paddy Power had backed down and wanted my reaction. I was very pleased; it shortened the journey home to Kerry. At the following Central Council meeting we moved to close the loophole Paddy had supposedly spotted, even though Liam and I had raised it at a management meeting previously. I wondered was it from there that the alleged loophole was perhaps broadcast?

The second ambush marketing saga involved a couple of Cork hurlers. They had branded a beer product (Corona) on their boots for the Sunday game. There was nothing about it in the papers on Monday, but it was splashed all over the media on Tuesday and the controversy raged for a week or so. Again, the first I heard of it was a phone call from Jim O'Sullivan, that respected and popular GAA correspondent for the *Irish Examiner*. It was estimated that for about €1,000, Corona had got €100,000 worth of free publicity. They stated that they were only interested in 'looking after the players'. I said if they were 'only' interested in the players, they should donate €100,000 to the Cork players' holiday fund in lieu of the free publicity they had received. Most people in Cork saw through the ambush and it too died a quick death.

Another controversy, this time of a different kind, emerged when in an interview with Tony Leen (13 April 2006) I suggested that I was amazed that while we had clubs called after every hero and martyr in Irish history, I was at a loss to explain why no club, no field or no Cup was named for 'The Big Fellow', Michael Collins. I pointed out that he had played and helped organise the game in London, that he was a close colleague of Sam Maguire and that when he was Minister for Finance he had donated the first grant to Croke Park—£10,000 to help it prepare for the Tailteann Games, a massive sum in those days. He also attended games regularly and if you go into the Poitín Stil Pub in Rathcoole, just inside the door is a big photograph of Collins and Harry Boland (who was Dublin County Board Chairman), at the Leinster Hurling Final on 21 September 1921. Without a doubt, Collins is the greatest martyr *not* to be honoured by the GAA. Ironically, the only club I could locate that was called after Collins was a soccer club in Belgium.

Of course, in typical Civil War fashion, when I mentioned Collins people said: what about the GAA honouring de Valera? Others thought

I was angling for a seat in the Dáil. De Valera was a very good man, but to suggest that if Collins deserved to be honoured by the GAA then so did Dev is absolute rubbish. Dev had no involvement in the GAA. Rugby was his game, although he went to very few international games— hardly the credentials of a rugby fanatic—and he also took PE out of the school curriculum in the 1937 Constitution. A good man, definitely, but hardly a great sportsman—not to mind a great GAA man. Like the opening of Croke Park, the GAA will have moved on and will be fully depoliticised when it gives 'Collins the Great' the honour he deserves. I think it will happen, too, and it will be a proud day for the GAA and for Ireland.

I suppose the most pleasant and most public function a president has to perform is to present the Sam Maguire and Liam McCarthy Cups to the All-Ireland winning captains each year. While all captains are great, I doubt if any president had the honour of presenting those Cups to so many sporting luminaries as I had. In 2003 the two best players of the modern era captained their sides to All-Ireland glory: D. J. Carey and Peter 'The Great' Canavan—something that has probably never happened before in the one year. Then in 2004 Ben O'Connor captained Cork to the first of two-in-a-row. Ben was perhaps the first captain to have his twin brother playing on the winning side. I am pleased I had the presence of mind to insist on Gerry being brought up for the presentation as well, causing the presentation to be delayed for a few minutes as Gerry modestly remained at the bottom of the Hogan steps. Some people got annoyed with me, telling me to get on with the presentation, but I wouldn't until the twins were together to receive Liam. Sure, such a historic occurrence may never happen again.

The following year one of the best and most popular sportsmen in the country, Seán Óg Ó hAlpín, accepted the Cup for Cork. Just before the presentation, in order to get a feel for how I should approach it, I asked Seán Óg was he going to speak in Irish, English or both. His reply was, 'Glan as Gaeilge' (totally in Irish), which set the tone for a great boost to our native tongue. A man born in Fiji accepting the hurling Cup and speaking 'Glan as Gaeilge'—beautiful, *ard-fhear*, Seán Óg.

In 2004 Daire Ó Cinnéide did likewise for Kerry. Daire is a brilliant fellow and came first in Ireland in Irish in the Leaving Cert. His native West Kerry *blas* brought poetry to Croke Park. In introducing Daire, I took a description of Diarmuid (in the great Fenian tragedy *Diarmuid agus Gráinne*) and presented Sam Maguire to '*Daire dea-fhoclach, dreach-sholas Ó Cinnéide*' (*dea-fhoclach* meaning sweet-worded or fluent; *dreach-sholas* meaning good-looking or handsome). Daire, being a Gaeilgóir genius, copped it straight away and he told me that a few in the Gaeltacht did likewise, especially Mícheál Ó Sé (Raidio na Gaeltachta) and Seán Mac Antsithig (peileador agus captaen na Gaeltachta). I doubt if many more knew or cared what I was saying.

My final Sam Maguire presentation went to the man with the human engine, Brian 'The Vet' Dooher, who had replaced Cormac McAnallen as captain of Tyrone. It was a happy but poignant moment (see page 197) and the fact that Tyrone beat Kerry made it even more historic (for Tyrone anyway).

Every Cup presentation was special and pleasant. I particularly recall wonderful moments when Waterford won the Munster under-21 All-Ireland Junior football and Munster Senior hurling titles. I had the privilege of being present for all three of those landmark games. I also had the privilege, when deputising for Joe McDonagh, of presenting Westmeath with the All-Ireland under-21 trophy in 1999. I said that, like Joe Dolan, they would go on to win 'more and more and more'. Likewise, when Limerick won Munster under-21 in football and hurling (and then went on to win three under-21 hurling titles in a row at All-Ireland under-21 level). The club titles are brilliant occasions and I will always treasure the memories of hosting the first club Junior and Intermediate All-Ireland finals in Croke Park—magnificent moments, long to be cherished. And then there was the Tommy Murphy Cup, especially when that prince of modern footballers, Declan Browne, accepted it when, against all the odds, Tipperary triumphed over Wexford in 2005. And what about the Christy Ring and Nicky Rackard Cups and the beautiful letters I received from Christy Ring's wife and Rackard's nephew thanking me for my effort. Wonderful memories and truly an honour.

One of the most important and worthwhile ventures I undertook as Uachtarán was to organise the first ever national club forum. This was an opportunity for representatives of our clubs to come together at INEC, in Killarney, for a full day's seminar. It had never happened before in the GAA. The social and awards committee spent many months organising the whole thing and on a bright November day the first gathering of GAA clubs took place in my home town. It was a historic and a great day. The feedback was excellent. Perhaps the one mistake we made was to pack too much into the day, but you will always learn from these situations. We had two enthralling and engaging guest speakers— the highly respected and competent Donal O'Grady and the father of modern football, the great Kevin Heffernan.

One of the messages that came through loud and clear from the club forum is that the fixtures schedule needs a major revamp if clubs are to survive and thrive. That process is easier said than done, but at least there is now recognition of this complex problem and steps are being taken to find practical solutions. We are all club members, so it behoves us all to pull together on this one. I believe that as the problem has now been well articulated, we will hopefully move towards a sensible solution quickly. If not, the clubs will tell us loud and clear at our next forum, which I hope will take place fairly soon and in Croke Park. Killarney was a good venue for the first one, but I did meet many members around the country who said that with club matches, etc. they just couldn't make the long journey to Kerry. That's a fair point, so let the next one be in Dublin.

Another important, but totally unpredictable function the President has to undertake is to attend funerals and sometimes give graveside orations. Funerals, not surprisingly, can throw your schedule out of gear completely, but there are many you have to attend and others you should attend but cannot for one reason or other. Graveside orations can be tricky. Who gets one and who doesn't? Who gives the oration? I have been asked to give orations on numerous occasions. I always wrote my own script because I operate on the basis that if I didn't know the person well, I shouldn't be eulogising him, regardless of what position I hold or the deceased held. I refused to give orations if I didn't know the person fairly well, but I never minded once I knew and admired the deceased. Thus I have given orations for great men like Seán Purcell, Joe Keohane, Tim Kennelly, Tim and John Kerry O'Donnell, Murt Galvin and Pa Doyle, Pat Healy and many more.

The President is also in constant demand as a guest speaker at social events, seminars, summer schools, breakfast briefings, political gatherings, society gatherings and annual lectures. Thus I have spoken to the Law Society, the Royal College of Surgeons (annual Doolan lecture), McGill and Merriman Summer Schools, the Progressive Democrats and Fine Gael, Kerry Associations in Dublin and Cork,

Vodafone, Skillnets, Harvard College Alumni, Chartered Accountants and numerous chambers of commerce, as well as book launches and university student groups. All these were very interesting and I found them very stimulating, especially when there was time for questions from the floor. Most questions would be well thought out and challenging and I liked the spontaneity of it all. Occasionally, some smart-ass would try to catch you out. At one breakfast meeting, before a couple of hundred people in the Burlington, I mentioned the voluntary work of the GAA. One guy asked what salary I was getting as Uachtarán and what travelling expenses I was on. He got quite a hop when I told him I got no salary as President *per se*, just my ordinary teacher's salary, and that my travelling expenses were the same as everybody else's—50c per mile. Still, the unpredictability is part of the enjoyment and when you are open, honest and not too worked up about impressing people, it can all be very enjoyable and rewarding.

When you are in the public eye it is amazing how people form an opinion of you and get to know you without ever having met you. By and large I have been lucky to get a positive reaction from most, and I suppose some of the awards I have received reflect that, including People of the Year (2005), Entrepreneur of the Year (2000), Business Person of the Month (April 2006), Honorary Doctorate (DIT 2007) and voted Kerry Person of the Year by the listeners to Radio Kerry (2006) and Star Personality of the Month (May 2006).

On the Monday after the England v Ireland rugby game in Croke Park in 2006, I was driving to Dublin when President Mary McAleese rang me to thank me and to congratulate the GAA on the magnificent occasion the previous Saturday. 'Seán,' she said, 'you were the real "man of the match" for without you, it would never have happened.' I was greatly honoured and humbled, especially as later that day she said the same thing publicly at the presentation of the Gaisce Awards. Ironically, I had changed my car the previous week and the hands-free mobile-phone set had not been fitted to my new car. Just as I was saying goodbye to President McAleese, I noticed a car with a flashing blue light behind me. An unmarked Garda car pulled me in and I was fined and got two points on my licence—the first I had ever received. Yes, Borris-in-Ossory at midday on 26 February has two reasons for being remembered: the President's call and the penalty points. The President's call was the more memorable!

The only other time I was 'fined' was in Auckland, New Zealand, in 2006. I was in Melbourne, Australia, and had to get up at 4.00am to catch the flight to Auckland. As I had had nothing to eat, I bought an apple at the airport. I was carrying the apple in my hand as I went through security in Auckland. There was no problem with the first security guard, but when I was going through the second barrier the officer pulled me in and said, 'In your customs declaration you wrote that you weren't bringing any fruit into the country.' 'That's true,' I replied. 'But you have an apple in your hand.' 'Yes,' I replied, 'but I am eating it.' 'And what will you do with the core?' he queried. 'I will put it into the refuse basket.' 'It's illegal to bring fruit into New Zealand. You made a false declaration. You are, therefore, fined $200,' he retorted. I argued and pleaded, but to no avail. It was an expensive snack. When I linked up with the Bank GAA teams, I learned that one of their members suffered a similar fate for an orange!

My role as Uachtarán took me overseas fairly frequently. Some places I visited had never before been visited by a President. New Zealand was one such place. Gay Kelly was married to a Kerryman and she asked me to call when in Australia with the International Rules Team as no president had ever gone there before. I was delighted to oblige and was thrilled with the strength and organisation of the game there. People like Gay, Mary Galway, Jim Connolly and Mick Fox put their hearts and souls into the GAA. Mike was a native New Zealander, but as Chairman he was as enthusiastic and as committed as any chairman in Ireland. I enjoyed Auckland very much, and seeing a place that was so far away and so cut off from mainstream GAA but so committed was very pleasing and impressive. Bank of Ireland and AIB visited there two years ago and they too received a fabulous welcome.

In Auckland, I said I'd like to see a New Zealand ranch. Gay organised a 'farmer' to collect me one morning and bring me to his ranch—all 1,500 acres of it. I discovered that the farmer in question had left Donegal at fourteen years of age, unable to read or write, but he now owned not only a 1,500-acre farm but three more ranches and a rash of property. He was the second richest man in New Zealand. He brought me to visit a development he had completed. All the roads were called after places in Donegal: Glenties, Raphoe, Rosses, Gweedore, etc. The second richest man in New Zealand, as modest as they come, but still so proud of his roots. A special man, Hugh Green— one of our thousands of resilient exiles.

I was in Australia for the International Rules, of course. I hope that the series can be resurrected. Indeed, I personally didn't agree with all the one-sided outrage following the last encounter. We had gone to a lot of trouble working on the rules of the game and the disciplinary procedures after Australia 2005. I said after Dublin 2006, and I still say, that if the referees had done their job properly, we wouldn't have had half the mayhem that ensued. I think we could also have sorted things out for 2007. After all, if we are going to sort them out for 2008, why wait two years? It doesn't take two years to talk and work out a few rules. I know Andrew Demetriou and the AFL want things to work. The GAA wants things to work. So let it be. It should happen and it will happen. Why? Because the players want it, and when all the huffing and puffing and shuttle diplomacy is done with, the players will have their way. Anything less would be a great injustice.

There are over 500 clubs worldwide and following the opening of Croke Park, the opportunity is there to grow that number appreciably. The worldwide publicity couldn't be bought and must be capitalised on now. The GAA has units in every continent, and I was always amazed and very proud to see the extent to which exiles and their non-Irish friends were prepared to go to play our games and develop the GAA in their countries of adoption. Witness David Olsen, a Swede I honoured with a President's Award in 2006. He almost single-handedly built up a thriving hurling community of all Americans in Milwaukee, USA. Look at the strength of Ladies Football in Australia as another example, they have teams there who could hold their own against any team in Ireland and are nearly all Australian born. See the magnificent successes of recent years of the Asian seven-a-side annual tournaments and the Europe-wide football leagues. Highly educated Irish young men and women are bringing their games to distant lands and sharing it with their friends. The changing patterns of emigration in Britain, America and Canada are now taking our games into the schools and developing 'native' talent to fill the void created by dwindling numbers of emigrants.

As Chairman of the Overseas Unit, I encouraged this development and Croke Park gave funding for same. And so it was that during my presidency the first North American Continental Youth Tournament

2004 took place in New York, and is now an annual event, whereby a few thousand young kids from under-8 to under-18 travel from cities all over the USA and Canada to compete in an annual under-age tournament. Such an event would have been amazing and unthinkable just a few years ago. I enjoyed all of those events and met some really great people. Yes, at home or abroad, the GAA attracts the best. Without a doubt, the future is bright and can get even brighter.

PART VII

Rule 42 and All That

The Debate

Rule 42 was the rule in the GAA official guide prohibiting field games other than Gaelic football and hurling being played in GAA grounds. An exception could be made, and indeed was made, for once-off games, such as American Football, which wouldn't be in direct competition with the GAA. An American Football game was played in Croke Park in 1999 between the American Navy and Notre Dame, which was well and good because the game was never going to pose a threat to the GAA. Tom Kane, now of Adare Manor, was one of the primary movers in that adventure.

Soccer and rugby were different, however. They were the garrison games, the games of 'the enemy' and for that reason had been hated and feared in equal measure for generations. So much so that up until 1971 members of the GAA were not only banned from playing either soccer or rugby but banned, under pain of suspension, from attending any of these games as a spectator. Many a great player paid a heavy penalty for having the temerity to defy the ban. Indeed, a vigilante committee was established in each county to prey on would-be offenders. Mick Mackey, one of the triumvirate of hurling legends, loved attending 'foreign' games. Proving himself tactically clever as much off the field as on it, he got himself appointed to the Vigilante

Committee so that he could attend all the foreign games he liked without fear of reprisal. I never heard of anyone being suspended as a result of Mackey's vigilance!

In many respects confining GAA grounds to Gaelic games made a lot of sense. The GAA bought the grounds, developed them and maintained them. GAA clubs are very busy places, with teams from under-age right up to adult level. The ladies' games are now growing as camogie and ladies' football enjoy increasing popularity and continuous participation. Indeed, most club grounds are over-stretched, consequently the vast majority of clubs need extra playing fields to cater for their own members. It would be the height of folly and quite absurd to try to cater for other sports on top of all this. Besides, the dimensions of the playing area for soccer and rugby are different from Gaelic games. You'd have some field and some fun if you were constantly changing the goalposts.

Croke Park is a different kettle of fish, however. For a start, almost every other ground in the country is used anything from 200 to 300 days each year; they are nearly all over-used. Not so Croke Park. It is used regularly at weekends during the championship season, but otherwise lies idle for long periods of the year. Once the All-Irelands finish in September, the field sees very little action for the next eight months—apart from an International Rules game or two and club finals on St Patrick's Day.

During my term as President, we introduced All-Ireland finals in hurling and football for intermediate and junior clubs. Despite some opposition, I succeeded in getting them fixed for Croke Park in February, which takes up two dates. People said, 'Where are you going with junior and intermediate clubs in Croke Park? Sure there'll be nobody at them.' Well, there may have been only 6,000–10,000 people there, but the atmosphere was electric and the players, who might never play there again, got a memorable day out, and some supporters who would never have been in Croke Park before came all the way to support their local village. The feedback I got from opening Croke Park to the junior and intermediate clubs was truly delightful and genuine: 'Fair play to you, you gave the small club a chance' and 'I never thought I'd see the day that my dear little club would play an All-Ireland final in the greatest sporting cathedral in the world,' were typical of the responses I received afterwards.

Of course, that still leaves Croke Park way behind all other GAA grounds in terms of usage. As soon as the Cusack Stand had been redeveloped, I came to the conclusion that this exceptional stadium ought not be strait-jacketed by Rule 42. The first day I walked in under the new Cusack Stand and looked out onto the hallowed turf of Croke Park, I said to myself, 'Amn't I lucky to be a member of this great organisation that can construct such a fantastic edifice? Isn't it a pity it isn't utilised more?' As the Canal End (now known as the Davin Stand) and the Hogan Stand were completed, I became more convinced than ever that here was a gem that the world must discover. Back when I was Chairman of the Munster Council, my colleagues on management and I were once taken on a tour of the new Hogan Stand (2000). As we sat on the upper deck, staring out at the empty stadium, I said to one of my party, 'Wouldn't it be a shame if this place were to be filled only once or twice a year?' 'What do you mean?' he replied. I answered, 'We should be renting this place out to soccer and rugby for their big games and using the income to promote our own games at grassroots level.' He raised an eyebrow. 'You must be joking,' he countered, 'that will never happen anyway.' But as each year passed and the arguments raged, I became more and more convinced that opening Croke Park was the right thing to do. Right for the GAA and right for the country.

In my first year as President I used to look out at Robert Ellis tending to the field like a mother tends to a baby, day after day, but no one set foot on the pitch for seven long months—only the seagulls. I couldn't understand the logic of keeping it closed. This was the GAA's primary asset and should be put to work for the Association. Even if there was never any talk of soccer and rugby having to play their home games abroad while Lansdowne Road was being refurbished, I would still have been in favour of opening 'Croker' for practical and business reasons.

I had long since got over the fear, the dislike, and, indeed, the hatred, that many GAA people inherited of soccer and rugby. Yes, we felt any advance made by either code was at the expense of Gaelic games. Soccer and rugby were challengers for the hearts and minds of the young generation, for media coverage, for sponsorship and for the admiration and love of the nation. Whether it was based in reality or not, that sense of threat was still there and indeed still is in many quarters. I dare say that there are an equal number of likeminded people in the other sports organisations, too.

Jack Charlton and Italia 1990 changed all that for me, although not in the way you might think. I confess I had very mixed emotions about Italia '90. Jack was a great character, who thought and spoke more like a Gaelic man than an Englishman. His style of play could be termed 'traditional Gaelic': kick the ball and put them under pressure was evocative of Kerry great, Joe Keohane. Charlton rallied the country behind the Irish soccer team in a way we had never seen before. The team did well. The country celebrated. The GAA trembled. Part of me, like many other GAA people I suspect, wanted Ireland to win; another part of me wanted Ireland to lose—simply because I feared a takeover by soccer. It was a great time and it was a terrible time.

However, in the aftermath of Italia '90 things slowly returned to normal. The crowds began to flock back to GAA matches. People who had ranted and raved during the World Cup began to compare Gaelic games to soccer and appreciated the Irish games more than ever before. Cork won the double in 1990 and the Meath/Dublin saga of 1991 ended all fears of the demise of Gaelic games. My inherited GAA bias slowly dissipated. I began to see 'foreign games' in a new light. I began to see all sports as important and admirable in themselves. In sport there could be no enemies. In fact, 'enemy' is a direct contradiction of what sport is all about.

I continued to be a GAA man first and foremost, convinced of the value of our games and culture and confident that they could grow and prosper, provided we endeavoured to work hard at promoting our games. The future was beckoning and it was only our own fears and qualms that were holding us back. We had no enemy without, only enemies within. And when it came to Rule 42, in particular, some of them were to prove very hard to overcome!

The Long Road to Change

In 1982 a man called Jerry Flanagan asked the Meath County Board 'to examine the possibility' of making more extensive use of Croke Park, but his appeal fell on deaf ears and that was the end of that.

My first public utterance of my new thinking came in Killarney, at the Kerry County Convention in January 1991. Speaking as Chairman of the Kerry County Board, I said that as Croke Park was such a fine stadium, we should be making better use of it and therefore should consider ways to make it work for the Association by renting it to other bodies. In my Chairman's Address I said:

Much has been written, even more spoken and a multitude whispered about such topics as a national stadium, the total re-development of Croke Park and the competition from other codes and sponsorship.

These questions have to be looked at in the light of the times in which we live. Competition is the life of trade and in the long term it will do us good not harm. We have nothing to fear. Rather than being self-defensive and over-sensitive we should be self-advancing and compromising. Ecumenism is as desirable in sport as it is in the churches, and I think an organisation so strong, so self-relying as the GAA, has within its scope the power to make at least occasional ecumenical gestures at national level towards other organisations without compromising our principles or creating all-embracing knock-on precedents. Friendly rivalry should be our motto, not open hostility. A calm business-like approach and mature reflection must be brought to bear on these major questions of the day and opportunities to help ourselves while helping others should not be spurned on spurious high moral grounds. Opportunities to avail of sponsorship, revenue and good-will must all be grasped and put to good use to promote our games at home and abroad.

(KERRY CONVENTION, 1991)

Little did I, or anyone else, think at that time that fourteen years later I would have such a pivotal role to play in bringing about those 'ecumenical gestures' towards other organisations and that 'opportunities to help ourselves while helping others' would be such a major debating topic during my presidency.

Tarbert, a club in North Kerry, took up my lead and tabled a motion for Congress along similar lines. It never really got off the ground, but the genie was out of the bottle and the debate was on.

A few years later there was much speculation about a national stadium. The great and generous J.P. McManus donated €50 million to the government to build such a facility, a truly colossal amount of money at that time. Bertie Ahern's dream of developing Abbotstown as an 80,000-seat stadium began to be floated in the right circles. As well as that, there was speculation of an English premier club being located in Dublin. Indeed, there were strong attempts made to bring Wimbledon FC to Dublin, and that and the proposed national stadium at Abbotstown became the hot topics of the sporting world.

At the time, I felt that if an 80,000-seat stadium were built in Abbotstown, it wouldn't do much good for the GAA. It would be in direct competition regarding concerts, for starters. Plus if an 80,000-seat stadium were available to soccer and rugby, they would never need an 82,500-capacity Croke Park. I feared Croke Park could even become a white elephant. A motion tabled by Shanahoe, Co. Laois, seeking changes to Rule 42 went before Congress in Galway in April 2000, but was referred to Central Council and died a quick death. The following year, Roscommon proposed the first major motion on opening Croke Park to soccer and rugby The wording of the Roscommon motion read:

[To Treoraí Oifigiúil/Official Guide]
    Riail 42 T.O. 1998 be amended by including the following section (c), 'Central Council shall have the power to authorise the use of Croke Park in certain circumstances, for field games other than those controlled by the Association. Sections (a) and (b) to remain unchanged. Rule 5 to be amended accordingly.

There were actually two other motions on the *clár* of Congress that year relating to Rule 42: one was tabled by Laois, which was withdrawn; the other was tabled by the Grattan Óg club, Longford, which was ruled out of order by Uachtarán Seán McCague on the basis that it did not quote Rule 5, as it should have done.

The Roscommon motion got the green light and was debated on the floor of Congress. Nobody expected it to get the requisite two-thirds majority. The debate was muted and not as high on emotion as it would be in subsequent years. Nevertheless, twenty-two speakers contributed to the discussion and, to everybody's surprise, it failed by just one vote to reach the magic two-thirds majority, receiving a total of 176 votes in favour and 89 votes against. If one person had changed his vote and voted in favour rather than against, the motion would have been passed. As it was, the vote was taken on a show of hands and when the result was announced there were calls for a recount as the counting procedure was anything but an exact science. Straight away Frank Murphy was on his feet, saying there was no call for such a procedure. Seán McCague, Chairman of Congress, acquiesced to this objection. End result: motion defeated.

Many commentators blamed Bertie Ahern for the failure of the motion on that occasion because the night before Congress Seán McCague had announced a grant of £60 million for the development of Croke Park, plus further funding for games development, coaching, etc. Undoubtedly that substantial cash injection had a profound influence; one of the major planks of the move to open Croke Park was based on income, i.e. the GAA needed to utilise the earning capacity of the stadium if it was to survive and prosper. The financial imperative now being greatly reduced took the momentum out of that argument.

While the media blamed the government and Taoiseach Bertie Ahern, in particular, for his sudden largesse, it has to be said that he was encouraged and indeed persuaded to do as he did by the higher echelons in the Association, who were totally opposed to opening Croke Park. Strangely, that fact has never been mentioned or commented on in the media or elsewhere. Nonetheless, although the day was lost, the plot was thickening.

As always in these closely run votes, there were some crucial voters missing, including myself. I had attended Congress on Friday night, but had to go home to Kerry early on Saturday morning for personal reasons. I informed the Kerry delegation of my dilemma and they willingly covered for me. I headed for Kerry at 6.00am and was back in Dublin again by Saturday evening, but alas I was too late for the debate on Rule 42. If I had been present, I would not only have voted in favour but would have spoken in favour of the motion as well. I'd surely have swung one vote in the hall. Well, if I had, it would have saved me an awful lot of bother and hassle later on as President—and a good bit of fun too, may I add.

Tommy Kenoy (Kilmore Club), who proposed the Roscommon motion, opined afterwards that 'the reason no one was trying to trip us up in 2001 is that nobody thought the motion had any chance of being successful.'

The drama was just beginning. The pro-lobby—buoyed up by their close vote but feeling cheated by Bertie's millions and the refusal to have a recount—vowed to return the following year. In the meantime, the anti-group gathered their forces and with a general election in the offing, the notion gathered currency that Congress 2002 wasn't an appropriate year to discuss Rule 42. So while the motions committee deemed the motion 'debatable', it was subsequently claimed that it was being debated only to engage the delegates! Wonderful semantics.

Thus two motions appeared on the *clár* of Congress in 2002, one by Kildare and a Clare motion that sought to 'authorise Central Council in respect of the use of Croke Park in certain circumstances for field games other than those controlled by the Association and to amend Rule 5 accordingly.' It was suggested from the top table that the motions be withdrawn. Kildare agreed to withdraw its motion, but Noel Walsh of Clare was having none of it. The upshot was that Congress was in no mood for change and a motion that had failed by only one vote a year earlier now got just a little over one-third of the majority. Only nine speakers contributed to the debate and the motion was lost: 197 against and 106 for. The irony was that any motion failing to get support from one-third of the delegates cannot be tabled again for at least three years. If five more people had voted against the motion, it would have got less than one-third (i.e. it would have been 100 against and 203 for).

As it happened, when Noel Walsh refused to withdraw the motion, Kerry were annoyed with him and were going to vote against, but I asked them not to. If they had, the motion would have got less than the one-third needed and would have been 'in limbo' for three years, the years of my presidency—which would have been forever! It would have made things much simpler, but much less challenging, and Croke Park would probably never have been opened.

The pro-group took a fair hammering at that Congress. In the space of one year the delegates' positions had changed so much that instead of two-thirds being in favour of change, two-thirds were now against it. It would be some task to turn it around again, especially as the IRFU, the FAI and the government grew in their resolve to build the 80,000-seat stadium in Abbotstown. On Friday 3 May 2002 the IRFU and FAI issued a joint statement reiterating their unequivocal support for Bertie Ahern's Stadium Ireland proposal in Abbotstown, saying it was 'impractical' to use Croke Park other than for one-off events. Both bodies stated that the pitch size at Croke Park was not conducive to a good atmosphere at any international fixtures that might be held there.

(How wrong this turned out to be!) They added that 'there is no doubt that Croke Park would be a suitable venue for once-off fixtures or tournaments, ie Euro 2008, Rugby World Cup finals etc.' but that a full fixtures schedule would be impractical—'the issue of the long-term availability of Croke Park to meet FAI and IRFU international fixture commitment and the size of the pitch and stadium itself make any sharing arrangement impractical.' As a result, they were committed to the proposal to build a national stadium—music to Bertie's ears, no doubt.

In light of this statement, would it be advisable to bother trying to open Croke Park at all? But would Abbotstown be built, especially if the GAA voted to open Croke Park? How could the millions and millions of euro be justified? Still, it was now definitely harder for the pro-opening group to progress. And so it turned out.

Would it, in fact, be impossible to stem the flow of the tide and re-channel it in a new direction? Some may have felt so at that low point, but they took solace in one development: my election as Uachtarán-Tofa. If I was prepared to stick to my stated position and to articulate my viewpoint honestly, things could be turned around, or so the thinking went. In interviews prior to my election I had made it clear that I favoured opening Croke Park to other sports, but in my year as Uachtarán-Tofa I wasn't anxious to either use or allow myself to be used to propagate a view contrary to the prevailing view of the establishment at the time. Indeed, in my acceptance speech to Congress, I made that very clear. I said, 'I have been elected as Uachtarán-Tofa, I am not Uachtarán and won't be for another twelve months.'

I had watched, with disapproval, previous Uachtarán-Tofa usurping or allowing themselves to be usurped as if they were already Uachtarán. I wasn't going to do that, especially to Seán McCague. He had another twelve months to go of his three-year term and I was determined to give him the space and time to fulfil his agenda. Besides, I had great respect for Seán and liked him personally. We might have held different views on various topics, but I found him to be honourable and fair. He was also the first Uachtarán to appoint me as Chairman of a national body—the Overseas Committee—and we had developed a great relationship in that role. So for my entire year as Uachtarán-Tofa, I politely refused to attend Provincial Council, County Board or any sub-committee meetings. I went to meetings of sub-committees only when asked to do so by Seán McCague. Ironically, two of those meetings involved the GPA and another one, the government.

During 2002, my year as Uachtarán-Tofa, things took a turn for the worse, or for the better depending on the way you looked at it. The PDS forced Bertie Ahern to pull the plug on a national stadium at Abbotstown, mainly because of the cost involved—although the location, out of town and in Bertie's own backyard, probably had a bearing on it, too. The upshot was that the GAA was summoned to Government Buildings to be told that Abbotstown was no longer an option and that the government's commitment to Croke Park was also off. Part of the deal for the 'Bertie Millions' had been that the GAA would commit to using Abbotstown a few times each year—a move I felt made no sense anyway.

So the GAA suddenly found that €38 million was being withdrawn, which naturally was a major blow to Croke Park. Minister for Finance Charlie McCreevy was very upfront and left no doubt that the position was as outlined, and gave little hope for a reprieve. When word of the turnabout filtered through to the membership, many felt cheated that a commitment entered into would not now be honoured, and due to no fault of the GAA. But such was the case. Personally, I looked on the bright side.

First, being relieved of the compulsion to put 200,000 bums on seats in Abbotstown was a relief. I had already made up my mind that when I was Uachtarán I would try to negotiate our way out of that clause. My thinking was: what was the point in building Croke Park only to pull some major games out of it and play them a few miles up the road? Secondly, with the plug pulled on Abbotstown, bang went a rival in scale and size to Croke Park, and bang went the notion of premiership football in Dublin. There was now a chance that a smaller stadium would be built, leaving Croke Park as the major edifice and allowing the two stadiums to complement each other. The bottom line was that neither Dublin nor Ireland needed two 80,000-seat stadiums. If the GAA played ball, it could be set up forever more. I made it clear that personally I was in favour of opening Croke Park to other sports. By so doing, I was sending a coded message to the government that business could be done for €38 million, which would also remove any reason to justify building an 80,000-seat stadium. It worked, too. Word was out that the 'next Uachtarán favoured opening Croke Park, and that a smaller, state of the art stadium would cater for all needs in that situation.'

I then went 'silent' again and gave every support I could to Seán McCague. Indeed, at one stage both he and Liam asked me to a meeting in the hope that my stated views would 'sate' Charlie McCreevy and encourage him to grant the €38 million, which was becoming a big bone of contention for many GAA officials. I went to the meeting they had arranged with Bertie and Charlie. But Charlie wasn't for turning.

Congress 2003 approached. In February of that year I attended my first meeting of the Motions Committee. Many motions were deemed out of order. Every single motion in relation to Rule 42 was ruled out of order, which was a bit strange as some of the exact same motions had been deemed in order in previous years. Still, I wasn't going to go against the Iar-Uachtarán, the Uachtarán and the Ard-Stiúrthóir, especially as this was Seán McCague's final Congress. If he was accepting it, I felt I should do the same. As a result, no motion dealing with altering Rule 42 appeared on the *clár* at Congress 2003 in Belfast. I felt no harm had been done as it would not have been passed anyway, but some people who had tabled motions were, not surprisingly, upset and vowed to come back again the following year.

Uachtarán

I took over as Uachtarán and in my acceptance address made no mention of Rule 42. It was a good tactic. I knew there were enough people who would mention it, and the media certainly wouldn't let the matter die. Besides, it would have been the height of folly, and insensitive to those who had supported me, to take up an entrenched position on such a divisive and emotional subject in my inaugural address.

As I suspected, the media were onto it like a shot. I rarely had to refer to Rule 42 in speeches, apart from club functions and guest speaker assignments. There was little need to as the media kept asking the questions and, of course, the editors highlighted my responses. Basically, my responses were simple. Yes, I was in favour of opening Croke Park and I wasn't going to change my position now that I was President. And yes, the matter should be debated at the next Congress. I thought this was very reasonable and naïvely believed my logic for opening Croke Park would be understood and accepted by a majority, from Coiste Bainistí down. I was in for a rude awakening.

The management team that year included many strong and determined opponents to any change to Rule 42, such as Seán McCague, Christy Cooney, Jimmy Treacy, John O'Reilly and Rory Kiely. It wasn't long until I perceived rumblings of discontent regarding the style and the substance of my leadership. It manifested itself early on when the matter was raised under 'AOB' at a management meeting. I was told that the Uachtarán's job was to defend policy, not try to change it. My stance on Rule 42 was fairly well criticised. Like Muhammad Ali, I absorbed the blows and then 'stung like a bee' with a counter-blow. I told them that I was quite entitled to point out where I thought the GAA should be going and that I had no intention of being derailed. I went on, 'Don't we see chairmen of provincial councils, etc., making all types of suggestions regarding GAA policy regularly?' That ended the discussion for the time being, but I remember wondering to myself: if this matter were put to a vote here at management, how many of the fifteen present would support my view on Croke Park? As I looked round the table of Coiste Bainistí members, I felt the honest answer was none—although one or two did give great support subsequently when it was needed, especially Tommy Moran of Leitrim. But that meeting was only a little foretaste of what was to come.

I continued working like a beaver for the Association, driving change in many different directions, but I couldn't escape Rule 42. Gradually it emerged that Lansdowne Road was the preferred choice for development by soccer and rugby. I often wondered how soccer and rugby could get along so well and how the rugby folk were so inclusive and accommodating of soccer. Surely some amongst them must have felt: 'Lansdowne Road is ours, let's develop it for ourselves and let soccer go and develop Dalymount Park or somewhere else.' But no, they seemed to have had no difficulty in working out an accommodation acceptable to both Associations. Ironically, when Armagh won their first All-Ireland in 2002, the 'welcome home' ceremony took place in Armagh Rugby Grounds. But the shelving of the National Stadium in Abbotstown threw up a completely different scenario. If Lansdowne Road was going to be developed over a period of two or three years, where were the Irish teams of both codes going to play their home internationals? Croke Park was the only alternative in Ireland. The debate intensified as the stakes got higher. It wasn't just two teams playing a game anymore; tourism, commerce and the economy all entered the fray and there was also that divisive nugget: the question of Ireland's image and patriotism.

How would Ireland look if soccer and rugby were playing their home games in Britain, while one of the finest stadiums in the world remained closed in Dublin? Who would be blamed? Not soccer, not rugby, no, the GAA would be blamed for its exclusivity and intransigence. I reckoned it would amount to a monstrous own goal by the GAA. Besides, as an Irishman, the thought of Ireland playing its home games in England was totally unpalatable to me—it would be irrational, short-sighted and unpatriotic to allow such a situation to occur.

As time went on my views became clearer, my determination greater and my enemies more numerous. I felt that the top echelons in Croke Park didn't support my opinion. Gradually, though, I was building up a picture of who I could trust—not many. I stopped discussing my true feelings with those I couldn't trust and got on about my business. I detected little mood in Croke Park for change. In fact, from reading the Ard-Stiúrthóir's report to Congress 2004, many got the impression that he was opposed to any change. This is what he wrote:

This issue probably got more publicity during the past year than any other item—other than the games—so I propose making a few points with regard to it.

Contrary to the opinion of some, ideology now plays very little part in the maintaining of Rule 42 as our policy in regard to use of Croke Park and our grounds generally. Ideology and the use of the term 'foreign games' is used predominantly by those whose experience or knowledge of the Association does not extend beyond envy of the GAA infrastructure and comparison with their own sport's lack of infrastructure.

The debate on Rule 42 has been taking place both internally and externally for a number of years. Internally there have been two distinct points of view: both formulated on the basis of what is considered to be in the Association's best interest. There is the view that opening Croke Park to other sports would be a hugely significant financial bonanza which would be of major benefit in eliminating the debt on Croke Park and which in turn would allow increased investment in games development and games promotion at grassroots level from any revenue accruing.

The second view is that it would not be in the Association's interest to allow Soccer and Rugby use Croke Park or other grounds. The general rationale supporting this point of view is that these two sports are the main competitors to the GAA and Gaelic games. As competitors they have all the advantages of the international dimension including unlimited indirect promotion at no cost to the domestic organisation. This applies to Soccer in particular, which is promoted on a multiplicity of television channels on a daily basis and which has access to the revenue that international television and competition can accrue. Against this, Gaelic Games are indigenous sports, the likes of which have not survived in any similar scenario anywhere abroad. They essentially do not have the advantage of an international dimension and its associated promotion or revenue. The GAA's only advantages are the passion and commitment of its members and supporters, the entertainment value of its games and most importantly the infrastructure of playing facilities which it has provided through generations of effort and a clear vision of a sense of place in Irish society and culture. This supports the view that to cede use of Croke Park or other grounds to other sports would eliminate one of the few competitive advantages that the Association has and would lead to the provision of a hard won infrastructure countrywide to our competitors with little or no capital commitment on their part.

Both points of view are genuinely and passionately held and it is important that both points of view should be put forward in a mature, business like way concentrating on the needs and best interests of the Association and no other.

The debate outside the Association has focused on the lack of suitable facilities for the two major international codes and on why the GAA should open its facility to accommodate them.

The following are the hard and dispassionate facts from my perspective. The GAA has provided a network of grounds and facilities countrywide at a cost of €2.6 billion at the last calculation. The competing professional sports, particularly

Soccer, have expended virtually no capital investment over the past thirty years. Yet, both sports are expending considerable resources in games promotion and games development at underage and schools level in particular. Neither make any secret of the fact that they are consciously competing for the hearts and minds of the youth.

The debt in relation to Croke Park will peak at about €100 million. We have spent €230 million of our own money and will spend €260 million before the stadium is complete. This is modest by comparison with any comparable stadium worldwide but massive for a voluntary non-profit making organisation. The Government have allocated €70 million from lottery funding for Croke Park, of which €19.5 million was spent on making the stadium ready to host the Special Olympics. It is important to point out that the Exchequer has been a net beneficiary in terms of taxes accrued as a result of the development. To date there is €38 million outstanding in respect of the grant aid commitment given in 2001, yet at the same time the government will be spending a minimum of €195 million on redeveloping Lansdowne Road and thus eliminating the need for either of our rival organisations to make any significant capital investment, as we have been required to do.

Many of the most powerful, most influential and most articulate administrators in the GAA were completely opposed to any change to Rule 42. Almost all the former presidents—a powerful and respected group—were against change, and almost all the Ulster counties were of a similar frame of mind. I knew all of this, but I had learned long ago from Shakespeare's Polonius, 'this, above all, to thine own self be true, thou cans't not then be false to any man.' I had to be true to myself. I was determined to do two things: one, let the membership know my feelings and the reasons why I felt the way I did, and two, get the matter debated at Congress.

I also knew that I was embarking on a dangerous tactic. If Rule 42 wasn't debated or was debated but was not passed, the critics would round on me and say I had been naïve and foolish. Indeed, Kevin Kimmage wrote as much in an article in the *Sunday Independent*. What would he and others have written if Rule 42 had been rejected in 2005?

But then, I'd rather fail attempting to achieve something I believed in than take the easy option and play it safe, sit on the fence and achieve nothing.

The matter took a strange twist at the Cork Convention on 14 December 2003. On Sunday night I got a call from Jim O'Sullivan, asking for my response to comments made by some delegates about me at that day's Convention. One said that he could have no respect for me as Uachtarán because of my position on Rule 42, and I was personally attacked in a way probably no other president had ever been attacked before.

Cork slams GAA President

'Croker debate intensifies' was the heading in the *Irish Examiner* on Monday 15 December 2003:

GAA President Seán Kelly came in for stinging criticism at yesterday's Cork GAA convention for espousing personal views on the opening up of Croke Park to soccer and rugby. Cork delegates took a firm stand against the President in an extraordinary attack—setting the scene for fierce internal debate on the matter. John Arnold said, 'He did not respect' the President and John Corcoran added, 'The President doesn't deserve the respect of ordinary gaels.' Dan Hoare added, 'I would not let anyone into the car park not to mention into Croke Park,' he blasted. Issue was also taken with the President 'for comments (favourable no doubt) made by President Kelly in relation to attending the Irish Rugby team's world Cup games.' [The rugby authorities told me that no GAA president had ever attended a rugby international before.]

Be this as it may, what surprised many observers was that no attempt was made by the top table to intervene out of respect for the office of Uachtarán, if not for the office-holder. It was also noted that at the Antrim Convention that same day, similar comments were made about my views on Rule 42, but with one major difference. The Antrim Board made it clear that while it disagreed with my position on Rule 42, it still respected and supported me as Uachtarán, something I greatly appreciated and admired.

The media swarmed around me for my reaction. I think most

people were surprised, and probably pleased, that I didn't take a whole lot of notice of the criticism. In a RTÉ interview I said that people were entitled to express their opinions in a democracy and that when you are in a position of leadership, you must take the good with the bad. I concluded by saying, 'It would be a very poor Kerryman that would allow criticism from a few Cork fellows upset him.'

I also got some very nasty phone calls and letters telling me that I was a 'traitor' and a 'disgrace', the insults embellished, of course, with choice language and threats. These I took in my stride, but it was a trifle tricky when people tried to accost me in public at functions or in bars. I usually wriggled out pretty quickly and didn't allow myself to be pressurised. One interesting development was that a letter criticising me and purporting to come from former president Paddy Buggy was read out at Ulster Council. Paddy was upset when he heard this and asked for a copy of the letter, but on 4 April 2005 I received a letter from Liam Mulvihill stating: 'I had a call from Paddy Buggy this morning (Monday) and he told me that he had failed to get a copy of the letter from the Ulster Council (which he was supposed to have written). He wanted you to know that there hasn't been any development.' Interesting, I thought. Dirty tricks, perhaps? We'll never know.

Anyway, I concluded that Congress would decide everything, or so I thought. I was certain that if I, as Uachtarán, wanted the matter debated at Congress, it would happen. I also believed that it would be a PR disaster for the GAA if all motions were deemed out of order once again. I honestly believed that the Iar-Uachtarán, all being men whom I admired and respected, would see things that way and that at least a majority could be persuaded to allow Congress to decide the matter.

I should have seen the writing on the wall. Jack Boothman, a very popular and committed president, had personally written a long letter to all county boards, Central Council delegates and members of management, outlining in graphic terms his complete opposition to opening Croke Park under any circumstances. His intervention wasn't well received by many as they felt such a direct approach by an Iar-Uachtarán wasn't desirable. It was also noted that one of the counties proposing amendment to Rule 42 was Jack's own county, Wicklow. Jack himself had played both rugby and cricket—indeed, I was forwarded photos of same by one of his former playing colleagues—which made his total opposition to 'garrison games' puzzling. The same could be said of another arch-opponent of change, Mícheál Greenan, who had been involved in soccer for some time. Still, everybody has their own logic and their own reasons, and I respected that.

Back at the first meeting of the Motions Committee, in February 2003, a strange thing had happened. One member noted that the final closing date for the receipt of motions was a fortnight away and proposed that we should deal with all motions other than those pertaining to Rule 42 'in case we rule them out of order and they could put another motion in before the closing date'. The meeting accepted this, although I couldn't quite see the logic of it as I felt some of the motions in relation to Rule 42 were in order and would be so deemed. If I had thought otherwise, I would have contacted a county board myself and worded a motion for them.

Indeed, I did exactly that for two other motions. I was very anxious to extend the five-year limit on the term of office to all provincial and Central Council delegates. Limerick had passed such a motion at its Convention, but the motion was either naïvely or badly worded because it was completely out of order and didn't include provincial delegates at all. The 'iar-uachtarán' who spoke of counties putting 'another motion in before the closing date' had given me an idea. I decided to draft a motion regarding the five-year rule and get a reliable official to put it through his county board. While driving up the M50 on my way to Newry, I rang a county official, gave him the wording on the five-year limit and asked him to get his county to sponsor it.

Immediately after 'sorting the five-year rule' on the M50, I made another call to another county asking them to put in a motion regarding mascots. Laois had been fined €1,400 for having two mascots in the Leinster Final—the twin sons of captain Joe Higgins. This was contrary to rule, so the fine was imposed—€700 for each child. Naturally, there was uproar. The first I heard about the fine was on my way to Dublin at around 6.00am one morning in August 2003. Maxi was on Radio One and she referred to it. By the time I had reached Dublin it was on every station, with Gerry Ryan offering to pay the fine himself (something he should have been left do and give the money to Joe Higgins). I heard one woman on CLR state, 'It's all that new President's fault.' I made up my mind it wouldn't happen again. When no motion came in to eliminate the 'ban' on mascots, I decided to avail of the window of opportunity and rang another county official and called out the wording of the motion for him, and he did the rest. So the 'five-year rule' and the 'mascot' rules were dealt with and conceived over the phone on the M50.

As I said, if I had suspected that the motions on Rule 42 were all out of order, I would have done the same for those, but even if I did, I doubt if it would have been given the green light. A fortnight later, after the final date for receipt of motions had passed, another Motions Committee meeting was held to deal with all motions in relation to Rule 42 and any other motions received in the preceding two weeks, including the two drafted over the phone on the M50. Thankfully, both of those were deemed in order—if they hadn't been, I would have been feeling rather silly.

Whatever about feeling silly, I soon felt a bit sick. In regard to Rule 42, we met a brick wall. No motion was deemed in order. I argued the cases, quoting the relevant rules. I pointed out that some of the motions did comply with the requirements to be in order. I reminded the meeting that Central Council had agreed to a suggestion of mine that the bye-laws committee be made available to help counties put motions in order. This they had certainly done for some of the motions. It was to no avail—the bye-laws committee, despite dealing and correcting bye-laws and rules every day, weren't deemed correct on Rule 42 either. There was no other resource available to counties to help them put motions in order. I then queried how these motions could be deemed in order in previous years, by the exact same committee, but were now suddenly out of order. I asked if they were aware of the upcoming fallout if all motions were again out of order this year. I said, 'There'll be f**king war if all the motions are deemed out of order again. It will be an absolute PR disaster. For God's sake, will ye put one motion on the *clár* because it's not going to get the two-thirds majority anyway.'

My pleading fell on deaf ears. For a full two hours the argument raged. They weren't for turning, though. Eventually, I realised that I couldn't get anywhere. There was no support whatsoever. In the end I decided I'd ask each one of them individually. Some had been hedging, but by Christ, if they were going to do me down, every single one of them was going to have to say so as I sat at the top of the table in Box 621 of the Cusack Stand. I went around the table to each one, asking each man for his decision. Every single one of them said 'No', making statements such as, 'If soccer and rugby are ever played in Croke Park,

I'll leave the Association' and 'We'd be turning our backs on all that the GAA stands for' and 'The sacred soil of Croke Park must never be tainted with the thud of boots of foreign games.'

I knew the game was up. A thought flew through my mind that I would go over their heads and appeal to Central Council, but this wasn't really an option. I finished the meeting, ordered taxis for some of the older Iar-Uachtarán and conveyed them down to the lifts. I had other business to conclude and at 10.30pm I left my office in Croke Park and headed on the long, lonely road home to Kerry, depressed, disappointed and dejected to my innermost soul.

I had stated all year that 'Congress will decide'. Now, Congress wasn't going to have any say in it. As I drove home alone—always alone—through that dark and wet night, I wondered what the fallout would be. I realised that as a member of the committee, and out of respect for the Iar-Uachtarán, I would have to present a dignified and calm exterior. But I also decided that I wouldn't throw in the towel. This was no way for an association to do business, strangled by its own rules. I'd simply have to work harder to win changes, including Rule 42.

In the *Irish Independent* Martin Breheny wrote:

Seán Kelly has been outspoken in his belief that the rule regarding the use of Croke Park should be amended and will be extremely disappointed that the matter won't even be discussed next month. However, he put a brave face on the decision of the vetting committee, which will come as a total shock to the rest of the GAA world … Kelly insisted on accepting collective responsibility for the decision to rule the motions out of order, but he must be privately seething over the failure to face up to one of the most contentious issues in the GAA … Despite that, it's likely that a proposal to amend Rule 42 would be beaten at the GAA's congress this year but the decision to stifle debate on the matter will anger many members of the Association who believe that it portrays them in a very negative light.

You're spot on, Martin, says I to myself, but the game isn't over yet. I would bide my time.

In the *Irish Times* (Tuesday 9 March 2004), Seán Moran summed it up as follows:

GAA Congress in Killarney will not be debating the use of Croke Park in the latest twist in a bizarre controversy dating back three years. The motions ruled as out of order are precisely the same as the one debated without quibble when proposed by Roscommon in 2001. It also passed the vetting process of the Motions Committee in 2002 before McCague entered his caveat on the floor of Congress (he had pointed out his reservations, but decided to take it anyway in the interest of debate). It undermines the democratic principles that underpin the Association. That will have to be addressed.

I got to bed at 3.00am, only to be awakened four hours later by a phone call telling me of the tragic and untimely death of Tyrone's captain, the great Cormac McAnallen. I was stunned. Without a doubt it was the lowest moment of my presidency. Cormac was an idol. He was not only a great footballer but a man of great talent, great values and great commitment. He was so strong, so independent and yet so popular. It was no wonder Mickey Harte, another really great man, selected him to be his captain. The turnout at Cormac's funeral said it all. From all corners, people came and they stayed for days. At least 20,000 people attended his funeral. Compare that to the small turnout at Charlie Haughey's funeral, he who was a former Taoiseach, minister and leader of the biggest party in the Dáil. People may not have known Cormac personally, but they knew enough about him to recognise that here was true greatness—the kind every mother and father would love their son to be.

I drew strength out of Cormac's death. If the failure to get Rule 42 on the *clár* for Congress was a bad reflection on the GAA, Cormac's life and funeral was, in many ways, a reflection of all that is good about it— genuine fellow feeling, generosity without thought of cost, willingness to do anything for someone you genuinely appreciated and admired. On that day in Eglish, Cormac's home place was sad but happy, turbulent but peaceful, empty but full.

Cormac's death took some of the attention away from Rule 42 for a while, but it didn't entirely spare some members of the Motions Committee from getting a bit of a lambasting in the media. This was something I genuinely disliked as no matter what the decision, it's always unedifying to see men, especially elderly men, being subjected to such criticism. But rightly or wrongly Tommy Kenny's observation that 'ordinary GAA members have been given the ultimate kick in the backside by diehards' was a fair reflection of grassroots feeling.

Most commentators felt that the Motions Committee was giving me a very firm slap on the wrist and, as a consequence, that my presidency would be gravely wounded and I'd be a bit of a lame duck. I certainly didn't see it that way and had no intention of becoming a lame duck— something that would have greatly pleased some in Croke Park, and elsewhere. Cormac McAnallen had never thrown in the towel and I had no intention of doing so either. In fact, in some ways I was pleased with the setback and the criticism. It was almost as if we were joining battle, but while the skirmish may have been lost, the battle was far from over.

Congress was approaching fast. It would take place in my own home town of Killarney. Everybody was saying it would be something of a damp squib given that no motion on Rule 42 was up for discussion. I had other things in mind, though. For a start, there were some very important motions up for discussion, including the 'M50 motions' and the hurling development motions to establish the Christy Ring and Nicky Rackard Cups and another, very important to me, regarding the setting up of All-Ireland competitions for Junior and Intermediate clubs.

Due to good preparation by the HDC and Paraic Duffy, these all got through safely. Cork were known opponents of the introduction of the hurling proposals, but we were ready for them. The 'weaker' counties were fairly well canvassed and I convinced Ger Loughnane to become a Clare delegate so that he could speak from the floor, if needed; Pat Fitzgerald (Clare Secretary) arranged that for me. The motions were well carried, despite some strong opposition from some counties, notably Cork, Kilkenny, Offaly and Antrim. No disrespect intended, but Cork have been noted for opposing many changes in the past. Apart from Rule 42, they also opposed the introduction of the Club Championship and were even a little unenthusiastic about ladies football. Their voice often carried great weight, but not on this occasion. The motions I wanted to get passed were passed. There was more to come and it came via my presidential address. As usual, I wrote it myself, got it typed up and put on DVD locally.

Before I rose to speak, Danny Lynch approached me all in a flurry. He was looking for copies of my speech to distribute to the assembled media. I told him the media could wait, that I had plenty of copies, but

I wasn't going to release them until after I had spoken. When I came to Rule 42, I said the following:

The fact that no motion on Rule 42 appears on the Clár despite being submitted by eight counties has disappointed and indeed angered many. The past Presidents have borne the brunt of much of this anger. This is unfortunate, as each of them has given life-long and distinguished service to the Association and they, no less than anyone else, are constrained by the rules of the Association. Nevertheless the fact that motions now out of order were deemed in order, in previous years, has perplexed many and has led to unsustainable conspiracy theories. As I indicated last year, when announcing the setting up of a Rules Revision Committee, our rules are too complicated and often too negatively written. For instance the Motion Committee's role is to judge whether motions are in order, not to put them in order and the President can rule a motion out of order, not in order.

It is particularly disconcerting that clubs and county boards have no support mechanism available to them that guarantees motions are in order. When top officials in the Association and even the bye-laws committee, known masters of the rules, can't guarantee that, despite their best efforts, motions are in order, it is time for a rethink. When and where are voluntary officials supposed to gain the necessary expertise to master the rules?

I would welcome a situation, where if motions are passed at County Conventions, a committee at national level would have the authority to put them in order. This would get rid of the convoluted system that we have at present and encourage our voluntary members to table motions, forward good ideas, happy in the knowledge that they will be discussed on the only floor that matters, the floor of Congress. How does it progress our association when a perfectly laudable, well-thought out idea can't be discussed because it's technically out of order?

Besides when knowledge of the rules is the preserve of a few, this confers a certain power on these few, which is unhealthy and undemocratic. Are there 40 people in this hall who could confidently put a motion in order for Congress? Are there 30? Are there 20? Are there 10? I emphasise this because it doesn't have to be like this, it's not like this in most other organisations and it mustn't be like this much longer. Hopefully the Rules Revision Committee, who have done much work over the past year, can re-draft the Rule Book and make it relatively easy for voluntary officials to master.

The Strategic Review Committee, having undertaken a comprehensive in depth investigation and an extensive market research process, made the following recommendation re the use of Croke Park: 'The GAA should, as soon as the surface of the Croke Park pitch has proved its stability, re-draft Rule 42 of its official guide to ensure that "the right to make decisions in relation to the use of Croke Park should be delegated to Central Council rather than being covered by general rule".'

This committee was, in the words of my predecessor Seán McThaidhg whose brain-child it was, made up of 'a cross-section of Irish Society best placed to comment of the needs of the Association' and some of the top administrators in the GAA, namely, two Iar-Uachtaráin, Peter Quinn and Joe McDonagh, two provincial Chairmen, Christy Cooney and Nickey Brennan, and the then four Provincial secretaries. Their recommendation makes good sense to me and I have said so when asked and indeed, I look forward to the day when this recommendation like other recommendations of this fine report, which have not already been dealt with, is debated at Congress.

Some individuals have questioned the right of the Uachtarán to express his personal opinion on this matter. One assumes that these critics are expressing their own personal opinions, while wishing to deny me, an tUachtarán, the right to express mine. Well, I have news for you gentlemen and it is this. When you have the same mandate as I got from Congress two years ago, then and not till then shall I be silenced by you or anybody else. I was elected to lead, not to be led, to praise not to be praised, to serve not to be served. As I said last year 'in endeavouring to serve all, I'll ask myself one question: "What is best for the Association?" I do not have any other agenda either sporting, personal or political. I'll listen carefully, consult widely, ponder deeply but ultimately make up my own mind and follow that without fear or favour.' That's what I've done and that's what I'll continue to do.

Like Johnny Cash, I intend to keep my eyes wide open all the time, keep a close watch on some friends of mine, but when it comes to walking the line, I'll walk no line but my own, the line that I think is best for the GAA.

Wouldn't it be a remarkable state of affairs if everybody in the country was entitled to comment on what changes the country needed except the Taoiseach, or if all the world could suggest policy changes for the Church save the Pope? Likewise, in our Association? How else are changes to be brought about, improvements made and debate initiated except by suggestions? People expect leadership from the top, people are entitled to know one's views and everybody is entitled to express an opinion and be respected for same, regardless of whether people agree or disagree with the articulated thoughts.

Criticism doesn't bother me too much. In fact, a little controversy now and then should be relished by the wisest men. It would be a dull world if we all agreed. Organisations like ours need and indeed can thrive on divergent views. But, ultimately, we're all serving the same cause and pursuing the same goals.

My speech was interrupted by sustained rounds of applause and calls of 'Hear, hear' from those who were surprised but pleased by my comments; the minority, who were equally surprised but very displeased, greeted me with stony silence. When I finished there was a standing ovation, but some, including some past presidents, remained seated. The eagle-eyed photographers captured these scenes, of course, and the telling photographs were carried by all the major media and television.

Many people regarded that speech as the defining moment of my presidency. I had thrown down the gauntlet to some of the most knowledgable, experienced and influential in the Association.

In the following Monday's *Independent*, Martin Breheny wrote:

With the debate on the use of Croke Park bound in a technical knot by archaic procedures, the 2004 GAA Congress seemed to be headed for a dismal cul de sac—only to be rescued by a spirited assertion of his authority by President Seán Kelly ... Kelly made it clear that he was deeply concerned over the difficulties involved in putting motions in order ... However it was the censure of his critics that made the most dramatic impact. His views on the use of Croke Park drew most criticism, including a sustained attack at the Cork convention. Kelly faced down all his detractors with a clear reminder that he was in charge and was not for turning ... It was a strong speech by Kelly who is clearly determined not to allow his Presidency be undermined by sniping from whatever quarter it emerges.

In *The Star* Damien Lalor wrote:

Kelly was in a fiery mood and anyone who thinks he is going to lie down and be happy to wear the President's chain with meekness is mistaken. When the ex-Presidents threw out the matter of a Rule 42 debate, Kelly finally knew where he stood.

Kelly received a standing ovation for his speech but many were unmoved. The Cork delegation for example, didn't exactly wave their handkerchiefs. There's no doubt but that some are out to soften Kelly's cough, but the Kilcummin man, although he was left wheezing some weeks back with the Rule 42 snub, promises to be in full voice again soon.

The question now was: could I deliver?

It was a tall order and a high-risk strategy. I think many people, encouraged by my stance, began to see Rule 42 as a far wider issue than just opening the gates of Croke Park. The battle was now firmly on between those who wanted the GAA to remain as it was—conservative, cautious and self-serving—and those who wanted it to move onwards to a brave new world of inclusiveness, openness and generosity.

My address to the Kerry Convention in January 1991 was now becoming a reality. The moral high ground was about to feel heavy tremors. For me, and indeed for almost everybody, Congress 2004 was an outstanding success. I had answered my critics—as one columnist put it, I 'gave them both barrels'—and had made it clear that while they were entitled to express their opinions, I too was entitled to express mine, and I wasn't going to be stopped from expressing them either. Also, to avoid 'f**king war in Congress', as I put it to the Motions Committee, I appeased Congress by getting a resolution passed that the terms of reference of the Motions Committee would be redefined at an upcoming Special Congress. The major hurling motions all went through, as did the five-year limitation on office. And while motions on Rule 42 were not on the *clár*, delegates did air their views when discussing the Ard-Stiúrthóir's report.

Killarney—Congress 2004

First to speak was a most respected and dedicated official, Jimmy Dunne of Wicklow. He said his county was deeply disappointed that their motion was ruled out of order by the Motions Committee, especially as the Bye-Laws Committee had helped them put it in order, as directed by Central Council. He said that some of the statements from those opposed to altering Rule 42 were hilarious and bordering on the ridiculous. They had heard references like 'the eight rebels' (the eight counties who tabled motions on Rule 42), 'the motions were planted', and 'they should not be allowed into the carpark'. He added that at times the very position of Uachtarán was being brought into question and being undermined, people expressing a view that challenged the status quo were considered almost anti-GAA. Pointing out that we couldn't be 'prisoners of history', he concluded by suggesting that the biggest challenge facing the GAA was 'to retain the goodwill and support of the general public'.

Speakers like Donal McCormack (Down) and Bob Honohan (Cork) strongly criticised those who had pilloried the Motions Committee with Bob stating that 'these men were attacked on the grounds of age as if they were simpletons and have no longer the power to make reasonable decisions.'

But Tommy Keroy (Roscommon) countered by saying that Rule 42 had taken many twists and turns since Roscommon had moved a motion in the Burlington Hotel in 2001 but the 'most savage twist of all came when the Motions Committee in one fell swoop wiped eight motions off the clár of Congress'. He added that it was a public relations disaster, especially as the Uachtarán had given them leadership, had advised them to submit motions to the Bye-Laws Committee, and the members had responded to the Uachtarán's lead, but now the motions could not be debated. He described the refusal to allow Congress the opportunity to discuss Rule 42 as 'one of the blackest days' in the GAA's history. He said the debate now was about the refusal to allow a debate.

He went further by calling for the suspension of standing orders to facilitate the calling of a special congress to debate Rule 42. He was seconded by Noel Walsh (Clare). The colourful man from Milltown Malbay also criticised the Ard-Stiúrthóir, saying he thought he was a little bit disingenuous in his summary of what the motion on Rule 42 was all about.

An interesting observation was made by Alan Delaney (Laois) who pointed out that Rule 4 of the GAA's official guide stated that the GAA supported Irish industry and that there was nothing more important than the tourist industry and, if Croke Park remained closed, up to half a million people would have to leave the island to view Irish teams abroad at enormous cost to the economy.

So now I had an unexpected development—a motion to suspend standing orders so that Central Council could call a special congress to debate Rule 42. What was I going to do? I could understand the frustration but this was the nuclear option. It would be highly divisive, the build-up would be enormous and the possibility of success highly unlikely. Nevertheless, in anticipation of this call I had prepared a statement which Coiste Bainistí and Central Council had adopted. It was time to play this card now, to avoid a fractious debate but also to appease the disenchanted. I said that what had happened in the last few months was unacceptable and 'it is my intention to ensure in the months ahead that the necessary steps are taken to ensure that nobody is put in that invidious position again. Coiste Bainistí intends to do a root and branch analysis of the current system and in so far as I can to ensure a system is put in place which facilitates every club and unit to address congress by way of acceptable motion.'

It did the trick. The disillusioned were pacified and while the motion to hold a special congress was put, it was defeated but without any acrimony. The vast majority were happy enough. I had appeased them without hanging anyone out to dry. But I would have to deliver. And besides it would all have to happen in the next twelve months. Any later would have been too late.

So Congress finished on a high and more importantly in a united manner (outwardly anyway, although I have no doubt some were smarting at my effrontery).

The Kerry County Board had done a great job in organising Congress and the banquet was a superb affair, with Liam O'Connor bringing down the house and our special guest, Minister for Sport John O'Donoghue, giving a marvellous speech. I had been working on the

Taoiseach, the Tánaiste Mary Harney, the Minister for Finance Charlie McCreevy and John O'Donoghue to consider paying the €38 million outstanding on Croke Park. Tommy Lyons, then Dublin manager, had told me that Bertie had said to him that they'd 'do business with Seán Kelly'. John O'Donoghue arranged for me to meet Charlie McCreevy and I found Charlie a most gregarious and engaging character. After going through the history of grants for the GAA, Charlie finished up by saying, 'Kelly, I like your style, I'll do something for you alright.' He even said that I'd have to get another job when my term as President was up, saying, 'You couldn't f**king well go back to teaching. 'Twould kill you.'

A meeting was arranged with Mary Harney, in her home. Mary was sweet, but was very anxious that Croke Park be opened: 'If you opened Croke Park, we could give you €50 million,' she said. I told her that it would be counter-productive to link the grant aid for Croke Park with opening it to soccer and rugby. She listened carefully and obviously took on board what I had said because, contrary to what many had surmised, when John and Charlie did come to delivering, Mary and the PDs rowed in behind them enthusiastically. John O'Donoghue kept in touch on developments and I knew he was making progress.

Not too long afterwards I was in my office in Croke Park when I got a call from Charlie McCreevy. 'Where are you?' he asked. I told him and said that I had a meeting at 3.00pm and another at 5.00pm. 'You can go into the meeting for a while,' he said, 'and f**k it after about half an hour. If you could be in my office around 4.00pm, John O'D and I will meet you.'

I followed his instructions and at the appointed time arrived in Government Buildings, where I met John O'Donoghue and Charlie McCreevy. I had been hoping for possibly €20 million, but they told me that with savings and juggling they were not giving us €20 million, not even €38 million, but two more on top of that: €40 million in all. I was delighted, but waited to hear the conditions, what strings were attached. I had made it clear all along, as I had to Mary Harney, that any funds for Croke Park couldn't be conditional upon opening it up. They respected that viewpoint and indeed, to the government's credit, from the Taoiseach down, they all said that opening Croke Park was a matter for the GAA. While they had their personal preferences, they weren't going to interfere with the GAA's right to decide. I really appreciated their understanding and observance of this point. This was crucial as many just wouldn't or couldn't believe that the government would give us €40 million without strings attached. Well, Charlie did attach one string! When I was leaving, he said, 'Don't forget me for a few All-Ireland tickets and I don't expect them for nothing. But there are always people that would drive you crackers looking for them.'

So that was it: €40 million to be paid in two tranches—€20 million in December 2004 and €20 million in December 2005. However, prior to Christmas 2004 the government decided to pay it all in one tranche, saving us about €1.5 million in interest alone. I wasn't in Croke Park the day they rang, but was the news greeted with delight and fanfare? No, they were simply told to send it over to Croke Park in a taxi. When the taxi arrived, no one from Croke Park was there to meet them. I was told this sometime after Christmas by a government official. I couldn't believe it. Could you imagine any other body telling the government to send over €40 million in a taxi, and not being there to meet them? Enough said.

With more certainty now coming into the picture regarding the intentions of the IRFU and FAI to develop Lansdowne Road, the question of opening Croke Park was never far from the headlines. Indeed, on a few occasions when we would be launching something or other, such as Inter Rules, Shinty, Inter-Provincials or Gaelic Telecom, journalists would ask me questions about Croke Park and I would reply, 'If I answer that question now, the headlines tomorrow will be all about Croke Park and Rule 42 and not about what we are launching. I will answer that question for you on another day.'

Special Congress October 2004 was approaching. It was to deal with the membership report, which had been in the making for over eight years and was chaired by Jack Boothman. It was a good report, but we availed of it to draft a special motion redefining the terms of reference of the Motions Committee. Liam Ó Maolmhichíl drafted a prospective motion first. I looked at it and saw that it might conceivably change nothing, so I said to Liam, 'That isn't worth a shite. We could be as bad as ever if that's all we are going to do.' He drafted a second motion which was much better, and it went on to be approved by the Ard-Chomhairle and brought before the Special Congress. The key clause here was that if motions were deemed out of order, 'Counties shall be advised in writing of the reason,' giving them an opportunity to submit a corrected motion. Special Congress was satisfied with the motion, therefore one of the promises I made at Congress in Killarney was fulfilled. The mechanism for tabling motions had now been changed, so what had happened in previous years would never happen again.

New Rule 80: Motions Committee
'A committee consisting of the President, the past President, and the Director General shall prior to Congress, examine motions submitted and decide whether these are in order. The committee may put a motion in order where there is a failure to quote the numbers of the rules affected or where there are minor clerical errors. In cases of motions submitted by counties being not in order, counties shall be advised in writing of the reason for a motion being not in order, and subject to a time-line determined by Central Council, shall be afforded an opportunity to re-submit an appropriately corrected motion for consideration of the Motions Committee. The President shall have the authority of Congress to rule a motion out of order.'

In many ways getting this motion tabled and passed at the Special Convention 2004 was the most crucial development in the whole history of Rule 42. Without it, one could be certain and sure that no motion on Rule 42 would ever again be debated at Congress because no motion would have got past the Motions Committee.

Christmas was approaching and with it the County Conventions. No fewer than twelve counties put forward motions on Rule 42—some to open Croke Park permanently, others to open it temporarily. The counties that submitted motions were: Meath, Dublin, Offaly, Sligo, Clare, Wicklow, Wexford, Roscommon, Laois, Longford, Cavan and Kerry. This breaks down as seven Leinster counties, two each from Munster and Connacht and one from Ulster.

Kerry's motion was strategic. The year before Kerry had considered putting a motion forward, but I, having discussed it with the sage of all sages, Gerald McKenna, had decided against it. Gerald said that it would have been bad if Kerry were seen to be pushing it so early in my presidency. This year it was different, however. There was no room for hiding in the woodwork. Kerry, and especially its Chairman, Seán Walsh, felt it was important that Kerry be seen to support my stance openly, especially in light of the public criticism of me from across the county bounds and elsewhere.

Going through the motions

So the counties submitted their motions and all was in readiness for the first meeting of the Motions Committee, on 31 January 2005 at 2.00pm. Once again, I was confident that some of the motions were in order. Surely twelve counties couldn't get it wrong? But to my surprise all of the motions relating to Rule 42 were again ruled out of order. This time, however, there was a second chance: counties had to be told why the motion was out of order. Many thought this would mean that the Motions Committee would spell out the exact wording required to put a motion in order. When I suggested this to the Committee, one said, 'Do they expect us to write it for them?'

Nevertheless, counties had to be told the reasons, such as failure to quote or amend another rule affected. If the reason was addressed properly in the re-drafting, the motion should get the green light—in theory, at any rate.

When word seeped through that all twelve motions relating to Rule 42 had again been deemed out of order, it set alarm bells ringing amongst the proponents of change. The media took great interest in the developments and it became widely known that counties were now consulting solicitors to ensure motions were in order. The Cavan solicitor and well-known expert on the rules, Niall Dolan, was in great demand for advice. Most counties got their motions in by the deadline, so the second and final meeting of the Motions Committee took place on 15 February.

I approached the meeting with a mixture of trepidation and determination. Even though I had been expecting Peter Quinn to attend, having called him in advance, he didn't make it. When I saw nearly all the Iar-Uachtarán turning up, I feared for the outcome. We had arranged lunch for them in advance and I had prepared myself mentally for a major showdown, if necessary. When I saw four or five of the older presidents coming up the corridor on the sixth floor, panting and out of breath from their exertions, I thought, 'God, it's like going to battle with my own father,' who was over eighty at the time. Still, despite my misgivings about taking on 'the elderly', I knew if it came to it, it had to be done.

We were all very civil over lunch, but after lunch Pat Fanning nodded off in his chair. The lift didn't come all the way up to the sixth floor, which meant he'd had to climb a couple of flights, which in truth his physical condition wasn't up to. Even though the meeting was due to start at 2.00pm, I suggested we let Pat sleep for a while. About 2.15pm he woke up and we adjourned to the next room for our meeting.

When the first two motions on Rule 42 were deemed out of order again, I began to agitate. Some were arguing against the validity of opening Croke Park, which had nothing to do with whether the motions were in order. I feared the worst and was prepared for a furious battle. But help came from an unexpected quarter. Suddenly Pat Fanning said, 'The Uachtarán is right, the substantive issues are matters for debate at Congress and while I agree with your views [the ex-presidents speaking against opening Croke Park], the motion before us is fully in order and it should go to Congress for delegates to decide.' It was the decisive intervention as some other Iar-Uachtarán agreed with him. The motion in question—the Cavan motion—got the green light. Boy, wasn't I lucky that I had allowed Pat to have his siesta? He would scarcely have had the energy or alertness required for the meeting otherwise. If passed, the Cavan motion would allow Croke Park to be opened permanently, so I knew it had little chance of getting the support of two-thirds of delegates at Congress.

I was afraid that all other motions would be ruled out of order. It was essential that at least one motion looking for the temporary amendment of Rule 42 went before Congress. A few minutes later the Wicklow motion advocating temporary opening got the go ahead. I was so relieved.

At least the delegates could now have their say and my oft-quoted statement that I wanted the matter debated 'on the only floor that mattered, the floor of Congress' was going to happen in April 2005.

At the end of the meeting seven of the fourteen motions (two more had arrived in the interim) submitted for the second meeting were deemed in order. In one sense it is extraordinary that seven were deemed out of order despite the best efforts of officials and solicitors to put them in order for a second time, but that wasn't worth dwelling on. Once more I conveyed the Iar-Uachtarán to the exits, but this year it was with a lighter and happier heart. It was agreed that no statement would be issued until the Ard-Stiúrthóir had had an opportunity to contact the counties involved.

The launch of the Páidí Ó Sé Tournament was taking place in the Burlington Hotel that night, so I headed over there. I was immediately surrounded by a posse of pressmen. I told them that I couldn't say anything at that point. 'Can't you give us a hint, Seán?' said Brian Carthy. I replied, 'Brian, no hints, no nods, no winks.' 'But,' says Tom O'Riordan, 'you are smiling, Seán. You seem to be in good form.' 'I'm always smiling,' I replied.

But Tom was right. I was in good form. In fact, I was in great form. I hopped into my car at 11.30pm and headed for the Kingdom. The long road home to Kerry was rarely so pleasant. I rang Juliette and told her the good news. I told nobody else until Liam gave the word, although I did whisper in the Taoiseach's ear at the launch that I expected Rule 42 to be debated at Congress.

The *Irish Examiner* got hold of the story pretty quickly, however, as Jim O'Sullivan revealed in his column. That's when all the speculation started. Would the Northern counties vote *en bloc* against opening Croke Park? What would the overseas units do? If it were rugby only being proposed, would that mean more supporters for change? Would Kelly rule that it would take only a simple majority to amend Rule 42 temporarily? The government, the FAI and the IRFU were all asked to comment, but wisely and diplomatically refused to be drawn, saying it was a matter for the GAA alone. 'We accept and respect entirely the fact that this is a decision for the GAA alone. We have not played any part in the debate, nor will we do so now. It is an internal decision for the GAA,' said John Redmond on behalf of the IRFU.

Yes, John, an internal decision, but one that would have to be taken in the full gaze of the public with major external implications. Now that the matter was to be debated at Congress, almost everyone in the country was interested in it and almost everyone had a view.

Mobilising the troops

I reckoned there were only two ways Rule 42 could succeed. One was by getting those in favour to concentrate on temporary opening while Lansdowne Road was being developed, the second was by mobilising the grassroots. I had clearly seen that the higher up you went in the Association, the greater the opposition to opening Croke Park. If rule change was going to be enacted, it could only come from the grassroots—those who talked the talk and walked the walk everyday for the honour and glory of their own villages.

This was easier said than done. In the previous year (2004), a motion by Roscommon to have a plebiscite, or referendum, was not allowed at Congress, being deemed a matter for Central Council. When it went before Central Council, it was said that only Congress could order a referendum as there was no provision in the rule book for such a process in the GAA. At a meeting of Ard-Chomhairle in 2003 (30 August), a motion requesting that a referendum-type consensus be taken at club level in 2004 was discussed. That meeting decided that there was no provision in the official guide for the carrying out of such a referendum and that such an exercise would be contrary to the rules/powers of the Ard-Chomhairle. That was their logic, but it meant there was no way an official referendum of the clubs could be called or held. Cuteness, real Kerry cuteness and cunning, was called for.

The only way I figured it could be done was for the clubs to debate and vote on the issue themselves, and then for each club delegate to bring its viewpoint to the County Board, which would then mandate their Congress delegates to vote accordingly. In many counties, and certainly in Kerry, the Congress delegates always had a free hand when they went to Congress and usually decided amongst themselves which way to vote. This was fine for most motions, but for a major policy change like Rule 42, it would almost certainly lead to defeat if all counties (not being as enlightened as Kerry!) were to conduct business in this manner.

How could we have a referendum without calling one officially—especially as a Clare motion to hold a referendum of clubs on Rule 42 was again rejected out of hand by the Motions Committee (February 2005)? The only way I figured it could happen was by asking clubs to discuss all motions on the *clár* of Congress, thereby proving in reality what the Association often boasted about—that it is one of the most democratic organisations in the world.

Once again it all happened on the M50. I had just cleared the toll bridge when I got a call on my mobile from Colm Keys, the tall, athletic journalist from Meath. In chatting with him, I outlined my strategy. He was of like mind—as an active club member, he was fairly *au fait* with grassroots thinking. The upshot was that he headlined my call for all clubs to vote on all motions. His article in the *Irish Independent* struck a chord with clubs around the country. The first county to take up my suggestion was none other than Armagh, who were against amending Rule 42. Gene Duffy and I had been good friends for a long time. Gene, like most people from Northern Ireland, holds strong views, but is also very fair and honest. He comes from Crossmaglen and like all those from that famous club, what you see is what you get. They tell you what they think, not what they think you'd like to hear. That's Crossmaglen, that's Northern Ireland and that's Gene Duffy.

A few days later Gene met me and said that the Armagh County Committee had discussed my call for the clubs to discuss Rule 42. He said they had decided to write to Croke Park for a copy of all motions, which they were going to send out to all their clubs so that they could discuss each one at the next county board meeting. I couldn't have asked for any more. They did so and, of course, voted against any change.

Nevertheless, Armagh had set the ball rolling. Every chance I got, I averted to Armagh's proactive exercise in true democracy. My aim was to encourage other counties to follow suit and sure enough, it wasn't long before the media was reporting on when each county was due to vote. The unofficial referendum took off like a prairie fire. The *craic* was mighty as club after club consulted its membership. In some cases big numbers turned up and the votes started stacking up on either side. Speculation was rife. A cliff-hanger vote was predicted.

I felt that if we got one of the Six Counties to vote in favour of change, it would be crucial. County Down went the closest. A majority of clubs were in favour, but at County Board level the executive also has a vote, which tilted the balance. When the votes were counted, it was a tie. It all came down to the Chairman and he gave his casting vote against change. He couldn't be faulted for this as chairmen often go with the status quo when votes are tied. When Down was lost in such a tight vote, I began to feel that that 'little bit of luck' that wins matches just wasn't with us.

Worse was to follow. New York voted against as well. Most people felt that the vast majority of overseas delegates would vote for change, but I knew quite a few of them were still clinging hard to the idea of 'Old Ireland' and therefore would vote against. Still, I was gutted when I read the result of the New York vote. Here was the GAA in the capital of the free world, voting against change and talking about things long gone. New York board didn't even own Gaelic Park. They had been at the behest of others to have some place to play their games for over 100 years, yet they wouldn't allow the GAA share their grounds in Dublin with sporting rivals who were going to be temporarily homeless, as New York and most overseas units had been for generations.

But following an impassioned plea from Chairman Seamus Dooley not to open Croke Park under any circumstances, New York Board voted 'no' by a 6:1 ratio. When I heard this I was truly depressed as there were three very good Kerry friends of mine on the Board—John O'Riordan, Anne Holland and Joan Henchy—but with Dooley leading off with 'ould Ireland and all that', they had no hope. At this stage the media has estimated that the 'yes' campaign was 56 votes short of a majority. After the New York vote, it was now over 60 votes in deficit.

The news from the North American Board was more encouraging and I was on very friendly terms and in regular contact with most of them. Following a conference call (America being too big to have a special meeting at a central location), it was reported that they were 'leaning towards opening it up'.

Luck sometimes comes unexpectedly, however, and another fortuitous meeting proved to be crucial, too. I was at a GAA function in Adare, Co. Limerick, where the topic for discussion was the Féile na nÓg competition, which Limerick was hosting that year—and they did a great job of it, too. At the end of the meeting I decided to have a quick word with their new Chairman, Denis Holmes. I asked him were they having a meeting to discuss Rule 42. He replied that they weren't having any meeting because their Convention had decided to oppose change to Rule 42. But I told him that that motion dealt with the permanent opening of Croke Park and clubs might view it differently if they were asked about temporary opening. I concluded that clubs at least deserved the opportunity to discuss it.

I scarcely knew Denis at that stage, but to his great credit he said he saw my point and would endeavour to have it debated by the clubs. He was up against it as a number of the Executive of the Limerick Board were totally against change, including their Central Council delegate, P. S. O'Riain, who was then touching ninety years of age and who had famously voted against change at Congress 2001, even though Limerick as a board voted in favour. Their long-serving Munster Council delegate, Rory Kiely, was also totally against any change. Rory is a shrewd operator and as Cathaoirleach of the Seanad carried a fair deal of weight. However, when Denis reported his discussion with me to his Executive, it was hotly debated, but fortunately for me I had a few great friends and loyal supporters in the Limerick Executive. They barely out-voted the 'No' group, which meant clubs in Limerick were allowed to vote on Rule 42. Ironically, one of the clubs that supported change was none other than Rory Kiely's club, where his son was the county board delegate. When the show of hands was called for at the Limerick meeting, Rory's son put up his hand as directed by his club. Limerick voted for change.

Waterford and Tipperary were in a similar position to Limerick, having rejected motions on Rule 42 at their Conventions. Again I had a word with their chairmen, Donie Shanahan (Tipperary) and Pat Flynn (Waterford). They did the needful and once again the clubs came up trumps, even though some of the most influential, most respected and longest-serving officials in both counties were vehemently anti-change. I was very pleased and greatly encouraged by this development. Now five of the six Munster counties were going to vote for change. In Connacht, Roscommon and Sligo had motions for change, Leitrim was very much in favour—again, that county has a tradition of backing the Uachtarán—Galway looked likely to support change, but Mayo decided to sit on the fence, being the only county in Ireland not to declare its hand prior to Congress.

In Ulster, all of the Six Counties said 'no' and were joined by Monaghan, where my predecessor, Seán McCague, strongly favoured a 'no' vote. That left two other counties: Cavan, which had a motion in favour of change, and Donegal. It took fair guts by Donegal, and especially by their Chairman, Charlie O'Donnell, and Central Council delegate Brian McEniff to vote in favour of change, given that Ulster Council Chairman, Mícheál Greenan, had argued vigorously for a 'No' vote.

In my three years as Chairman of the Overseas Committee I had successfully introduced the concept of twinning overseas units with units at home. Ulster had a twinning arrangement with Canada and, of course, New York, which takes part in the Ulster Hurling Championship. My overseas contacts kept me informed of the 'pressure' being brought to bear on them to vote the right way, i.e. Greenan's way. However, it was heartening to see so many people standing up for what they believed in and not allowing themselves to be pressurised into a stance to which they did not subscribe. So that was Ulster.

In Leinster all twelve counties seemed to favour change and, of course, over half the motions in favour of change came from Leinster. And then there was Cork—the People's Republic of Cork. However, the people of the republic weren't given an opportunity to vote on the motions as they were in all other counties. The previous year Cork Convention had voted against any change to Rule 42, with one delegate famously remarking that 'he wouldn't let them into the car park', echoing Mícheál Greenan's comment that the GAA wasn't in the business of 'housing the homeless'. Cork took the view that as no motion on Rule 42 had been received for their Convention in 2004, the previous year's policy stood because only Convention could change 'such a fundamental policy issue' (13 April 2005).

This was a smokescreen, of course. First, there was a world of difference between permanent and temporary opening and there were motions coming up on both. Secondly, every county can submit motions to Congress. If counties could take a position only on motions discussed by their own Convention, how were motions from other counties going to be dealt with? Thirdly, it is Congress, not County Conventions, that changes rules and makes 'fundamental policy' decisions. When the motions for a particular year's Congress are released, all counties and all clubs should have an opportunity, if they so wish, to discuss them and have a say on how their county votes. While Cork argued that the county is so big that not all clubs are represented at County Board level, they are represented at Divisional Board level and their votes could have been taken at that level and their delegates mandated to vote in accordance with the clubs' wishes, as expressed at Divisional level, when they went to the County Board meeting.

Cork County Board took a different view, but somebody must have forgotten to inform the clubs because across the county clubs were holding meetings and voting. When a sudden halt was called to these proceedings, the county at large was not impressed, especially as rumour had it that the guillotine had been applied because it seemed likely that a 'Yes' vote was in the offing. Such developments set the alarm bells ringing and so Cork did what Cork does: no vote, no need to vote as they were going to vote 'No' when the vote came. That stance backfired badly because, rightly or wrongly, they were lambasted around the country. Headings such as, 'Is Everyone Wrong Except Cork?' (*Irish Examiner*, 14 September 2005), 'Vote should have been taken on Rule 42 say clubs' (14 April 2005) and 'There is a communication problem here that must be addressed', focused much attention on Cork and disturbed many people around the country.

It was a fine build-up: the tension was being ratcheted up and the fires of emotion were being stoked. I had other matters to contend with, however, such as: how was I going to handle the debate? What time would it take place? Was it going to be a simple majority or a two-thirds majority? Was it going to be a secret ballot or a show of hands? All these things were crucial and the handling of them was in my hands. One thing I was determined to do was to be fair, and to be seen to be fair.

The simple majority, or two-thirds majority, was a bone of contention. It could be argued with a fair degree of conviction that a simple majority was all that was required to set aside or change a rule temporarily. After all, that is what applied when the 'temporary changes' to the knock-out championship system were introduced, and that constituted a fairly fundamental change in policy. Nevertheless, I felt that to go down that route would be problematic. As my views on Rule 42 were well-known, it could also have been interpreted as opportunistic, so I would not be seen to be fair. Plus, if the vote was passed on a simple majority, there was a grave danger of creating major division, or possibly a split, in the Association. I concluded that as this was a major change in policy—temporary or otherwise—a two-thirds majority would be the correct and the fairest criteria to apply. Just to be sure, and to have ammunition against those who might argue otherwise, I decided to seek legal advice. Our legal advisors concurred with my view. It was a wise move and was accepted with little demur—naturally, it suited those against far more than those in favour.

The decision as to whether the vote would be conducted by secret ballot (paper ballot) or by an open vote (show of hands) was a far more emotive and divisive issue. Many, including myself, favoured an open vote. As most delegates had already been mandated, it was important for them and for those who had mandated them that no questions be asked about their voting afterwards. While there were many who had personal votes, including members of Coiste Bainistí and the ex-presidents, it would be no harm at all to see how they voted. The downside of this was that people could be ridiculed or 'fingered' if they voted contrary to expectations. The paper or secret ballot would mean that nobody could be ostracised, but it would also mean that it would be very difficult to ensure that those mandated to vote one way or the other fulfilled their obligations.

The matter came before Central Council on the eve of Congress. There was a heated debate. I made it clear that I favoured an open vote, for which opinion I was rebuked by my fellow countyman, Gerald McKenna. He chided me by asking, 'Are you saying that you can't trust delegates to vote according to their mandate?' To tell the truth, that was probably true—for a handful anyway! I didn't say that, of course. Eventually, after further discussion, it was decided that Central Council would recommend to Congress that the vote be conducted by paper ballot and that Central Council members were expected to support that at Congress. I had lost round one, or so I believed. I retired a little perturbed and one delegate, a friend of mine, said, 'What's McKenna at, Seán?' As always, McKenna was about to prove that no fox was cleverer than he. But at that stage, I felt a bit rattled. Most supporters of change felt likewise, and *The Star* headline the following day (16 April) captured the mood very well: 'Kick in the Ballots for Yes Side'.

I felt even more rattled when I said to another friend, Munster Council Chairman Seán Fogarty, 'I suppose you'll be voting yes tomorrow, Seán?' 'Oh God, no,' he replied. 'The Munster Council decided I should vote against.' This amazed me, because five of the six counties of Munster were supporting a Yes vote, yet here we were with a majority of Munster Council delegates telling their Chairman to vote No—proving what I had already seen for myself: the higher up you climbed in the Association, the higher the percentage of people set against change.

There wasn't much time for pondering these matters as Congress weekend is a pretty hectic schedule. I had to go straight into Congress and chair it all for two full days, which demanded full concentration on the here and now. Rule 42 was fixed for the following afternoon. We had decided that immediately after lunch was the best time to debate the famous motion. Delegates, the media and the nation knew that the historic, decisive debate was to commence at 2.00pm on Saturday 16 April 2005. And so it did. In Croke Park itself.

I wasn't long in office in 2003 when a letter came in from Cork seeking to hold Congress 2005 in Cork. When Liam showed it to me he saw no problem, but I asked him, 'What's on in Congress in 2005? Election of the Uachtarán-Tofa. And who is going to be a candidate— Christy Cooney from Cork?' 'I suppose you are right,' he said, so I kicked for touch, hoping that the hotel (Jury's Croke Park) might be ready and that it would be the 'right' venue for Congress. Towards the end of 2003, Christy Cooney and Seán McCague began to pressurise me for a decision to hold Congress in Cork (the hotel being not due to open until 2005). But I procrastinated until they were off management (April 2004), then in May 2004 I recommended Croke Park as the venue for the following year's Congress, saying that it would be totally wrong to hold Congress in Cork or Kilkenny or in any county that had a presidential candidate.

It was a lucky job I did because if Congress had been held in Cork, it would in all probability have made the passing of Rule 42 much more difficult, and perhaps, impossible. Nickey Brennan mightn't have been elected Uachtarán-Tofa either.

The debate
The appointment of tellers was also an important decision, especially if the vote was going to be on a show of hands. It has been traditional at Congress that the provincial chairmen act as tellers. I didn't want that, but I had to be very careful, so I got over it very nicely by saying, 'The tellers shouldn't be people who have votes themselves.' The provincial chairmen in 2005 were Mícheál Greenan, Seán Fogarty, John Lacey, Tommy Moran and Nickey Brennan. Tommy Moran was the only one of them to state that he was voting for change, so I suggested that the provincial secretaries, who don't have a vote, should act as tellers. I also included the Chairman of the GAC, Tony O'Keeffe, and the Chairman of the Coaching and Games Committee, Paraic Duffy, who acted as returning officer. I was happy with this set-up.

Before discussion began on the motions themselves, we had to decide whether the matter was to be by a show of hands or by secret ballot. I had to do my duty as Uachtarán. Even though I preferred an open vote, the fact was that Central Council had decided it was recommending a secret ballot and I was obliged to inform Congress of this and vote accordingly. Many delegates weren't willing to buy into this, however, and there was a proposal by Noel Walsh (Clare) that it be a show of hands. The matter was hotly debated and, to my surprise, Congress voted for a secret ballot, backing Central Council's recommendation by 165 votes to 153. I feared the worst, as did many others who were hoping for change. I think most journalists and the packed public gallery believed the day was lost. But like a great All-Ireland Final, things can swing and change in the blink of an eye. At this stage the ball was in and the game was on.

I advised Congress that, instead of taking all motions on Rule 42 separately, we should debate the substantive issue and then decide on the order in which we would subsequently vote on the motions. I felt this was the easiest and the best approach. Basically, people were either for or against opening Croke Park and it was simpler to let them have their say. I was determined to be scrupulously fair, but firm.

That morning, I made sure I was first to arrive at the venue. I did so for a specific purpose. Croke Park staff always organised the top table and I wasn't happy with the seating arrangements, so I just went up to the rostrum and changed some of the place-names around to get the positioning I wanted. Nobody noticed, nobody knew. I was particularly interested in the placing of Tommy Moran (Chairman of Connacht) as he was instrumental in my strategy to keep long-winded speakers at bay: a bell. This thought had come to me years earlier, when I had noticed that while standing orders stated that a speaker to a motion could not speak for more than three minutes, the actual length depended on who was speaking. Fr Leo Morohan, a wonderful, sincere Mayo man, got up to speak one year at Congress and his opening remark was, 'I promise I'll be brief.' I timed him and when he was finished I stood up and said, 'Fr Leo promised to be brief and he spoke for seventeen minutes, despite standing orders only allowing three.' There was an 'ooh' in the hall, but in fairness it wasn't Fr Leo's fault. He should have been checked. I thought a little bell would do the trick nicely, thank you. I always had a 'bell-boy' to perform this function. My 'bell-boy' this year was Tommy Moran, so I made sure he was sitting near me. I made a few other small adjustments that weren't noticed but were important, as they allowed for a little marking to take place on the top table—an important but unnoticeable detail! We got through the morning's work without any great acrimony. We broke for lunch and resumed our seats.

The clock struck 2.00pm and things got underway. The debate turned out more or less as I had requested. I had asked people to put forward their views without castigating or deriding other individuals or organisations. I was particularly fearful that in the full gaze of the cameras, some might go for glory and have a right cut off the FAI, the IRFU or the government. As it turned out, my request was heeded by and large and for two hours there was a superb, passionate, calm and strongly worded but fair debate. As tends to happen in these matters, one side gets a run, then the other side.

I introduced the debate by saying that I wanted to make a few points on behalf of Coiste Bainistí and Ard-Chomhairle. As long as I was simply clarifying matters raised at Coiste Bainistí (Management) or Ard-Chomhairle (Central Council), no one could say I was interfering with the debate or steering it in any one direction, even though those points of clarification could be very important to dissuade some genuine doubters. I started with two points that would favour those opposed to change.

First, I informed Congress that on behalf of Central Council I had sought senior counsel advice as to whether a simple, or a two-thirds, majority was required to change a motion temporarily. The counsel's advice was to operate a two-thirds majority because it was a fundamental policy change. This was very important because if we had to debate this on the floor of Congress, it would have been highly fractious and divisive and the principle would almost certainly have been clouded by people's preferred outcome. However, when the Uachtarán, backed by senior counsel, stated that it had to be two-thirds, that was that. Nobody could accuse me of bias—being in favour of change, a simple majority would have suited me better.

Secondly, and again to the apparent disadvantage of the 'Yes' vote, I had informed Congress of Central Council's recommendation to have a paper ballot rather than an open vote by a show of hands. That was challenged and lost by only twelve votes (165 for, 153 against), which was astonishing as all fifty members of Central Council were obliged to support the Council's decision. So, for instance, I raised my hand in favour of a paper vote, even though I would have been against it at the Council meeting. The vote was passed: paper vote it was.

Now for the crucial points for Congress.

I informed Congress that all the motions before them referred to Central Council making the final decision. If passed, it did not mean that every team could automatically play in Croke Park. In other words, Council would have to decide on the basis of the risk involved, availability of the stadium and the benefits accruing to the GAA. Again, no one could take offence here, but this point would subtly assuage those who might be prepared to vote Yes, but were of two minds due to fear of a sell-out.

Next, the key clarification: 'temporary' did not mean indefinite. Temporary would have to be defined clearly, and it certainly wasn't ten or twenty years. I also explained that once 'temporary' had been defined, the status quo would prevail at the end of that specified period. I told them that it was just like a player being suspended for two weeks or two months, as the case may be, and then at the end of that period automatically reverting to his previous status and being allowed to play again. So it would be for Croke Park—it would revert to the status quo then. Then I said I did not wish to make any further comment.

I called on Sligo to propose Motion 23 on the *clár*, to amend Rule 42. To be in order and pass the vetting process of the Motions Committee, the motion was over a page in length, but the crucial point was Section (a): 'Central Council shall have the power to authorise the renting or leasing of Croke Park for events other than those controlled by the Association during a period when the Lansdowne Road Football Grounds is closed for the proposed re-development.' Kieran McDermott, Sligo's Central Council delegate and a practising solicitor, formally proposed the historic motion. He made some interesting points, saying that Croke Park had kick-started the building industry in Ireland because when the redevelopment work had first started, 'there wasn't a crane to be seen in Dublin'. He added that as fine as the stadium was, it hosted only twenty-eight games a year and that whether or not Croke Park was open, the rugby and soccer matches were going to be played anyway. He also pointed out that if a request was made for the use of Croke Park by other sports, it would only be for three or four games per year. He concluded by suggesting that any rental income accruing should be used for the development of training grounds and coaching within the counties. Seán Quirke (Wexford Chairman) formally seconded the motion and waited to speak his piece later on.

The debate took off in earnest. First on his feet was ex-president Con Murphy (Cork), one of the very best and most respected administrators in the GAA, a man who was uniquely honoured with the Freedom of Cork City and, indeed, a man I always held in the highest esteem and affection. Con pulled no punches, though, and he didn't now either. He strongly opposed all the motions, saying that if passed, the Association as operated for 120 years would be put out of existence and that we would in effect be forming a new Association that 'caters for everything and anything and stands for nothing'.

He was supported in quick succession by powerful anti-change speakers in P.S. O'Riain (Limerick), Eamonn McMahon (Antrim) and John Connolly (Monaghan). All three were opposed to any alteration of Rule 42, with Eamonn saying any change would put us on the slippery slope: 'Croke Park today, could it be Semple Stadium next week, Parc Uí Chaoimh … Clones … Casement Park?'

Then Con from Cork was on his feet again. He wanted me to enlighten them as to which motion was being discussed. He wasn't going to get any enlightenment from me. I wanted a general discussion because there were seven motions on the *clár* dealing with Rule 42 and I wanted only one debate and one vote at the end of that debate. Any complication leads to confusion and if confusion set in, it would mean almost certain defeat. So I merely told Con that I would be asking the counties that submitted the various motions to clarify that for Congress. Con was not happy with this and retorted that 'the Uachtarán was the person in charge of the Association,' therefore the one to lead them and tell them why exactly they were discussing these motions. I did not reply, but I knew exactly what I was doing because I had spoken to Kerry Chairman Seán Walsh and told him to speak at the appropriate time and withdraw Kerry's motion, on the basis that it was for permanent rather than temporary change. I hoped that once Kerry did this, other counties would follow suit. I wanted it down to one motion—the Sligo motion—because it was the most clear-cut and succinct proposal and therefore had the best chance of being passed.

Con had now spoken twice when standing orders dictated that each person could speak only once. He was to get to his feet a third time, and I was going to show him who was really in charge—just not yet.

Instead, I saw the Clare Chairman on his feet and called on him to speak. Michael McDonagh said that the GAA would get the goodwill of the people of Ireland if it temporarily set aside Rule 42, thus being seen to put the past behind them. While not forgetting history, Michael argued, we could 'make history this very day'.

Pat Fanning (ex-president, Waterford) then opposed the motion, saying that if it were passed, it would amount to 'abandoning a principle on the altar of expediency'. He asked delegates not to 'sell the past by allowing Croke Park to be used to promote other games in competition with the GAA'. However, Seán Hackett of Lancashire countered by stating that we should consider the future of the GAA, not its past, and that ultimately we were 'masters of our own destiny'.

Joe McGurn (Fermanagh) agreed with Con Murphy, adding that when Con asked the question, 'What motion are we debating?' he had not received an answer. He concluded by suggesting that what we ought to do was 'buy an incinerator, throw the rule book into it and get rid of it altogether, because we are doing away with the constitution of our Association.'

Things were getting hot and bothered now, so before Con or somebody else had a chance to muddy the waters further by again asking which motion we were discussing, it seemed the perfect moment to play the Kerry card. Right on cue, Seán Walsh (Kerry Chairman) got to his feet and said that in order to allay the fears of Con Murphy, Kerry was withdrawing its motion 'in favour of the Sligo motion'. Nice one, Seán, I thought to myself, steady now and we're back in business.

Seán was steady alright. He said that Kerry trusted Central Council as 'Central Council aren't an independent republic divorced from the GAA'. He then spoke about 'helping neighbours in difficulty' and Kerry's legendary reputation for generosity. Then it was tit-for-tat as another half-dozen speakers spoke for or against, almost every second one. I was happy with the way the debate was progressing. Indeed, it was riveting stuff and I concentrated on every word the speakers uttered and enjoyed the style and substance of their arguments. Nonetheless, I was still scared stiff of the eventual vote and outcome. Then I was taken by surprise when Seán McCague (ex-president, Monaghan) stood to address Congress. Instead of outlining his own views, he said that under standing orders No. 5 he was asking that the question now be put to the delegates. He complimented all the speakers and suggested that Kieran McDermott now be asked to sum up and the vote taken.

Seán was absolutely entitled to make this request, but I felt it was too soon to cut off the debate and besides, only one county—Kerry—had withdrawn its motion. If I agreed with Seán, I would have one unholy mess on my hands trying to decide which motion we were going to vote on. Almost certainly, defeat would be the outcome. So I politely replied to Seán McCague that I felt there were a number of speakers who wished to contribute and it would be unfair to deny them the opportunity, and for that reason I was going to allow the debate continue for another while.

Often at debates like this, delegates sit back and then burst to get in at the end, sometimes when it is too late. Seán's request that the matter now be put to a vote galvanised people and those holding back probably said to themselves, 'I better get in quick or I mightn't get in at all.' And so the debate continued apace. Then Mícheál Greenan, Chairman of the Ulster Council, spoke from the rostrum and outlined his total opposition to any change to Rule 42. He said that people who held such views had been 'vilified and demonised' for quite some time, but had been 'very dignified about it all'. They hadn't jumped on the media bandwagon as other people, 'not sitting too far from me', had done for the last while. When he said this, there was a gasp from the floor because everyone knew that he was having a cut at me. I didn't react. He went on. In a whisper, I asked Tommy Moran how long he had been speaking for. Tommy whispered back, 'Over three minutes' and then asked apprehensively, 'Will I ring the bell?' 'Ring it now,' I whispered. Tommy Moran rang the bell and Greenan nearly hit the roof, saying he had stayed silent long enough and wasn't going to be silenced now; he almost suggested to Tommy what he could do with the bell. He continued to make his points and concluded by advising that 'if you want to play in Croke Park, it seems that you have a better chance if you play soccer or rugby'.

Some present were probably delighted with his speech, especially his jibe at me, but I met many afterwards who were fuming and some who had planned to vote against change but, after Mícheál Greenan spoke, had changed their minds and voted in favour. When he was finished, I could tell the tide had turned somewhat from the body language in the hall, so rather than being upset by his jibe and refusal to abide by the bell, I was secretly very pleased.

The next speaker was T.J. Ward of Longford, who said he was disappointed with 'one or two speakers so far', but added that he was withdrawing Longford's motion in favour of Sligo's. Things were heading for a climax now, when one of the big movers behind Rule 42 from the outset, Tommy Kenoy from the Kilmore Club in Roscommon, weighed in. He stated that the decision 'today will be a defining moment for the Association. It will demonstrate our willingness or otherwise to serve this nation in a time of need—to do what Irish people were always proud and happy to do—to help a neighbour in a time of need.' Then he, too, withdrew his motion in favour of Sligo's. Things were moving along nicely now. Con Murphy was finally getting the clarification needed on which motion we were voting on—at least three had been withdrawn.

After that Seán Quirke (Wexford) said that Wexford had submitted a motion as well, but it didn't get the approval of the Motions Committee and so wasn't on the *clár*, but that Wexford supported the Sligo motion. By way of levity he said to those who said soccer and rugby being played in Croke Park would lead to children taking up soccer and rugby in their droves, 'American Football was played in Croke Park and I guarantee you, it hasn't caught on in Wexford, yet, anyway.' He added that Gordon D'Arcy, who was from Wexford, had been selected on the Lions team that day and he looked forward to seeing him play on the green sod of Croke Park because 'he is a good Irishman, like all the fellas playing soccer and rugby'. He concluded by saying that 'if a neighbour's house burned down and you had a spare room, you wouldn't leave him out in the cold.' He felt we owed that much to the Irish people.

Other speakers had their say, including Bob Honohan (Cork, against), and Cathal O'Donaill (Dún na nGall), A. Delaney (Laois), N. Walsh (Clare) and Phil Brady (Cavan), all in favour. The latter two, Noel Walsh and Phil Brady, withdrew their motions in favour of Sligo.

It was now down to two, but before that could be resolved, I had to answer a query from Cathal Seoighe (Meath): 'Does it take a two-thirds majority to undo if the Sligo motion goes through?' I replied that I thought I had clarified that in the beginning (although it was good to have the chance to do so again to reassure wavering souls). I said if it went through today, it would revert to the status quo when the agreed time span had elapsed. That's what 'temporary' meant.

We were down to two motions now, but to my surprise Michael Murphy, the Wicklow Secretary, stated that Wicklow was letting its motion, No. 25 on the *clár*, stand because they had been approached by a number of counties during the week who said they would only support the Wicklow motion. This was correct. I had become aware at lunchtime, before Congress resumed to debate Rule 42, that some powerful figures on the anti side had approached some delegates who were mandated to support Wicklow's motion, but who themselves personally were against, and had told them that if they supported the Wicklow motion, they would be free to oppose all the others. The Wicklow motion read:

> ... during the development work on Lansdowne Road stadium that AC be given the power to consider on a match by match basis any request to allow games be played in Croke Park other than games controlled by GLC. That when Lansdowne Road stadium is officially reopened that Rule 42(a) revert to its original format and that this Rule 42(c) be deleted.

The Wicklow motion spelled out clearly what temporary meant. The big difference was 'match by match basis', which would render it practically unworkable as the FAI and IRFU might only be able to do deals on a yearly basis. Thus, by the time each match had been judged on its merits, the games could be gone elsewhere because the big games are decided twelve months in advance. Furthermore, you could see that the Ard-Chomhairle would be far more likely to accept some countries above others. For instance, Ireland playing France would be more palatable than Ireland playing England; and a rugby game would have more support than a soccer international because the Irish rugby team is a thirty-two-county side, while the international soccer team is

'Republic of Ireland' and therefore twenty-six counties. The FAI and IRFU couldn't possibly stand over that.

I was in a right dilemma now and had to think quickly to resolve it. When Kerrymen are in a fix they often play for time by asking a question. So I asked Michael how his motion differed from Sligo's. He said it was written into their motion that when Lansdowne Road was reopened, their amendment, Rule 42(c), would be deleted automatically. He added that two other counties were mandated to support Wicklow's motion alone, so they wouldn't support any other motion.

I replied that what they were spelling out in their motion wasn't necessary because that was what 'temporary' meant. Thankfully, neither Michael nor anyone else referred to 'match by match basis' as a difference between both Sligo and Wicklow motions. Still, this was difficult. I wanted to avoid confusion at all costs and having got each of the other five counties to withdraw in favour of Sligo, here I was, stuck on Wicklow. But I could see Michael Murphy's point perfectly: lose those two counties mandated to support the Wicklow motion and you lose the vote. It was bound to be that tight. It was that simple.

Michael Murphy insisted that while Wicklow supported the Sligo motion, he was mandated to put forward his county's motion. I replied that, essentially, that would mean voting twice on the same issue. Michael asked if we could vote on both motions together, to which I responded by suggesting that both motions together was really one motion because in essence it was the same thing. Phil Brady (the car dealer from Cavan) had summarised it very accurately—you were either in favour of temporary amendment or you were not. If you were mandated to vote for temporary amendment, you should vote for it. Temporary meant temporary and there was nothing stopping Central Council from putting a time limit on it by way of clarification. Then I told Michael that Wicklow was only complicating matters and making things worse by insisting on proceeding in this manner. Michael took the admonishment, and to his eternal credit, he withdrew the Wicklow motion, advising 'counties mandated to support Wicklow to support the Sligo motion.'

I now called on Kieran McDermott to reply to the debate, but just when I thought everything was clear-cut, fully explained and confusion eliminated with a single motion before Congress, up jumps

Con Murphy to seek further clarification. I knew if I allowed him speak, all would be lost. If I got into a debate by way of trying to clarify matters, others would probably weigh in and there would be bedlam in no time. I had often seen that very thing happen at meetings. But it wasn't going to happen now. Even though I didn't like doing it on a personal basis, I cut Con off, telling him he had spoken twice already (standing orders permitted each speaker to speak only once) and that the matter had been debated fully and there was one motion before the meeting: the Sligo motion. Con had to sit down without saying a word; he now knew who was in charge of Congress! He was not a happy camper and neither were others who were, I suspect, surprised by my audacity.

Nevertheless, I called for the distribution of the ballot papers. The votes were distributed, ticked *Tá* or *Níl* and collected. Paraic Duffy and the tellers withdrew and I moved to the next motion on the clár— Motion 30, dealing with the appointment of a Safety Officer. I felt I could do with a safety officer for myself! We were in the middle of Motion 34, dealing with the establishment of an Audit Committee, when there was a shuffle in the hall, a murmur of excitement as the tellers emerged and Paraic Duffy made his way to the rostrum and handed me the slip of paper. The audit motion was passed quickly— you could have got any motion you wanted through at that stage because people just wanted it out of the way to hear the result of Riail 42, Motion 23, the real audit that day. I opened the slip of paper. It read: Votes Distributed 326, Votes Returned 325, Spoiled Votes 1, Valid Poll 324, *Tá* 227, *Níl* 97. I looked up at the delegates and said, 'The motion, having received over a two-thirds majority, is passed.' There was an unmerciful outburst of loud cheering and clapping from the floor and the packed public gallery. I was elated, of course, but also deeply conscious of my role as Uachtarán. My job now was to bring the 30 per cent who had voted against along with me and not alienate them by gloating, so I said that when a game is over, players leave it on the field. We should do similar in this debate at Congress—leave our differences on the Congress floor:

We have put our faith in Central Council, so let them get on with it. Let us get on with our core business of promoting our games, helping our clubs and developing our counties. The ball is now firmly in the court of our would-be tenants. It's now up to them to play ball and we await return of serve.

The great debate that had exercised the minds of the country in every town, in every village, in every hall and in every pub had ended in a historic change of policy for Ireland's biggest and finest sporting organisation. Ecumenism had come to town. The reaction in the media and in the country at large was extraordinary.

In the *Independent*, Martin Breheny waxed lyrical.

The atmosphere was as tense as an All-Ireland final dressing-room when GAA President, Seán Kelly, who handled the entire debate superbly, moved on the motions to amend Rule 42 ... The secret ballot proposal won on a 165–153 vote and immediately a mood of pessimism drifted over those who wanted Rule 42 changed. They felt that in a secret ballot some delegates who had been mandated to vote for change might defy the instruction ... Almost immediately, former President Con Murphy was on his feet contending that a vote for change was a vote to put the GAA out of existence ... And so it went ... P. S. O'Riain, a veteran of opposition to changing the rule, insisted that the calls for change were media-driven ... While former President Pat Fanning said that he hadn't heard a single cogent argument why it made sense to open Croke Park to other sports ... Former President Dr Mick Loftus was concerned that allowing rugby and soccer into Croke Park would further fuel the drinks culture.

'How many times do I have to explain that temporary means temporary?' asked Seán Kelly wearily, although one suspects that he knows better than anybody if Croke Park hosts soccer and rugby for a few years, it will remain open for bigger international occasions ...

When the bell sounded to indicate that his [Mícheál Greenan's] time was up, he told the time-keeper that he would be going on for a few more minutes. 'We've kept quiet long enough,' he said. Some of the anti-change smirked contentedly at the sight of the Ulster Chairman, who is also a Vice-president of the GAA, declaring that he was planning to ignore procedure. They may have thought that after victory on the vote to decide how the ballot would be conducted, the wind was whipping up in their favour. Not so ... Kelly warned delegates that toilet needs could wait until the vote was over ... The tellers disappearing for what seemed like an age. When they returned Paraic Duffy handed the result to Kelly and Liam Mulvihill, neither of whom showed any emotion, although Kelly's voice seemed chirpier than usual when next he spoke ... And then the result—'Motion carried,' said Kelly quietly. It was rumoured that the one spoilt vote arose when one delegate ignored his county's mandate. On spotting this, the County Chairman is reported to have spoiled the vote rather than let it count on the other side.

A pigeon ... swooped across the pitch, soaring high as it disappeared through the gap between the Cusack Stand and the Canal End ... It may have been on its way to announce to its rugby and soccer friends in Lansdowne Road that they would be living in more salubrious surrounds in a few years. They would have to rent it, but so what? Wouldn't it be better than heading across the Irish Sea?

In *The Star*, Damien Lalor wrote under the heading 'Kelly Rules with Iron Fist':

Seán Kelly's reputation was on the line. He knew it and we knew it. So on Saturday he took no nonsense ... After listening to former President Con Murphy speak on the Rule 42 debate and try to come back into the debate two further times, Kelly ruled with the iron fist and cut him short. There was more: he warned delegates that there would be no trotting out to the toilets during the voting. Bladders were on hold; this time, there would be no million dollar slash. No delegate was allowed to stand up except the tellers and if you voted with your arm in the air it was to be in the air and none of this 'and up around your shoulder' business, as the boss (Kelly) said ... Kelly had his homework done, you see. His watchdogs were on full alert, throughout the hall. This time there would be no arse-boxing with the voting, no half-raised arms, no mistake in the computing. It was an experience to be there, looking on as the GAA's decision-making road-show swung into operation.

In *Ireland on Sunday*, John Fogerty wrote: 'Kelly leads sport out of the dark ages'. Donal Keenan headed his article with 'Seán Kelly plays down the hero role, history shows otherwise' and went on,

> Yesterday, just as in 1923 (when Kerrymen who a few weeks earlier had fought on opposite sides in the Civil War downed their weapons and took to the football field together in pursuit of All-Ireland glory) the GAA once again rose majestically above petty politics and jealousies. They, and all of us, can be justifiably proud.
>
> Kelly's triumph means that his Presidency will be remembered in history as a defining period for the GAA. Despite fierce resistance, outright resentment, disgraceful attacks on his office, he courageously led a campaign for the modernisation of minds in the GAA and got his reward yesterday.

The front page lead in the *Sunday Tribune* said: 'GAA votes 227 to 97 to open Croker' and quoted the Taoiseach saying it was, 'an historic and momentous day for Irish sport'.

John O'Brien in the *Sunday Independent*, under the title 'Croke Park prised open', wrote: 'Extraordinary scenes as delegates take the historic step to amend Rule 42,' adding, 'Shortly before a quarter to five, Seán Kelly called out the result and, incredibly, the "yes" camp held sway. Faces looked around to be sure. Where was the classic GAA fudge? Where was the sting in the tail? There wasn't any and the hall erupted.'

Paul Keane in an article in the *Sunday Mirror* headed 'Ruled In' wrote: 'The gates of Croke Park were sensationally flung open. It was one of the most difficult decisions the GAA has ever had to make ... but yesterday's historic vote to change Rule 42 showed the organisation acting with self-confidence, strength and dignity. This was the right decision.'

And for good measure, Seán Ryan in *The Voice* wrote: 'Seán Kelly is the GAA's answer to Pope John Paul II—while I can't vouch for Seán's holiness (you're wise there, Seán) I can say that he has brought a new dimension to the President's role, just as John Paul did to the Papacy.' (And let the comparison stop there!)

Crossing the divide

When the media reaction died down, we had to wait for what I had described as the 'return of serve' from the would-be tenants, namely the IRFU and the FAI. Some people had suggested that the two bodies would never seek to use Croke Park, that they'd rather play the games abroad than come to our patch. Undoubtedly there were some people in those organisations who were as opposed to playing in Croke Park as there were in the GAA to opening it up for play, but if there were, they were very much in the minority and they kept their views to themselves.

The FAI and the IRFU had greeted the decision to open Croke Park with expressions of gratitude and delight, and it wasn't long before they sought meetings to clarify what exactly had been passed and how they should proceed, especially as plans for the revamping of Lansdowne Road were moving swiftly. The government had rowed in financially with them and it was generally planned to apply for planning permission for Lansdowne Road in 2006 and start the redevelopment work in 2007.

A number of preliminary meetings, involving personnel from both sides, took place to clarify these points. Some of these meetings took place in my absence, with Danny Lynch and Liam Ó Maolmhichíl representing the Association. It was only when I met members of the IRFU and FAI casually that I learned some confusion and uncertainty had crept in. I calmed their fears and apprehension by saying, 'Leave that to me and I'll check it out.' As usual, I kept my own counsel, but I did receive a 'note' from Liam regarding progress, and of course Coiste Bainistí had to be updated by Liam on what was happening. In the ensuing discussion it was even suggested that the IRFU had no intention of coming to Croke Park and that Philip Browne was only going through the motions so that the GAA would get the blame when rugby eventually played their games abroad.

I intervened at this point, stating that this was a very unfair slur on Philip Browne. I said I didn't like people being criticised when they weren't in a position to defend themselves and that from my knowledge of Mr Browne, he was a very honourable and competent man who wouldn't engage in this kind of double-dealing. I added that I had found Philip, and all at the IRFU, very honourable and gracious and fully believed that they had every intention of coming to Croke Park. I suggested we needed somebody from management to attend these meetings in future. Quick as a flash, Mícheál Greenan offered to attend the discussions on behalf of management. Ninety-nine per cent of the time when someone volunteers to do something on behalf of management it is accepted, but this was different. Sending Mícheál Greenan out to discuss the accommodation of the IRFU and the FAI in Croke Park would be like sending a fox out to discuss bedding arrangements with hens, so I politely thanked Mícheál for his 'very kind offer' but said, 'I think I had better go to these meetings myself.'

And I did. I told them exactly what the wording of the Sligo motion was and they informed us of their plans. We told them it would be very useful if they could get some assurance, verified independently, of the likely timeframe involved both in submitting and acquiring the necessary planning permission. We had a very positive meeting and I think they left knowing that they were welcome to Croke Park and that, within the remit of Congress, we would do everything to help them out.

It wasn't long until we had the relevant documentation in hand. A letter from Tom Philips and Associates on behalf of Lansdowne Road Stadium Development Company to the GAA's planning consultants, Kieran O'Malley and Co. Ltd., stated: 'I am writing to you to set out why I believe that Lansdowne Road will be closed in the period from late 2006 onwards to facilitate works in relation to the procurement of and/or subsequent exercise of a planning permission.' It outlined that they hoped to apply for planning permission early in 2006 and that the entire process would take about a year given that, after Dublin City Council deliberated, it would inevitably go to An Bord Pleanála. One of the most pressing points for the FAI/IRFU was an early decision from the GAA. As their games are international, involving so many countries, venues, hotels, television stations, etc. they needed confirmation twelve months in advance of the venues and dates. I understood their dilemma, so instead of forcing them to go all over England provisionally booking various venues, I agreed to put their request to the Central Council meeting of 10 December 2005. Quite frankly, I didn't foresee any great problem as we were only putting into effect what Congress had already decided—or so I thought. I didn't see any obstacle, and that was the rock on which I almost perished. Albert Reynolds said it all when he declared, 'The little things trip you up.' Well, I nearly tripped up.

I knew that some people were getting very animated about planning permission, saying it had to be granted before Croke Park could open to other games otherwise 'redevelopment' was meaningless. But there was no reference to planning permission in the Sligo motion, nor in any other motion. I was damn relieved when I checked this out and believed everyone would accept it. But I was hoping in vain. Some also questioned the accuracy of the planners' judgment, which was reasonable, but as I pointed out, no one can say with certainty 'that planning is going to be granted on or before a definite date'. Those things just don't work like that; but you have to accept the bona fides of reputable people.

Knowing that Bob Honohan (Cork) and others held these opinions, I did some homework for the Central Council meeting and tipped off a few influential delegates, including Gerald McKenna of Kerry and Bernie O'Connor of Galway, as to what might happen in order to be ready for it. However, I did no such preparation for Coiste Bainistí because I assumed that the vast majority would be prepared to recommend to Central Council to allow negotiations to begin.

So on Saturday morning, 10 December 2005, I updated management on the situation and recommended that we ask Central Council to allow negotiations to begin, with a view to opening Croke Park in 2007. Following some discussion and an explanation of the IRFU's/FAI's need for an early decision, a vote was called for. To my surprise, it was tied—five votes each. One more vote against and my goose was cooked. I would have to go into Central Council and recommend that Croke Park remain shut. My God, that would have been a bitter pill—the ultimate humiliation, the supreme irony. Thankfully, somebody up in heaven was looking after me when I wasn't cute enough to do it myself. I was alarmed by this turn of events and more or less said to management that we shouldn't be going against the wishes and spirit of Congress. At this Mícheál Greenan stood up and questioned the correctness of having a second vote, then promptly walked out.

I am not sure whether I was supposed to be upset by this

development, but I was very pleased to see him walk out because it meant I would in all probability win the second vote. The bould Mícheál had, unwittingly, come to my assistance. The words of Oscar Wilde ran through my head: 'What seems to us bitter trials are often blessings in disguise.' No wonder one Northern delegate remarked to me, 'Seán, Mícheál Greenan is the best friend you have.' I knew exactly what he meant. Now, back to business. I explained once again that the IRFU and FAI had applied in writing to use Croke Park and that a decision was needed soon, and I again called for a vote. It was carried this time. I could now go into Central Council and ask for permission to start negotiations so that soccer and rugby could be played in Croke Park in 2007.

I went to Central Council that very evening and personally recommended that approval be given to allow the negotiations to begin. Some objected, saying the goalposts were being shifted prematurely. Frank Murphy had written to Liam Ó Maolmhichíl stating this point strongly, saying 'The "closure" of Lansdowne Road grounds can only be interpreted to mean "after the planning process for the proposed redevelopment has been completed and not before"', but I retorted by saying that 'if we don't act now, we won't be able to comply with the decision of Congress, as the international bodies have to be given twelve months' notice of fixtures' intentions.' Gerald McKenna rowed in then and said we had decided in good faith to help the other organisations when they were in need, and in good faith we should let our negotiators deal with the issues arising therefrom.

Bob Honohan (Cork) proposed a direct negative, but in the ensuing vote Gerald McKenna's proposal was carried by an overwhelming majority. Once again a bit of homework had worked a treat. At the end of the meeting Nickey Brennan (Uachtarán-Tofa) said that the issue would be watched very carefully during 'my watch' and that with 'two senior officials like Liam Mulvihill and Danny Lynch and myself [Nickey], we have enough expertise around to guide us through the process.' In the *Irish Times* (12 December 2005), Seán Moran noted:

President Elect Nickey Brennan didn't speak until after the vote was carried (by a margin of about 6 to 1 among the 50 delegates) but he then said that he would trust Liam Mulvihill and Danny Lynch (and himself) to conduct these talks. This is a change of emphasis from current president Seán Kelly, whose comments to this newspaper suggested that Stadium Director, P. McKenna, who has conducted rental negotiations for other events such as concerts and even this year's Ulster Final, would lead the negotiations.

Nickey was entitled to his view, but I had a different plan. In fact, I had already selected my negotiating team to talk to the FAI/IRFU. We had called a meeting for Saturday morning, 26 November, at 10.00am, the morning after the All-Stars Banquet in the Citywest Hotel. I wanted as much input as possible from the Stadium Executive, thus Hugh Cawley, Paddy Wright, Peter McKenna and Brendan Waters were nominated to conduct negotiations on behalf of the GAA. I suggested that neither Liam Mulvihill, Nickey Brennan nor myself should involve ourselves in the discussions, so Nickey then suggested Danny Lynch. I concluded that we needed someone from the Management Committee on board, too, and before Nickey or anyone else could recommend someone, I suggested Tommy Moran. Tommy had voted in favour of opening and would be a great man if tensions rose too high because he has a great way about him, has a wonderful sense of humour and commands a huge amount of respect. Before we concluded our meeting I told my negotiating team, 'You must conduct robust negotiations, but at the end of the day you are expected to do a deal—that was what the Congress motion was all about.'

We had our negotiating team and now, after the Central Council meeting, we had a mandate to proceed. Once again the media celebrated widely and banner headlines appeared in every newspaper. Under a huge heading and accompanying picture of Croke Park, in an article entitled 'The Gates Are Open', Dermot Crowe wrote in the *Sunday Independent* (11 December 2005):

Croke Park could be hosting rugby and soccer internationals in little over a year after Central Council yesterday agreed to start negotiations with the IRFU and FAI. In a statement after the meeting the GAA said that the Lansdowne Road Development Company had confirmed that an application for planning permission is to be lodged with Dublin City Council early next month. The company's planning consultants also gave assurances that Lansdowne Road will be closed for all of 2007. After yesterday's meeting, Seán Kelly, who had been a supporter of opening up Croke Park, stated that he was pleased that Central Council had taken a positive decision on the IRFU and FAI applications … Kelly has been to the forefront on the Rule 42 debate and last year said it made sense to relax the rule, 'but there are those who are against it … and all the arguments in the world won't sway them'.

How right I was! The following night, Sunday 11 December, I was guest of honour at Tyrone's All-Ireland medal presentation and banquet. I was, as always, made most welcome by the officers of the Tyrone County Board, but the Ulster Council representative gave a frosty reception to me, my wife and my ten-year-old daughter, Julie. Noticing this, and sensing that the Ulster Chairman might use the occasion to have another 'swipe' at me, I asked the Tyrone officers about the order of speakers for the night. They told me there were just two speakers—the Chairman of the Tyrone Board, Pat Darcy, and myself. I was happy with this because I expected Mícheál Greenan, as Chairman of the Ulster Council, to speak and if he was, I was going to make sure I was speaking after him, not before.

Pat made his speech and, like all chairmen of clubs and counties in Ulster, he was most welcoming and appropriately proud of Tyrone's achievement. Then I spoke. As Kerry had been beaten in the All-Ireland Final, I had some good-humoured banter with the Tyrone audience. Tyrone had also taken the McKenna Cup (an Ulster competition) and Mícheál Greenan, as Chairman of Ulster, was asked to present it. He took the microphone, however, and had a right pop at me and at Central Council. My wife and daughter, not having experienced that kind of thing before, were taken aback and were very upset and in tears. I told them not to react to it as I wasn't one bit perturbed or surprised by his outburst. Indeed, I got a bit of a laugh out of it when I presented the medals to Brian Dooher, Peter Canavan, Stephen O'Neill, etc., and they said to me, 'Seánie, we thought we would have to jump to your defence there for a while. What the f**k was up with that guy?'

A done deal

Most observers expected the negotiations between ourselves, the IRFU and the FAI to take a long time. Some thought we would extract an exorbitant rent, but as the *Examiner* quoted me under a heading one day: 'We aren't going to screw anybody'. And we didn't. Indeed, it was a win-win situation because we all stood to gain handsomely from any deal. The only hiccup was that details of the negotiations were leaked to the media. Many assumed the IRFU, or particularly the FAI, was leaking the information. The two bodies were naturally alarmed about this as bad feeling could cause havoc and jeopardise a deal. They rang me to assure me that they weren't responsible. I told them they weren't under suspicion, because the first day I read the 'leak' in the paper, I knew from the tone and content of the article exactly where it was coming from. The expert leaker came from the GAA side, and he was also fairly good at covering his tracks by pointing the finger of blame elsewhere. But by then I could have written the script and I assured the IRFU/FAI not to worry, just to get on with the business and whatever deal was done, I'd stand over it. I also told the GAA negotiators that they weren't to tell me or anyone else the details of their discussions until a deal had been finalised. They were to revert to me only when a deal was almost done, so that I could approve the general thrust and perhaps help to spot any flaw or omission. And that's what happened. When the deal was done, Hugh Cawley rang me to get my imprimatur. They had covered everything. It was a great piece of work and all sides could hold their heads up high. Thus in a little over a month after Central Council gave its positive decision, the deal was done.

The first 'foreign' game to be played in Croke Park would be the Six Nations game between France and Ireland on 11 February 2007. This was the one request I had made: realising the sensitivities of the occasion, I wanted the first game to be the least divisive possible. In this respect, the thirty-two-county nature of rugby won the day. I also asked the rugby authorities if it could it be France, not England, in the first game. I mean no disrespect to England, but historically France and Ireland have been mutually supportive and friendly and for that reason it was a better fit. The IRFU listened, understood and through quiet, diplomatic consultations with their international board, it was arranged.

It was important that a deal be cemented early in January because otherwise Philip Browne, and possibly John Delaney, would have to go all round the stadia of England and provisionally book venues for their matches. The fact that the deal was completed and announced in early January meant they were spared these unnecessary journeys and probably some embarrassment, too. (Unfortunately, they had to do exactly that in early 2007, the year after I left office, because it was decided that no decision would be made by Central Council until 17 February 2007, thus causing exactly the situation we had studiously avoided in 2006.)

Once again the media were euphoric. The *Irish Examiner*'s front page led with the headline, 'Croker deal nets GAA €7m bonanza. FAI and IRFU sign historic deal' (18 January 2006), and I was asked to write an article headlined: 'Clubs must benefit from Croker cash.' John Delaney (FAI) described the agreement 'as an historic day for soccer and for sport in Ireland'. Philip Browne (IRFU) said: 'The agreement represents a significant milestone in Irish sporting history—it is a major celebration for Irish sport and indeed for the general public in Ireland.'

The media in general concurred, devoting not only acres of space on the sports pages to the agreement but also in the news columns, even carrying editorials celebrating the occasion. In an editorial entitled 'Brave Game Won', the Irish *Daily Star* wrote:

Congratulations to the GAA, the FAI and the IRFU, who have managed to accomplish what many have described as Mission Impossible. All three organisations have struck a historic deal which will see soccer and rugby played in Croke Park for the first time ever. This is a highly controversial move—but it is the right move. GAA President Seán Kelly deserves particular praise for his bravery in advocating the opening of Croke Park in the teeth of considerable opposition. But he has managed to do it in a fair, open and democratic manner. Now let the games begin.

The Irish *Daily Mirror* editorialised as follows:

GAA score huge with Croke play. The GAA is to be congratul-ated—their deal with the IRFU and FAI is a milestone in Irish sporting history and means the dreadful Rule 42 will never again divide Irish sport. It is not before time that the GAA came out of their time warp and woke up to the real world. Most youngsters don't discriminate between soccer, Gaelic football, rugby or hurling. They love them all. GAA president Seán Kelly deserves much praise for his far-sighted leadership, as there are many in his organisation who are still opposed to 'foreign' games at Croke Park. It would have been a national disgrace if Irish soccer and rugby fans were forced to travel abroad to watch Irish teams play their 'home' games. The decision is not only good for the country, it finally gives the GAA the chance to show off their super stadium to the rest of the world.

And in the sports pages the *Mirror* headlined, 'Croker Opens Up— Irish sport forgets the past and starts new era. HISTORY MAKERS—GAA prove good neighbours and give FAI and IRFU use of stadium—Croke of gold for Irish Sport.' You can't beat the tabloids for drama!

Under the heading 'History at Croker', the *Irish Times* editorialised as follows:

The agreement is a milestone in the history of Irish sport . . . Nothing was an absolute certainty until yesterday's announcement . . . For so long criticised as being too conservative and inward-looking, the GAA has shown an enlightened approach in recent years . . . Much of the credit for convincing the grass-roots that there was more to be gained than lost by opening the gates of the stadium must go to outgoing president Seán Kelly. His tenure at the helm of the GAA has been marked by a refreshing honesty and openness that has percolated through all areas of the Association's activities. Yesterday's agreement is a fitting tribute to his astute handling of the most delicate issue in the GAA's recent history. He deserves credit for delivering what he describes as an all-inclusive Ireland in sport. Yesterday's accord reflects a new maturity that will have economic, social and sporting benefits for years to come . . . they have served up the thrilling prospect of watching history being made on the famous turf of Croke Park in 2007.

There has been much speculation about the deal and what it was actually worth to each party. The agreement itself, called 'The Stadium

Letting Agreement', ran to fifty-five pages, much of it legal necessity or, in layman's language, legal jargon. Obviously some of it is confidential, but the more salient points are as follows:

The GAA would receive a minimum of €1.25 million per game in rent, payable twenty-one days in advance of the event period. In other words, if nobody turned up for the matches, the GAA would still pocket the princely sum of €1.25 million. But that was the minimum as that calculation was based on 26 per cent of tickets sold at a base price. Any ticket above the base price meant that 26 per cent was higher also. So the GAA guaranteed minimum of €1.25 million was in reality far below the actual figure. In fact, the first two rugby games played in Croke Park netted €2.2 million each to the GAA.

Some of those who had been against opening Croke Park had argued that it would cost the GAA millions to prepare the grounds for soccer and rugby fans, having to pay for segregation and other specific measures. In fact, the GAA doesn't pay anything at all to prepare the grounds to accommodate soccer and rugby games. The 'event period' referred to three days before a game and two days after a game. The respective bodies would have this period to prepare the stadium for their games and to clean up afterwards.

- Other responsibilities the tenants would assume were paying Dublin City Council to clean up the surrounding area after each game, to hire and pay for security, stewards and gardaí, with GAA stewards being given first option.
- To alleviate fears that either the FAI or IRFU would flood the schools with cheap tickets, it was agreed that no ticket would be sold for less than face value.
- To appease residents' concerns about noise, etc. it was agreed that no event would continue later than 10.00pm. No sideline seating was to be permitted at any event.
- Premium seat-holders would be given first option to buy tickets in their area and the GAA would be given a number of complimentary tickets for use in the GAA box and Ard-Chomhairle area, which meant that many of those opposed to opening Croke Park were now going to be given two complimentary tickets for soccer and rugby matches there. Interesting to observe the take-up!
- Some of the anti group had said that Lansdowne Road could be

declared closed and then open again once the big games had started in Croke Park. Well, the IRFU and FAI were hardly going to engage in those semantics and readily agreed to a clause that stated the IRFU acknowledged as a 'condition and fundamental term' that Lansdowne Road would not be used for sporting or covenant purposes during the period specified in the agreement.

Thankfully, I secured the agreement of Central Council to negotiate and conclude the deal without having to call another meeting to have it ratified. Accordingly, once the agreement was reached, we were able to approve it, announce it, draw it up legally and sign it. It all came to a quick conclusion thanks to good negotiating teams all round, and each party came well out of it. It was, as the papers said, a win-win-win situation for everybody.

That was it then, all done and dusted and accepted. Well, not quite. Recalcitrant elements still persisted and some continued to say that if planning permission had not been granted by February 2007, the matches couldn't go ahead. Brian Carthy of RTÉ radio put that very point to me in an interview and I replied that it was not the case at all. What were we going to do? Wait until the day before the first match and pull the plug because planning permission wasn't granted? Or pull the plug a week or two before that and then, if planning permission was granted the day before the first match was to be played, where were we then? Tell the IRFU that it was okay, France and Ireland could play the following day? Then overnight the French followers could fly in, the Irish followers come from all over, sell 82,500 tickets, put up goalposts, print programmes, summon stewards and gardaí, etc.? Such a scenario made absolutely no sense. So I told Brian that the decision had been made and there was no reference to planning permission in the Sligo motion, that Central Council had given the go ahead to that motion and that I certainly wasn't for turning at this late stage of the game.

Some objected again and Bob Honohan of Cork became fairly animated about the whole business and was quoted widely in the media. But as Seán Moran wrote in the *Irish Times* (Wednesday 29 March 2006), under the heading 'Croke Park—hardly any ground for objections': 'It's hard to explain the desire of so many to emulate the Black Knight in *Monty Python and the Holy Grail*, gamely fighting on and taunting his opponent in combat, as King Arthur serially chops off all of the knight's limbs with a broadsword.' Moran went on to point out that there was no reference to planning permission in the Sligo motion and that of the twenty-five delegates who spoke on the issue, 'at no time did the question of planning permission arise'. Still, the criticism and the questioning persisted all the way to Congress in Killarney, where Bob Honohan raised the matter at both Central Council and Congress levels.

As Ian O'Riordan wrote in *The Irish Times* (21 March 2006): 'With the issue of opening Croke Park to other sports refusing to go away, there is now little hope of Seán Kelly enjoying his last month as GAA President … as certain members are still questioning the validity of suspending Rule 42 if planning permission is not granted for Lansdowne Road.'

Bob mentioned that some of those who had voted in favour of change were now opposed to what was happening and he mentioned Gerry Mahon (Leitrim) as one of these. Gerry couldn't be at Congress himself, but had written to me apologising for his absence and also dissociating himself from any comments made by Bob, adding that he fully supported the manner in which I was dealing with the Croke Park issue. I produced Gerry's letter and read it out at the meeting, which fairly cut the ground from under Bob. At Congress, it was apparent there was very little support for his views.

Handing over the reins
Congress passed off without rancour, and I handed over to my successor as Uachtarán, Nickey Brennan. Rule 42 had been amended and the agreement with the FAI and IRFU was signed, sealed and delivered. There was no going back: 11 February 2007 was fixed in stone as the historic day that Ireland and France would play the first international rugby game in Croke Park, with the Ireland v England match taking place two weeks later, on 24 February, and the first soccer international scheduled for 24 March 2007, when Ireland would play Wales. It should all be plain sailing from here on, and with the closure of Lansdowne Road in 2007, arrangements for 2008 should be little more than a formality.

Even though I was still a member of Coiste Bainistí (for one year after my term as Uachtarán), I didn't think it appropriate for me to comment one way or the other on these matters. It was noted, however, that Nickey, Liam and Danny had several meetings with the IRFU and FAI that weren't as 'cordial', as the press reported. The FAI, in particular, was pulled over the coals—in my view somewhat unfairly—over a few developments. A big deal was made over Bobby Robson, Steven Staunton and John Toshack coming to visit Croke Park. Now, if either had ever criticised Croke Park and said it was built by 'a crowd of bigots', as one individual is supposed to have said, there might be some cause for complaint. As it was, they all declared it a fantastic stadium and said they were looking forward to playing there. Sir Bobby beamed at the prospect and said that he had been all over the world, and Croke Park was as good a venue as he'd seen anywhere.

In fact, Bobby and Steve had visited the stadium during my term as Uachtarán. I didn't know that they had sought and received permission to come and visit, but if I had been asked I would have said, 'Yes, certainly, they're welcome'. Indeed, as it transpired I was in Croke Park the day they came and I was asked to meet them. I was delighted to do so and told Bobby Robson that I was probably the only Newcastle supporter in Ireland—Alan Shearer is my favourite player, with Shay Given running a close second. I found both Steven and Bobby to be perfect gentlemen and I presented them both with a memento of Croke Park before they left. Steve had actually played a lot of Gaelic football himself, and it was quite obvious that he was up to speed on all matters Gaelic. Now, six months later, when I had left office, it was a bit rich to be criticising John Delaney and the FAI for the visit. As for John Toshack, as Ireland were due to play Wales, wasn't it only natural that he would come to check it out?

A big deal was also made about the FAI's request to train in Croke Park. It was seen as a cheap publicity stunt, but in fairness to the FAI it said it would prefer if rugby trained there first. John Delaney had asked FIFA to change the soccer schedule so that a rugby match could be played in Croke Park first as well. The FAI got no credit for this, but everybody deserves fair play. Of course, it's always a great sign of 'strength' when you attack the weakest link. The FAI has suffered over the years from some unfortunate own goals and it's become a bit of a tradition that if you want to show how tough you are, they are the crowd to kick because very few will come to their assistance.

Personally, I couldn't understand this obsession with the FAI and

IRFU at all. Why is Croke Park the great stadium it is? Didn't officials from the GAA visit every stadium in the world worth visiting so we could learn from them? Weren't we welcomed with open arms wherever we went? Haven't we welcomed all types of people to Croke Park? During my presidency I had the pleasure of welcoming several unionist and loyalist politicians, and people of every persuasion have visited and been welcomed to Croke Park, even if many came incognito. And remember, too, that on the night of the Special Olympics we had a cortege of PSNI motorcyclists driving around the pitch—the first time since Michael Hogan was shot dead in November 1920 that the Crown forces had set foot on it. Sir Hugh Orde, the PSNI Chief Constable, was there. Yes, I was President that night, too, and thoughts of Michael Hogan were going through my mind. But it was a special moment and I don't recall anyone objecting to it. Yet here we were, in 2006, making things somewhat uncomfortable for our fellow Irish sportsmen.

It reminded me of an article written by that incisive writer, Eamonn Sweeney, in the *Irish Examiner* (17 February 2005). Commenting on the 'True Gael', he said:

> For the old style GAA administrator nothing but 100 per cent affection for the Association is acceptable. And, in time honoured Irish fashion, this affection is not only displayed by love but also by hatred. It's not enough to glory in the achievements of the GAA, to be a True Gael you have to also disparage soccer, rugby and any other foreign games you come across—if you're on top put the boot into the underdog.

The GAA was on top now. Soccer and rugby needed our stadium, and those who had voted to open Croke Park had done so not out of a sense of superiority but out of a sense of generosity. I sometimes got the distinct impression that those who remained largely silent during the debate, and were probably against it, hoped it would be unworkable. If the vast majority of GAA people knew that, they would be appalled and disgusted. Generosity had opened Croke Park, and that 70 per cent are still generous and would have no time for posturing and putting the boot into the underdog.

The first rugby game in Croke Park

Anticipation was high as the New Year, 2007, drew close. The historic first 'foreign game' to be played in Croke Park was fixed for 11 February and everybody was looking towards that day: the majority with keen excitement; a minority with loathing and trepidation. The search for tickets began early and quickly gathered pace as the weeks went by. Tickets were like gold dust; I received enquiries from all over Ireland and as far away as England, America and even Australia. The request was always the same: 'We would love to be at the historic occasion and would travel all the way home if only we could get tickets.' It was the same everywhere. A headline in an article by Justine McCarthy in the *Sunday Tribune* summarised the unfolding scene well:

> Nowhere are feelings more mixed about today's historic rugby match than in the North. Some feel betrayed, others are keen to set foot on Croke Park for the first time. One thing everyone agrees on, though: 'It's as hard for a Catholic to get a ticket as it is a Protestant'.

All the media outlets went into overdrive on the significance of the upcoming Six Nations games and most saw it as more, much more, than just a game. An editorial in the *Irish Examiner* said:

> In overcoming vociferous resistance were voices which urged greater inclusiveness and sportsmanship, led by Seán Kelly, a man of vision. He steered it [the GAA] towards its momentous decision. Kelly was right in saying that it was a generous decision reflecting confidence and a desire to help out people in need for which history would judge them well.

An editorial in the *Sunday Times* described it as follows:

> Moving the goalposts isn't always a bad idea. This afternoon's Six Nations clash between Ireland and France marks a momentous and laudable change in Irish life, a revolution in the configuration of a mindset as much as a sports pitch. The playing of rugby on the hallowed ground of Gaelic games' headquarters is a potent symbol of a new national pluralism and self-confidence. The occasion

should be applauded by all as a celebration of a truly modern Ireland ... The GAA has proven once again to be in touch with the spirit of the times ... All within the Association who drove through the process of reform deserve immense credit. Particular praise is due to Seán Kelly, the former GAA President, who argued convincingly throughout his tenure for repeal of Rule 42 ...

The real test of whether Ireland has become a self-assured sporting nation will be in two weeks, when the English rugby team appears in the GAA's inner sanctum, and 'God Save The Queen' is played alongside 'Amhrán na bhFiann' at Croke Park. Only when they too are afforded a sporting welcome will the process of transformation be complete. Today, however, there can be no losers – except, let's hope, the French.

The international media also took great interest in the event. Radio and television stations from all over the world featured special programmes about Croke Park and Irish history. The BBC, Sky and CNN all did special programmes; I was interviewed live on CNN after the English game. Newspapers such as *L'Équipe*, *Le Monde*, *The Irish Echo* and the *Washington Post* were all looking for information and interviews. Even the *Financial Times* (10 February 2007) devoted much space to the games in Croke Park. In an article entitled, 'Croke Park lay ghosts of history to rest', written by Simon Ruper, it said, 'More than just a game. This is the day that the wounds of Irish history can be proclaimed more or less healed.' Then he went on to describe Gaelic Football as 'Europe's last great medieval folk game' (I must talk to Simon about hurling) and observed:

If Ireland rather than Britain had colonised the world, we'd all be playing Gaelic now ... On 24 February, when England's rugby team visits, the once unimaginable will happen: the British flag will fly over Croke Park ... on Irish terms, by invite. Now that Ireland is no longer paranoid about Britain, Hogan's ghost can be buried.

And so the build-up reached a crescendo. All viewpoints got an airing. Those opposed to opening Croke Park got more than their fair share of coverage. In an interview with the media in Dubai, during the

Vodafone GAA All Stars Tour, Mícheál Greenan fumed, 'We have not only been sold a pup, but a whole litter.' John Arnold from Cork wasted no time in pointing the finger at me. I was contacted by Tony Leen, Editor of the *Irish Examiner*, to write a column on my thoughts and feelings coming up to the big game. It appeared in the paper on Saturday 11 February:

> History is written every day but occasionally an event can transfix a nation. Some of these momentous events can occur suddenly such as a great calamity like a volcano eruption, a major terrorist attack or a destructive hurricane. Other historic events, usually of a pleasant nature, are a long time in the planning.
>
> Such a joyous occasion kicks off at 3 p.m. tomorrow in Croke Park—the first rugby match to be played at GAA headquarters.
>
> It has been a long hard struggle for those who believed that this was the right thing to do. While the debate began by way of motion to Congress in 2001, it really gathered steam during my Presidency. This was something I hadn't anticipated, but there were so many twists and turns, attacks and counter-attacks that it was always on the agenda right to the last day of my three-year term, which ended at Congress in Killarney last April with the signing of the agreement with the IRFU.
>
> Well, while I was president and had a role to play especially in getting the motions into the Clár (agenda) for Congress other lone rangers were always in the front line. GAA stalwarts, because that's what they are, like Tommy Kenoy, Noel Walsh and Anthony Delaney were bravely challenging and fighting for a cause they believed in. These are great men, men of conviction and courage. Those who opposed them with equal candour are also great GAA men, men of conviction and courage too. It was the worst of times and it was the best of times, we took a lot of stick but continued to fight the good fight.
>
> And it all came to a climax when over 70 per cent voted to open Croke Park to rugby and soccer internationals while Lansdowne Road is closed for re-development. Seventy per cent is a substantial majority and in a democracy it has to be accepted.
>
> Some people, who see a different reality to most of us, still oppose, confront and ridicule. They selectively quote out of

context and give us two cent worth of logic. They think they are representing the 30 per cent who voted against. They were proven wrong in April 2005 and they are wrong again in 2007. There is no 30 per cent against opening Croke Park now. I believe a majority of those who voted against now accept the decision and have moved on. Most of those who voted against were intelligent, dedicated and conscientious. They are well used to winning and losing, that's what the GAA is all about. They have moved on. Indeed if I had a euro for every time someone criticised the decision to me, I wouldn't fill a poor box.

So things have moved on, let's move on with them. France and Ireland play in the Six Nations on Sunday then, not by accident I might add. We wanted a rugby game first and we got it, Ireland's rugby team represents all 32 counties of Ireland.

We wanted France to be the first team to play Ireland and the IRFU respected our wishes and delivered. Indeed, I must compliment Philip Browne and people like Noel Murphy and Tom Kiernan for their honourable demeanour, forbearance and sense of gratitude.

France was the perfect fit. Always our ally, never our enemy. History shows that from Killala to Kinsale they were always our friends. It will be special when the battle of the Tricolours takes place tomorrow. Two nations, different countries, similar flags.

The occasion itself will be fantastic. A win for Eddie's boys would be heaven. Hopefully.

Then England! Well, at least these games are being played on Irish soil. What sort of atmosphere would pervade the country now if Ireland was on its way to England to play our home matches? The GAA might not be to blame per se, but would be targeted for the criticism. What's more, people would understandably vote with their feet and turn their back on the GAA in droves, disgusted at our lack of generosity, lack of vision, lack of true sportsmanship. Thank God 70 per cent voted yes. We have saved the country deep embarrassment and earned it a fortune. And we haven't done too badly ourselves either. If no one at all turned up for the games, the financial agreement is such that the GAA would still pocket more than a million euros. But with a sell-out crowd, the GAA will make substantially more.

One thing I said in the debate was that the money from the rent would have to filter down to the counties and the clubs. That has been agreed at management level although the mechanics have still to be worked out. Still, you can do an awful lot of promoting your own game on €7m plus. Not bad for renting out your ground when otherwise it would've been idle.

We gave, now we receive. I often heard my mother say that 'God loves a cheerful giver'—mothers are always right. So now that we have given Croke Park to our fellow sportsmen, let's be cheerful about it. That's my wish—that everyone who comes to Croke Park will feel welcome. Be they French Quakers or English Presbyterian—it's immaterial. They are all welcome in Croke Park.

My hope is that Croke Park will reflect what Ireland used always be known as—Ireland of the welcomes. Welcome all. Welcome to Croke Park of the welcomes. History.

There were many requests for interviews from TV, radio and the print media. I was reluctant to do them at first because at the previous management/Ard-Chomhairle meeting Nickey Brennan had asked for endorsement for a number of items coming up to the 'foreign games' in Croke Park, one being that only he himself would speak on behalf of the Association. However, when I saw the interviews being given by Mícheál Greenan, Liam Ó Maolmhichíl, Peter McKenna, Seán Fogarty, Tommy Kenoy, *et al*, I didn't see much point in refusing reasonable requests made to me. Indeed, there were so many media outlets at home and abroad looking for a piece of the action that a posse of people was required to satisfy them. I decided to do my best to oblige.

I agreed to a request from Richard Coffey of Bantry Blues GAA club in Cork to appear in Croke Park at lunchtime on Friday 9 February, as part of the club's corporate fundraising venture. That morning Colm Murray of RTÉ rang me and asked for an interview for the one o'clock news, live from Croke Park if possible. As I was going to Croke Park anyway for the Bantry Blues function, I said it would be okay. I was due to meet Colm at around 12.45pm. When I arrived in Croke Park the Irish rugby team was just coming off the pitch, in ones and twos. Word had just come through that Peter Stringer and Brian O'Driscoll were both out through injury. It was a devastating blow, especially to

O'Driscoll as he was not only missing the historic game but was also losing out as team captain. Despite this disappointment, which had only just been announced, Brian had the good grace and generosity to come over to me and thank me for all I had done to get them into Croke Park. In returning thanks to him, I sympathised with his enforced absence and added, 'It will be much sweeter when you lead out Ireland to meet and beat England in a fortnight's time.' He smiled in agreement.

The players and officials couldn't have been nicer and it was a joy to be able to welcome greats like Paul O'Connell, John Hayes and Eddie O'Sullivan to Croke Park. Indeed, John Hayes and I recalled our first meeting, which had taken place in Bruff School over eighteen months earlier. I said then that I hoped John would have the honour of playing for Ireland in Croke Park. He said he hoped so, too, but that he mightn't be still on the team by then as he was thirty-four years of age. As events transpired, not only was he on the team but he had the game of his life against England on 24 February and was later voted Player of the Championship. Some boy, Hayes!

The build-up continued, as described by an editorial in the *Irish Times* (10 February):

> When the rugby players of Ireland and France run onto the field of Croke Park tomorrow, they will bring the curtain down on one of the most contentious issues in the cultural and sporting life of the island of Ireland over the last 90 years . . . All strands of Irish life . . . witnessing . . . a historic event that will be recalled for generations to come . . . Irrespective of the match result, it will live up to its billing as one of the greatest days in Irish sport.

The historic Saturday night before the historic Sunday, I was invited as a special guest to a lovely ecumenical function held in the Burlington Hotel. It was Babs Keating's idea. He and the Tipp supporters GAA club invited three of the greatest teams in the history of their respective codes to a reunion in the Burlington. They were the Tipp three-in-a-row All-Ireland winning teams 1949–1951, the Mayo double All-Ireland champions 1950–1951 and Ireland's last team to win the Grand Slam, in 1951. It was a beautiful night and to share a table with the great Jackie Kyle, captain Karl Mullen and the other surviving members of those great teams was enriching and inspirational. It was a memorable night and when Tommy Fleming, that brilliant entertainer, forgot to sing 'Slieve na mBan', the evening was rounded off with Babs himself doing the honours.

The Sunday morning of the match I did an interview for 'Sportsbag' with Robbie Irwin, was on the panel on the 'Marian Finucane Show' and for good measure did an interview *as Gaeilge* for TG4. Then we made our way to Croke Park.

The atmosphere was fantastic as we approached the gates. Some cheered, others pulled my leg—including the great Mick Galwey, who jokingly called out when he saw me, 'There he is, good God, Seán Kelly, what have you done to poor ould Ireland. It's all your fault that foreign games are being played in Croke Park today. Shame on you, Kelly!'

The IRFU had invited me and Juliette to a pre-match luncheon. It was a pleasant occasion and everybody was wild with excitement and in awe of the great stadium. As usual, Philip Browne and Peter Boyle and their officials were the essence of courtesy and good manners. John Delaney (FAI) was also there, as were the French officials. When I was introduced to a French lady I said, 'Bonjour, Madame', but she quickly replied, 'Bonsoir, Monsieur.' It was 3.30pm and French women are noted for precision.

Match-time! The national anthems were respectfully honoured and the game began.

David Skrela of France had the distinction of kicking the first rugby ball in Croke Park. The French also scored first as the Irish, despite all efforts to the contrary, were obviously affected by the occasion. Enough has been written about the game itself, but a few little things stood out. Many GAA people noted the lack of flags, colour, women and children compared to an All-Ireland Final. This can be partly explained by the difficulty in acquiring tickets and the time of the year the game was played. Still, the atmosphere was electric and good humour resonated everywhere. If people forgot where they were, they were quickly reminded when Skrela approached the first rugby penalty kick in Croker. Silence descended on the stadium, but then a lone voice from the Cusack Stand shouted out, 'Take your point'—a great cliché in Gaelic games. Skrela did take his point, in fact all three, and France dominated proceedings before Ireland fought back bravely and with great spirit.

When Ireland went ahead and still led with time almost up, we were ready to party. But even though no cockerel appeared on the field, the French stole a march on us and nabbed a try and conversion at the death to deny us victory. I felt sick. I have an absolute dread of and hatred for last-minute defeats—my mind went racing back to college games in 1978 and 1979, to Munster Minor games in the mid-1990s, to the All-Ireland Final and the Darby goal in 1982, and to the Munster Final and the Tadhg Murphy goal in 1983. Every country man and woman could have quoted their own litany of lousy leaks at the death. It was a sickener, and it came from our friends the French. History should have warned us—the French always came late to Ireland!

Still, we recovered quickly and when Gavin Cumiskey of the *Irish Times* rang me for a reaction, I said given a choice of beating either the French or the English, no disrespect intended, but we'd take beating the English any day. For once the occasion was just too good to be completely spoilt by a last-minute goal or try. Still, I was worried and began to think that if Ireland didn't beat England and if the soccer team was beaten as well, Croke Park would quickly be dubbed 'Choke Park' for Irish rugby and soccer teams.

The media waxed eloquently about the whole historic occasion. Many tributes were paid to the GAA and I got special mention in a number of articles and editorials. In an editorial in the *Sunday Tribune* (11 February 2007), under the heading 'Opening of Croke Park should point way to new future for Ireland', it opined:

> The GAA has shown us all that we can remember and commemorate the past, but we do not have to be prisoners of the past. History is ours to write. Others should follow. Ian Paisley and Gerry Adams have an opportunity to break new ground in Northern Ireland. The leadership of the Democratic Unionist Party is not being asked to disregard the past, but rather to create a new future. Through sport and politics these are really good times to celebrate Ireland in all its traditions.

Yes, the feeling was wonderful and the encouragement satisfying. Personally, I couldn't believe the number of rugby players, and especially the parents of those from Northern Ireland (like the Best and

Boss families), who introduced themselves to me and thanked me for helping to make their days in Croke Park possible.

In between the French and English games was a very important meeting of Coiste Bainistí and Central Council. We were making a decision, at last, on extending the opening of Croke Park into 2008. I say 'at last' because I couldn't understand why it hadn't been done in December 2006, as we had done in December 2005, thus saving the IRFU and the International Rugby Board an awful lot of bother in booking provisional venues abroad in January. After all, nothing happened between December and February to alter the landscape. Management were to meet to discuss the matter on Friday night, 16 February. Unfortunately, by the time I realised that, I had already committed to presenting awards for the Kerry Education Services at Manor West Hotel in Tralee. I also knew that Liam Martin, a good friend of mine, would also be absent. Remembering how I was nearly tripped up the previous year, I approached Nickey Brennan and alerted him to the situation. I told him I was prepared to drive to Tralee for the awards night and drive back up again afterwards if he would put back the decision until Saturday morning. He saw the danger and agreed.

So I did exactly that. On Friday evening, 16 February 2007, I drove to Tralee, attended a lovely awards night under the direction of my long-time friend Eamonn Fitzgerald (ex-Kerry goalkeeper), and at midnight hopped into my car and headed straight for Dublin. I was in bed at 4.30am and was at the management meeting at 9.00am the following morning. I was relieved to see Liam Martin was also there. When it came to discussing Croke Park's availability in 2008, Mícheál Greenan gave us the 'pups and the litter' again. But I pointed out that the bona fides of the IRFU/FAI had been well established:

This time last year people were saying that they (IRFU/FAI) had no notion of developing Lansdowne. The IRFU/FAI said that they'd be lodging an application for planning permission in January—they did so. We asked the foremost planning authorities in the county how long the process would take—they said at least a year—that is happening. They said that they expected a decision from Dublin City Council sometime in the autumn—they received full planning permission from Dublin City Council in August last. They said Lansdowne Road would be closed early in 2007. It is closed. Everything they said they'd do they did, and so we should, in the spirit of Rule 42, extend the decision for 2008.

I also wanted the friendly, or ranking, games schedule to be included as well, but Nickey and Liam had decided to postpone that decision for another day. Thus the request for 2008 was granted, and it was even more emphatic at Central Council level. Indeed, at Central Council I complimented Bob Honohan and Cork for coming down the road a good bit from the previous year's total opposition. Bob had said he'd accept it, provided full planning permission was granted for Lansdowne Road in 2007. Thus 2008 was agreed and I happily hopped into my car and headed for Stewartstown Harps' (Tyrone) Golden Jubilee function.

Like all Northern nights, it was a gala affair and brilliantly compèred by the Dungannon dynamo, Adrian Logan (UTV). In the course of the evening an auction was held to raise funds for the Stewartstown GAA club. Ironically, but perhaps not surprisingly, rugby tickets and Irish rugby jerseys were the most sought after items. There are people who still believe all of Ulster was against opening Croke Park. Well, if they were, and I know they weren't, they went along with the decision pretty quickly. The fact that I am still invited to more functions in Ulster than any other province would appear to support that thesis. The honesty and commitment of Ulster was best summed-up by Armagh County secretary Paddy Óg Nugent when, at the announcement of the result of the debate on Rule 42 at Congress 2005, he said, 'we will abide by the decision. It was definitely democracy at its best.' And Ulster at its best as well. But others wouldn't or couldn't agree.

On the way home to Kerry on Sunday 18 February, I tuned in to RTÉ Radio 1, where I heard John A. Murphy in discussion with Jo Jo Barrett about Jo Jo's decision to take his father's medals out of the GAA museum in protest at the playing of 'God Save The Queen' in Croke Park. Jo Jo informed us that he had come out of a church in Spain, where his grandson was being baptised, to talk on the programme. John A. disagreed with him as only John A. could, citing his own father's achievements for Cork and for Ireland, and adding that one All-Ireland medal in Cork was worth ten in Kerry.

Barrett's actions spawned a media frenzy that lasted the whole week before the English game. Those who supported the opening of Croke Park were classed as traitors in some quarters. There was talk of a sell-out and martyrs for old Ireland turning in their graves. There was no escaping it—it was the talk of the airwaves. Would there be trouble when the English came to town? When interviewed, I appealed for dignity, courtesy and respect for both anthems and this plea was carried in many news bulletins and papers. In the *Star* it appeared under the catchy heading, 'Let them sing their song'. Former Uachtarán Mick Loftus also publicly urged similar restraint. Many others, including President Mary McAleese, did so as well. I particularly noted the courageous stand of Michael Hogan, who was quoted in the *Examiner* as saying he had no objection to 'God Save the Queen' being played in Croke Park and he hoped both anthems would be shown respect. Michael Hogan, nephew of Mick Hogan who was shot dead at GAA headquarters by the colonial British Forces on 21 November 1920 (Hogan Stand is named in his honour), said he was against opening Croke Park to soccer and rugby but 'accepts the democratic decision' and 'the English team and supporters are our guests so we will have to welcome them. We have to respect their anthem as well. If the Irish team was over in Twickenham, they'd respect our anthem.' And as for the planned protests in Dublin, 'I wouldn't have time for any of that.' It took great courage to speak out like that and I have no doubt it had a big influence on others.

An even more moving newspaper article appeared in the *Sunday Times* (11 February). David Walsh, that brilliant and observant penman, interviewed Oliver Hughes, Vice-chairman of Wolfe Tones GAA Club in Bellaghy, Co. Derry. Oliver's brother, Francis, became a revered martyr when he was one of those who died during the hunger strike at the Maze prison in 1982. At least another half-dozen Bellaghy Club members lost their lives in the Troubles, including Colm McCartney, who was shot dead near the border in 1975 as he made his way home from a match in Croke Park. One of Bellaghy's best footballers, Willie Stratheern, was shot dead by a sick sectarian killer, who tricked Willie into opening his pharmacy in the early hours of the morning by claiming he wanted medicine for his sick child. How low could one stoop! And then there was the great and lovely gentleman Seán Brown, who was snatched and killed by more sectarian killers as he locked the gates of his beloved Bellaghy on the night of Monday 12 March, more than ten years ago.

Seamus Heaney, the Nobel Prize-winning poet, also comes from Bellaghy and in his poem 'The Augean Stables' he wrote:

> ... and it was there at Olympia ... that we heard of Seán Brown's murder in the grounds of Bellaghy GAA Club.
> And imagined hose-water smashing hard back off the asphalt,
> In the car park where his athlete's blood ran cold.

Not surprisingly, when it came to a vote on Rule 42 in 2005, Bellaghy had voted against it. 'I don't know if there was any need for a debate at our club,' remarked Ollie. 'We knew how we felt. Our two delegates were told to vote no.' Now, almost two years on, with the first rugby game in Croke Park fast approaching, Ollie must have felt sad and perhaps bitter. No, wait a minute. This is a man who has lived through it all, no long-distance republican here, a man of deep thought and soul:

> And then he thinks of England in Croke Park, a strange religion in his Mecca ... He smiles inwardly at the recollection of where he has come from in so short a time ... a month ago he was dead against it but 'when I look at the television or pick up a paper and see what is being said about Croke Park I feel good about it ... Some GAA people will find it hard but not me. Croke Park belongs to the Irish people. We're now out of the trenches, we're off our knees, a risen people who don't need to look over our shoulders any more.'

God, when I read that I nearly cried with admiration and joy. How could a man who had seen his brother and friends die in tragic circumstances during the recent Troubles in Northern Ireland be so open to change, so forgiving, so modern? But opening Croke Park and playing 'God Save The Queen', surely he couldn't stomach that? Wrong again. Look at Oliver Hughes' answer:

> It's not a problem for me. It is customary to play the anthems of the competing teams in international sport, so that's what should happen. I hope everyone inside Croke Park respects England's anthem. People will be surprised I am saying this, but it is how I feel.

Yes, indeed, I for one was surprised, but was also delighted. When I read David Walsh's article on Oliver Hughes and the *Irish Examiner*'s interview with Michael Hogan's nephew, I relaxed for the very first time as I knew then that there'd be little or no trouble when England came to town. Like Oliver, I hoped that everyone inside Croke Park would respect England's anthem. With people like Oliver saying so, it made it much more likely to happen. In my book, Oliver Hughes is a big, big man, a true Gael, a true Irishman and a man of our times. It takes a man of intelligence to change his mind, especially on a very emotive issue that is close to his heart. It takes a man of great courage to admit to that change publicly. Even though I have never met him, Oliver is obviously such a man—intelligent and courageous. It's just what you'd expect from a man from Bellaghy. After all, you don't win All-Irelands without those two qualities. Bellaghy folk have them in abundance.

A few weeks later I had a similar experience in San Francisco. Seamus Canning and Joe Duffy invited me to the Ulster Club's Golden Jubilee celebration in the Golden Gate City. While there I met a man who had spent six years in jail in 'the Kesh', and had been harassed and beaten up by English soldiers all his life. His name is Paul Campbell. He told me that opening Croke Park was a good thing and he had no objection to 'God Save the Queen'. The charismatic and charming Paul Campbell said to me, 'We did what we thought was right in those days, what you have done in Croke Park is the right thing to do now.' We had a long chat over a few drinks in the Gold Dirt Bar in downtown San Francisco and by the time we were finished I was calling him 'Glen Campbell' and he was calling me 'Chuckie' Kelly. He still answers to it, as well! Paul 'Glen' Campbell.

And so the debate on whether 'God Save The Queen' should or should not be played in Croker continued all week. Some of those who were opposed to it organised a protest march in the vicinity of Croke Park on the big match day. There were fears of trouble, but the Gardaí were well on top of the situation and the protest passed off peacefully. I got a few nasty phone calls during the week as well, one telling me, 'You'll pay for this yet, you English-loving bastard,' but I just pressed seven on my mobile phone and deleted those messages and didn't say anything about them to anyone. I did note, though, in a photograph in one of the Sunday papers, a big placard carried by one of the protestors proclaiming 'Seán "Judas" Kelly, West Brit, No foreign games in Croke Park'. Another referred to me as Dermot McMurrogh (the King of Leinster who invited the Normans to Ireland in 1169) and some protestors burned an effigy of me.

Such are the ups and downs of public life. Only a fool thinks he can win them all. But then, how could you win over, or why should you try to win over, people who protest about 'foreign games' in Croke Park while wearing Celtic soccer jerseys on their backs? The mind boggles.

The mind boggled even more two months later, after I had finished my five-year term on management (one year as Uachtarán-Tofa; three as Uachtarán and one as Iar-Uachtarán). It is customary to mark the retirement of outgoing members of management with a function to which they and their wives/partners are invited. Accordingly, my retirement function was held in Dunboyne Castle on 12 May 2007. Between members of management and their partners, there were about forty people present. It was a lovely intimate affair, well organised by Joan Cooney of Pairc an Chrócaigh. All was going along beautifully, until Mícheál Greenan rose to speak. Reading from a prepared script, and referring to Croke Park and to me in particular, he said that there had been a reference made to Judas in the run-up to the England game in Croke Park. Bullishly he stated that the comparison was unfair to Judas because 'at least Judas had the decency to hand back the money and do away with himself'.

My wife, and indeed others, were greatly shocked and upset on hearing these words. Juliette wanted to leave immediately, but I whispered to her, 'Don't let him spoil the party for everybody.' Indeed, I was in two minds myself whether I would go over and floor him with a southpaw's upper-cut, for I felt that was just the medicine he needed, but I kept my cool. When it came to my turn to speak I simply said, 'Tonight is a social occasion, it is not appropriate to dwell on disputes or contentious issues.' The assembled gathering applauded and later everybody, including the Uachtarán and Ard-Stiúrthóir, apologised to me for the embarrassment caused. But it just goes to show, there's often a price to be paid for spearheading change.

But back to the great day—match day.

Match day

In some respects, the protests were at best sideshows. The real action was within the stadium and in the pubs and homes of Ireland. Saturday

24 February was as close to perfect as one can possibly come in this life. A packed crowd gave England a rousing welcome and, lo and behold, during the playing of 'God Save The Queen' there wasn't a single jeer or shout or boo. This was a defining moment in Irish sport and a defining moment in modern Irish history. Then when it came to our own 'Amhrán na bhFiann', it was sung with such gusto and such deeply felt pride that tears were seen in the eyes of such 'hards' as John Hayes, Paul O'Connell and Jerry Flannery. Ireland did a great marketing job for itself in those few moments and I got phone calls from exiles all round the world who were watching it on TV, thrilled by the spectacle. There was many a tear shed from Plymouth to Perth, from Liverpool to Los Angeles, from Sydney to San Francisco at that momentous scene. I was asked to sum up my thoughts about the day by the *Irish Examiner* and this is what I wrote under the heading, 'Proud to be an Irishman':

Nobody told us they'd be days like this. I don't know what day Van the Man was referring to, but it is the perfect summation of Saturday, 24 March in Croke Park. Because on last Saturday the fulfilment of an Irish dream came to pass before our eyes.

It was billed as a game of rugby but it was more, much more than that. Firstly, it wasn't just any game of rugby—this was Ireland v England, enough to attract the attention of those with less than a fleeting interest in sport. Any contest against 'the auld enemy' has added significance for Irish people and a victory against England is always treasured even if it was only tiddly winks. Ireland versus England, yes but *Ireland versus England*, for the first time ever in Croke Park not only captured the imagination of the Irish public but of the media all around the world as well. How would the Irish react to the first official visit of an English team to play in Croke Park since they came uninvited, unannounced and with such devastating consequences on Bloody Sunday, 21 November 1920?

Could we forgive and forget? Could we look them in the eye and welcome them as equals? Could we then go on and show our prowess by beating them at their own game? Or would we still show them that they weren't just 'the auld enemy' but still 'the real enemy'—ever to be hated, never to be respected?

I was a proud Irishman on Saturday last. Indeed, I have rarely been prouder or more conscious of my country and my nationality. Firstly, honesty was a real winner on Saturday in Croke Park. Those who couldn't 'stomach' the English national anthem being played and saw it as a sell-out to fallen heroes had the freedom to protest peacefully—always an essential right in a mature democracy. We didn't agree with their point of view but they were entitled to it and were able to express that view honestly and openly. I was proud of the Gardaí and security personnel for ensuring that the conscientious protestors weren't hijacked by extreme elements who like to latch on to the causes so that they can cause as much trouble and anarchy as possible. But above all I was proud of what happened In Croke Park. Firstly, a magnificent crowd created a brilliant atmosphere. It was smiles and good humour all the way. The real winners on Saturday last were the 82,300 people who attended the game. The eyes of the world were on them and they represented all 32 counties to the outside world. Ireland played a blinder in the stands and on the hill. When the English came out on the field for the first time since 1920 they got a rousing reception all around the stadium. When Ireland came out the roofs nearly lifted off the stands. Then the most seminal moment, in symbolism anyway, since the foundation of the state arrives—the playing of 'God Save the Queen' in Croke Park for an English team. To the great delight of the vast majority, and probably to the disgust of a small minority, the British anthem was treated with respect and courtesy and I didn't hear a dissenting voice right up to the last note. Ireland's fans did Ireland proud in those few minutes and did wonders for Ireland's image and the whole Peace Process. Yes, the war was over. We respected our history but we weren't prisoners of it. Then we proved how truly proud we were all over again by singing with gusto right to the very end of our own 'Amhrán na bhFiann'. I don't think I ever heard our national anthem sung so well and so proudly as in Croke Park last Saturday.

It was the talk of the place afterwards. One northern Unionist came up to me afterwards, thanked me for Croke Park and added, 'Today, Ireland grew up as a nation. It was the first time in my life that I felt I was truly Irish. Thank you and the GAA for providing me with this day.' How uplifting.

And it was uplifting for the players too. How they rose to the occasion! How well they played! It was easily the most enjoyable rugby game I have ever seen and one of the most memorable days in my life. History and sport rhymed in Croker last Saturday. Sport taught politics a lesson. And sport is the new 'warfare'? Not bellicose, vitriolic or hateful. Not sport, true sport, where one pits one's ability against another and fights for honour and glory of the little country or little village. Our players did that last Saturday. We welcomed the 'Brits' with courtesy and dignity and then proceeded to teach them a lesson at their own game. How sweet, how wonderful! Ireland beat England fair and square and the players were truly magnificent—every single one of them. They brought pride to the green jersey and redefined Irish nationalism with a style and commitment that was truly breathtaking.

Saturday vindicated those who worked to open Croke Park. It was a long emotional and acrimonious debate. There were, and still are a lot of hard words spoken. But Saturday last made it all worthwhile. Ireland, all 32 counties and all shades of politics and creeds within it, was united in a way it may never have been before. Things will never be the same again. After last Saturday there's no going back. Emotionally we have caught up with the economic progress the country has achieved in the past ten years. We are seen now as a progressive, inclusive country—a great sporting country and a welcoming country. A country to be proud of. It can only do us good.

In the lead up to the game somebody compared me to Dermot McMurrogh—he invited the Normans to Ireland in 1169. The insinuation was that I was a 'traitor' too. There's one big difference though. McMurrogh invited the English to Ireland in 1169 and they stayed for over 700 years during which time they inflicted many heart-breaking defeats on the poor Irish. The English were invited to Croke Park last Saturday, they stayed for one or two days and while here the Irish inflicted the greatest defeat on them in the history of the game. They retreated with heavy losses. Hard luck England, well done Ireland.

Yes, Van the Man was right, 'nobody ever told us they'd be days like this'!

Yes, indeed, it was a glorious day and Ireland played some brilliant rugby. The penalty kicking of Johnny Wilkinson and Ronan O'Gara was extraordinary. O'Gara kicked eight 'frees' in all and scored all eight. The great Johnny Wilkinson was equally impressive and their two kicks from the 'wrong' angle on the Hogan Stand side were absolutely breathtaking. I said to Ronan O'Gara afterwards, 'When you were taking that conversion from the sideline on your "wrong' side", I said to myself, if he kicks this, he is as good as Maurice Fitzgerald.' Ronan, modest as ever, smiled and replied, 'God, that's some praise, Seán, thanks.' Yes, a marvellous day and a great victory for Eddie O'Sullivan's Ireland. And what about the tries, especially Shane Horgan's—without doubt the best Gaelic football try ever scored, and it happened in Croke Park!

All the reaction afterwards was positive. But then, there was nothing remotely bad to be negative about. The *Irish Examiner* called it a 'victory' for sport, sanity and unity and 'A great day to be Irish'. And that is exactly what it was. A great day, a happy day, 'God save the Irish'.

The first soccer game in Croke Park

The Republic of Ireland faced into its international games next, facing Wales on 24 March and Slovakia on 28 March, both games being played in Croke Park. The Irish soccer team were going through their worst patch in over twenty years. Poor performances, especially against San Marino and Cyprus, had drawn the wrath of the media and the public on the heads of manager Steven Staunton and CEO John Delaney. It's amazing that in soccer and rugby it's the CEO who is the public face of the organisation, whereas in the GAA it's the President who creates the public image.

Regardless of how the soccer team were faring, the games were going to be historic events. I hoped Ireland would win for everybody's sake, but also as the Irish athletes, rugby and cricket teams were all doing well, soccer was getting a fair ould bashing for failing to follow suit and live up to expectations. It could do with a bit of a breather from the criticism.

The soccer team trained in Croke Park for the first time on Tuesday 20 February. I had an Integration Committee meeting that evening and met some of the soccer people coming out, including John Delaney. I was pleased when John expressed full satisfaction with the pitch and the co-operation they had received from Peter McKenna and the stadium staff. All was taking shape nicely. But I couldn't get over how small the soccer pitch looked, compared to the rugby pitch in Croke Park. They are actually both about the same size, but the long posts of rugby had a natural look in Croke Park, whereas the soccer goalposts looked almost dwarfed in the middle of the gigantic stadium. It would be interesting how it would look when the game was played before a big crowd. However, the bucket seats specially installed in the Hill 16/Dineen End looked terrific and many GAA people hoped they'd be left there permanently. Wouldn't that be a nice epitaph: 'The completion of the redevelopment of Croke Park came after twenty years of work with the installation of bucket seats on Hill 16/Dineen End courtesy of the FAI.'

On the night before the Wales v Ireland game, the FAI held an historic function in the Burlington Hotel. They invited all the soccer stars who had played for Ireland to a commemoration function. I was invited along, too, and John Delaney told me it was the players— Johnny Giles, Terry Conroy, Eamonn Dunphy and the like—who had requested that I be invited, which I considered a great honour. My daughter, Julie, was being confirmed the same day, but my wife said that I should leave after the Confirmation and go to Dublin. I was lucky that there was a flight from Farranfore at 6.50pm. So, having attended Julie's Confirmation, I left the church grounds after photos at 6.00pm, caught the flight and was in the Burlington Hotel at 8.20pm. Thank God for Pádraig Ó Céidigh and Aer Arann!

It turned out to be one of the most enjoyable and relaxing nights I have ever attended. International soccer players came from all over Ireland, England, Scotland, Wales, South Africa and even New Zealand for the historic get-together. There was no music, no partners, no media and no Kerrymen as, perhaps unsurprisingly, no Kerryman was ever capped for Ireland's soccer team! Jimmy McGee did MC in his own wonderfully unique style. Almost every former international I spoke to had either played in Croke Park for their school or played inter-county with their county, Packie Bonner, Kevin Moran, Niall Quinn, Steve Long and Con Martin among them. I did hear some harrowing tales of the days of the 'ban' and how many had suffered. For instance, Con Martin won a Leinster Senior medal with Dublin in 1942, but he didn't receive his medal until 1973 because of the strict enforcement of the 'ban'. Another player told me that he played hurling and football for his Dublin school in Croke Park and was also selected on the Ireland under-16 soccer side and was named as captain. On the day he was named as captain of Ireland, he was immediately expelled from the school—a unique way to mark a great honour—but such were the ways then. Liam Brady had a similar tale to tell. It's no wonder such resentment built up between the GAA and soccer. But thankfully, that function and the soccer international the following day in Croke Park helped put those dark days to bed.

I received great acknowledgment from all the speakers for my part in helping to open Croker. First, David Blood, the FAI President, mentioned me specifically in his address, then Jimmy McGee and Minister John O'Donoghue did likewise. Johnny Giles was made a special presentation as some time previously he had been voted Ireland's Best Ever Player by UEFA, a decision with which I wholeheartedly agreed. We discussed it at our table. We were fairly divided between Giles, Roy Keane and Paul McGrath, but I opted for Giles. I was particularly chuffed when, in his acceptance of his great award, he went out of his way to mention me and the part I had played in facilitating the opening of Croke Park. Yes, it was a wonderful night and one for which John Delaney and the FAI got deserved credit. For my part, the function took place during Lent, something I found difficult during the evening, but was mighty glad of the following morning!

In July, when the FAI held its AGM I was invited along and presented with a framed Irish jersey with the results and scores of the two soccer games in Croke Park engraved on it—a thoughtful and much-appreciated gesture.

The following day, 24 March, the first soccer international to be played in Croke Park took place before a full house. It was a game Ireland had to win and, unfortunately, the build-up was more about the alleged ineptitude of manager Steve Staunton and his players than the significance of the occasion.

I noticed that there were far fewer of the GAA hierarchy present at the soccer international than at the rugby games. In his GAA President's message for the first rugby game, Nickey Brennan had written: 'I particularly welcome Peter Boyle and Philip Browne of the IRFU,' and added, 'I hope that the Croke Park experience will be both fruitful and memorable for the Irish (rugby) team and its supporters.' For the England game Nickey had written, 'I am pleased to again welcome Peter Boyle and Philip Browne.' But for the soccer matches, no such mention was made of President David Blood or CEO John Delaney nor like sentiments expressed. Interesting, I thought.

Once again the Welsh and Irish anthems were treated with respect. There's a lesson here for all GAA fans—listen to or sing the national anthem until the very end instead of the current trend for cheering and shouting well before it is finished. The best ever rendition of 'Amhrán na bhFiann' for a Gaelic match in Croke Park was for the All-Ireland final between Tyrone and Armagh in 2005, something I commended both counties' supporters for when I was presenting the Sam Maguire to Peter. The greatest.

Finally, the landmark game between John Toshack's charges and Steve Staunton's kicked off. Ireland played well in the first half, with Steven Ireland putting away a fine goal. It turned out to be the only goal of the game; the second half was terrible. I was happy that Ireland won, but most commentators and fans were disappointed with the performance. As a consequence, rarely, if ever, has a team been criticised so heavily in victory. Indeed, in a humorous piece written by Eamonn Sweeney in the *Sunday Independent* (25 March), he said the opening of Croke Park to soccer internationals was part of a cunning plan by the wily Kerryman, Seán Kelly. Kelly, he said, knew that Ireland would play so badly and the game would be so boring that, instead of being a promotional tool for soccer, it would become one for the GAA! After that performance, most felt Slovakia would be too good for the Irish team and would end Ireland's qualification dreams and Steve Staunton's career as manager. I hoped not and felt if Ireland could only play with GAA-style pride and passion, they could be a lot better.

I was sorry for Staunton, too. He got some lambasting. They say it goes with the territory, but it was unrelenting and far too personal. The players got the brunt of it, too, and when some of them went along to support Bernard Dunne in his European title fight at the Point, instead of being applauded some fans booed them—an appalling act of bad sportsmanship. Ironically, though, all that unfairness may have triggered some 'fight' within the team because when they went out to play Slovakia a few nights later, they gave their best performance in years.

It was a hugely entertaining game and Ireland, like they did under Big Jack, kept putting the Slovaks under pressure, with players like Kevin Doyle, Stephen Hunt, Richard Dunne, Paul McShane and John O'Shea being kept particularly busy, and Shay Given as solid as ever in goals. The crowd were delighted and minute after minute, Mexican wave after Mexican wave, the fans grew more appreciative, the team grew more confident and once again we were on the right side of a one goal to nil result. *Olé, olé, olé* once again. I was delighted for Staunton and John Delaney and for the players. Afterwards I went down to the players' lounge to congratulate them. They were all in great form and I think they can now grow as a team. The spark was back and if they can hold onto their belief, a glorious new era could yet be in store for Irish soccer.

The atmosphere after the game against Slovakia was in marked contrast to that after the game against Wales. The media gave due credit to the team and even said Ireland still had a chance to qualify; Steve Staunton got a stay of execution and John Delaney had tears of joy and relief. Everybody was thrilled and it was a fitting way for the last of the spring spectaculars to end.

Thus, after the famous first four games in Croke Park, Ireland won three and were pipped at the death in one. There were no unsavoury incidents. Both visiting and home crowds were brilliant in the stadium and on the streets of Dublin. Ireland was portrayed in a most positive light, the sky didn't fall in and Gaelic games are as popular, if not more popular, than ever. I must say I was truly delighted as everything I had predicted and hoped for had come to pass. It worked like a dream—except for that French try at the Davin End deep into injury time.

The future of the Park

At half-time in the second soccer international, as Ireland led 1-0 and were playing well, I jokingly said to my pals, 'If the soccer team win here tonight, they will never leave.' They won. So, what of the future? Will we see the soccer and rugby teams back again on the field in Croker in years to come? Personally, I don't see why not. There will always be big games that well in excess of 50,000 fans will want to attend. I'd like to see the GAA keeping that option alive. I was always in favour of opening Croke Park, long before there was any talk of closing and redeveloping Lansdowne Road. I would like to see it being made available, if required, long after Lansdowne Road is developed, which should be some time in 2009.

The only cloud on the horizon, and it is one we need to be cognisant of, is a waning of enthusiasm or cooperation on the part of the GAA. Much ground has been gained, but it could be lost again if conditions change. In 2005, at the Ard-Chomhairle meeting on 10 December, the GAA took a decision to start negotiations immediately, and these were concluded in early January. This was done with one eye on the clock in order to give the IRFU and FIA plenty of notice to confirm and arrange their games—a mammoth task in itself. If we hadn't obliged in this way, the IRFU would have had to book venues all over Britain as 'Plan B' options.

In a memo to the members of Ard-Chomhairle for 10 December 2005, we stated that the IRFU and FAI:

> ... are required by their respective international boards to confirm the venues for their international fixtures a year in advance, i.e. December 2005/January 2006. If these sporting bodies cannot get confirmation of the availability of Croke Park for their internationals in 2007, or if the terms and conditions cannot be agreed by early January 2006, they will have no option but to seek an arrangement with alternative venues abroad. This will happen in the event of the application before Central Council today (10 December 2005) being refused or a decision deferred.

This was agreed and followed through. However, as the minutes of the Ard-Chomhairle meeting of 9 December 2006 show, this did not happen for 2008:

> An t-Uachtarán (Nickey Brennan) reported on discussions held with representatives of the IRFU and FAI on 27 November and he said the two organisations were looking for a decision with regard to the games in 2008 but that . . . we were not prepared to take a decision until after the commencement of games in 2007 (11 February being the first game). He said that there were difficulties for the rugby people in particular with regard to their schedules, and that An Coiste Bainistí was proposing that we

allow negotiations to commence with regard to 2008 on the clear understanding that nothing would be approved until the meeting of Ard-Chomhairle on 17 February 2007. He also said that the two organisations had been told to arrange an alternative (venues) for 2008 in case Ard-Chomhairle refused to give permission.

Thus the two organisations were told to have other venues ready, in case Croke Park was refused for 2008. The IRFU had to talk to Murrayfield, Cardiff and Twickenham, which must have caused great embarrassment all round. It wasn't good for the image of Ireland and it wasn't in keeping with the spirit of the Rule 42 amendment. It meant that the Six Nations international meeting had to be put back and the IRFU had to try to explain to French, Italian and other television stations, as well as sponsors, what was happening, i.e. they wouldn't have word on Croke Park until after 17 February 2007.

Central Council had approved the major 'leap of faith' in December 2005 by a margin of six to one, so it could easily have approved the same arrangement in 2006, if asked to do so. After all, the IRFU and the FAI had fulfilled all their promises of 2006. They said they would apply for planning permission in early 2006, and they did so. They said they expected a decision from Dublin City Council in the autumn of 2006, which they did and got a very good planning permission (for the redevelopment of Lansdowne Road) in August 2006. They said it would be appealed to An Bord Pleanála and that that process would take them into the first quarter of 2007, which also happened. And they said they would close down Lansdowne Road in 2007 and they did so, with some memorable moments as the players and public said goodbye to the old Lansdowne at the end of 2006. They did everything as they had said they would, and it would have been far preferable if negotiations had been concluded in December 2006 or early January 2007 so that the way forward in 2008 was certain for all concerned.

I never wanted the Bertie Bowl, because a second 80,000-seat stadium in Dublin would be like a man with two wives—a luxury, or a noose, you couldn't afford! A 50,000-seat and an 82,500-seat stadium is perfect for Dublin, offering the possibility of not only major international competitive games but many more besides, such as major friendlies, champions leagues, etc. A whole new opportunity is there for

Dublin to become the sporting capital of Europe. It could only be good for Dublin, good for Ireland, good for sport and good for the GAA. The redeveloped Lansdowne Road will cater for 50,000 supporters; Croke Park can cater for 82,500 supporters. If we all pull together in a spirit of sportsmanship, the future looks bright for sports lovers! All in favour, *lámha suas.*

INDEX